1978

The Discovery of Peace

Also by R.V. Sampson

The Psychology of Power

THE DISCOVERY
OF PEACE

by
R. V. Sampson

PANTHEON BOOKS

A Division of Random House, New York

First American Edition

Library of Congress Cataloging in Publication Data

Sampson, Ronald Victor.
The Discovery of Peace.

Includes bibliographical references.
  1. Tolstoi, Lev Nikolaevich, Graf, 1828-1910—
Religion and ethics.   2. Power (Social sciences)
3. War. I. Title.
PG3415.P4S2 1973   891.7'3'3   73-7008
ISBN 0-394-48507-6

Manufactured in the United States of America

Contents

Preface

I belong to the generation that was born at the end of World War I and was myself born on the first day of 'peace'. We had not had quite time to reach maturity when World War II claimed us for its own. For although I had frequently vowed that I would yield to no force compelling me to go to war and kill my fellows, when the war came I took the oath of allegiance to the Crown and became a soldier.

> When there was peace, he was for peace,
> When there was war, he went.

I have no wish to palliate in any way the gravity of my offending; but the reasons for my self-betrayal concern others besides myself. I had read and been strongly influenced by the spate of anti-war literature of the thirties; but when the time came (not without painful inner struggle) I went to war. I went to war, saying to myself that I would have refused to go to any other war in history, but that this one was different—the Nazis were unique in their evil. Although I had been convinced that war was wholly evil, I had not been convinced that there is not, and never can be a just war. In short, I had not learned to understand the real cause of war.

This I did not begin to understand until 1956 when the deliberate and calculated aggression of the British Government (and others) against Egypt had the cathartic effect of enabling me to question anew basic assumptions about the nature and cause of war. I had gone to war in 1940, in spite of my anguish, because essentially I had believed not only that the Nazis were brutal and cruel racialists (as indeed they were) but also that the 'British' were essentially 'decent' and just. But in 1956 the 'British' in violation of their own binding treaties began to murder Egyptian people because the Egyptians wished to administer the canal running through their territory. Why, I now asked myself, why was I in 1939, although fully aware that war was evil, indeed the greatest evil in the world, defenceless against the age-old argument that, while war in general is evil, the particular one in which I am called upon to fight is the exception, the one valid example of 'the just war'?

I came to the conclusion that the generation previous to mine had not understood the matter aright—notwithstanding their experience of World War I and their sincere hostility to war. The mistake that they had made, I concluded, was in supposing that the issue of war and peace is essentially a political issue, a matter of defending a good way of life against a bad one or at any rate a less bad one against a worse one; that ultimately the test of validity is pragmatic and lies in the assessment whether there is sufficient at stake to warrant the predictable evils and risks of resistance. The issue of war and peace, I came to realize, is not of this order, and can never be rationally resolved on this plane; the issue is always a religious issue, and can be correctly resolved in no other way.

Among the most influential books on war published in England after World War I was G. Lowes Dickinson's *War: Its Nature, Cause and Cure* (1923). It has the great merit of lucidity and sincerity. But the author does not succeed in reaching the heart of the matter. Lowes Dickinson argues that war is caused by the existence of sovereign States armed against one another; that this condition arises from the desire to hold on to what one has got and if possible to take in addition whatever others are not strong enough to hold onto; and that finally, the armaments necessitated by these inter-State relations themselves become an important contributory cause of war through the fear and distrust they generate and exacerbate in an unending vicious circle. In the past, he says, that was the whole of the matter. Today, owing to the emergence of 'democracy' there is the added factor of the need to manipulate public opinion. Whereas Frederick the Great could simply pounce when he decided the moment was ripe, today when whole peoples are required for enlistment in the military machine, it is politically important to manœuvre for position in such a way as to create a plausible impression that oneself is the victim of aggression and not the aggressor. The strength of Lowes Dickinson's analysis lies in his ability to make clear that war—World War I is his particular example—is caused not by the blunders of statesmen and diplomats but flows from the overall situation existing over a prolonged period both within the separate States and in the nature of their consequent mutual relations. But the sentence in which he states this also reveals the inadequacy in his analysis:

> And unless a real and successful attempt had been made to alter radically both the purposes of Governments and their means of achieving them, the war would have been ultimately precipitated in some other way, even if the crisis of 1914 had been overcome.[1]

---

[1] G. Lowes Dickinson, *War: Its Nature, Cause and Cure*, London 1923, p. 53.

The result clause is impeccable, but the *protasis* in the above sentence reveals the fatal weakness in the inter-war generation's analysis of the cause of war. It reveals the assumption that it is logically possible to 'alter radically' the purposes of Governments and the means they adopt to realize those purposes. It is not so possible. The purposes and logic pursued by all Governments then and now was stated clearly by Thucydides in the argument which he put into the mouth of the Athenian envoy to the threatened Melians:

> But you and we should say what we really think, and aim only at what is possible, for we both alike know that into the discussion of human affairs the question of justice only enters where there is equal power to enforce it, and that the powerful exact what they can, and the weak grant what they must.[1]

It could not be more succinctly put. It is unfortunate that Lowes Dickinson did not understand that. That is the logic which all Governments obey and must obey; and no man can change it. It is not possible to change it because of the intrinsic nature of government and because of the nature of the moral universe in which we all perforce must dwell. The issue of war and peace, I repeat, is a religious question. Brave Bishop Hugh Latimer put it very clearly when he wrote:

> . . . for God will not have it [the Truth] defended by man or man's power, but by His Word only, by which He hath evermore defended it, and that by a way far above man's power and reason.

No government by its very nature ever has or can ever accept the truth of Latimer's statement; for if it did so, it would immediately cease to be a government; it would be ousted by those possessed of insufficient moral and religious insight to understand that all governments are acting *ultra vires*.

As Latimer would appear to have perceived—at least in the above-quoted address—the very heart of true Christian teaching is contained in Christ's injunction to 'resist not evil', but on the contrary to try to do to all alike that which we would wish to have done to ourselves, even to those who persecute us. And the reason why we do not need to fear the consequences of relying unconditionally upon this simple precept is, as Latimer says, that God's Word alone is in truth a

---

[1] *Thucydides*, translation by Benjamin Jowett, second edition, revised, Oxford 1900, Vol. II, p. 169.

A*

sufficient defence of the Truth. The Truth is so uniquely powerful because no other force can vie with it as a means of kindling the human soul. An understanding of this religious truth is, moreover, not only a sure defence against all war; it is the only defence.

At this juncture, it is commonly objected that even if true, obedience to this principle would make impossible demands upon the weakness of our common human nature. Men are simply not brave enough to place their entire reliance on a principle which would deprive them of the right to resort to time-honoured if violent methods of self-defence. It is arrogance, we are assured, to suppose that we can succeed in changing human nature where endless generations of our forefathers have failed to do so. To which I reply that it may be when I am put to the test that I do capitulate to my fears, that my human nature is as weak as so many people are anxious to insist that it is. But if in the event I should prove to be not strong enough to act up to my own highest insights, that is no reason why I should not now and subsequently continue to honour the Truth with my word. And that itself is all that is necessary. However difficult it is to act it out under all circumstances, it is not impossibly difficult to admit that Christ's injunction to *resist not evil* and the conviction that God's Word (if we honour it by giving it utterance) will of itself defend us from evil is the Truth. If it is not the Truth, why is it that after two millennia no one has ever succeeded in demonstrating the invalidity of the proposition. Examples are not easy to find, since most writers of whatever complexion studiously avoid the subject altogether. However, some are brave enough to attempt theoretical justification of well-nigh universal practice—with disastrous results.

First, Trotsky. Who governs in any given State, Trotsky recognizes, is determined not by paragraphs of the constitution, but by the employment of all forms of violence. War, like revolution, is founded upon the intimidatory effects of violence. The quest for power at home or abroad does not necessitate the killing of everybody, only as many as are needed to intimidate the majority who survive. Trotsky then felt compelled to add:

> The State of terror of a revolutionary class can be condemned 'morally' only by a man who, as a principle, rejects (in words) every form of violence whatsoever—consequently, every war and every rising.

But this admission is felt to be too damaging even with the quotation marks and the 'in words' parenthesis. Therefore he adds the following sentence: 'For this one has to be merely and simply a hypocritical Quaker.'[1]

Secondly, Beatrice Webb. She, too, concedes the morality of non-resistance, but immediately adds that she does not, however, believe in it:

> ... there may be morality in refraining from any physical force whatever, whatever the provocation. I don't believe in non-resistance. Physical force does not differ in morality from mental force: both alike are dependent, for their rightness, on the purpose for which they are exercised— is the purpose consistent with love or not? The act of killing may be a manifestation of love. It is only right to add that it usually is not.[2]

The argument that it is morally permissible to resist and kill another person, provided it is done as an act of love, refutes itself. The argument that 'mental force' does not differ in morality from 'physical force' is extremely vague. If it means that a good example acting upon another's conscience is a form of 'mental force' and this does not differ morally from an act of violence to another, the argument is false. The former does not coerce another; the latter does.

Thirdly, J. D. Mabbott. The following argument is not posed directly in the context of 'non-resistance' but it is very close to that argument, in that it purports to show that authorized 'legitimate' coercion is a necessity of the human situation.

> An 'individual' on whom every law is a restriction, an 'individual' who, in the absence of all these laws, would be tempted by all the evils they abolish, yet fall to none, and by his own efforts resist them and so

---

[1] Leon Trotsky, *Terrorism and Communism: A Reply to Karl Kautsky*, University of Michigan Press 1963, pp. 58–9. Trotsky is by no means alone in his need to confine the argument only to 'hypocritical' Quakers. Compare with the above argument that of F. Melian Stawell, Newnham College, Cambridge, in her *The Growth of International Thought* (London 1929, p. 139). She too, attributing the command 'Resist not evil' to Quakers, continues: 'If they countenance the use of force by a government, even though they would not employ it themselves, if they take the benefit of living in an ordered community which relies upon force as a necessary, though dangerous instrument, they are open to the gibe that, like a new and more exasperating sect of Pharisees, they make ready to enter the Kingdom of Heaven through the sins of other men.' If her opponent is not caught in the 'hypocritical Quaker' net, he is sure to be caught in her 'benefit-taking' net, since nowhere on earth is any individual permitted to live outside the State or 'ordered community'.

[2] Diary entry for 28 August 1914 in *Beatrice Webb's Diaries, 1912–1924*, London 1952, p. 30.

strengthen his character and further the good of his community at all these myriad points, such an 'individual' is the ideol of a mythology which makes the hundred-eyed Argus and the hundred-handed Briareus sober biological specimens in comparison.[1]

This would appear to be an oblique way of saying that the morally good man, leading a moral life in the absence of all coercive legislation, does not exist. But even if this dubious proposition were true, the passage seems tacitly to concede a standard of goodness, while at the same time exempting us from the obligation to aspire towards its fulfilment on the grounds that it demands too much of our frail human nature. If we were to make difficulty of fulfilment a test of validity of moral standards, it is hard to believe that the concept of obligation itself would ever have been born.

My plea is not that mankind can overnight change their customary behaviour; only that we should acknowledge that the principle, *Resist not evil*, is morally incontrovertible, as is demonstrated by the endlessly abortive attempts to refute it; and therefore that it is true and morally binding on us to strive to fulfil, however great the difficulties. We may not be capable of becoming heroes; but we are capable of honouring the truth, so plainly indicated by our intellect and heart, with our word. And the Word shall, we will find, suffice. The very depth of the resistance to admitting the truth is indicative of the suspicion that the Word is indeed powerful.

As soon as we consider the issue of war and peace we become aware of an evident paradox, namely, that while wars have succeeded one another with but brief pauses in between throughout history, almost all people at all times are seemingly united in their apparently sincere protestations of their love of peace. As Erasmus put it in his *Querela Pacis* (*The Complaint of Peace*, 1517)

> As peace, am I not praised by both men and gods as the very source and defender of all good things? What is there of prosperity, of security, or of happiness that cannot be ascribed to me? On the other hand, is not war the destroyer of all things and the very seed of evil? What is there of prosperity that it does not infect? What is secure or pleasant that it does not undermine? No greater enemy of goodness or of religion can be found.[2]

But the wars continue just the same. And the reason lies ultimately with the Word—or rather with our failure to give utterance to the

[1] J. D. Mabbott, *The State and the Citizen*, London 1947, p. 70.

[2] *The Essential Erasmus*, translated by John P. Dolan, New American Library 1964, pp. 177-8.

word. We are either dishonest about the issue of war or we deceive ourselves and others or we genuinely fail to understand the nature of the cause. Or perhaps it is that our will to not understand is so great that we genuinely succeed in not understanding. F. Melian Stawell, from whose *The Growth of International Thought* (1929) I have already quoted, may fairly be held to represent characteristic liberal thinking about war and its cause even today. She concludes her survey of the voices from previous generations allegedly contributing to man's developing quest for peace with the following passage:

> As we looked along the perspective of history we saw a succession of isolated thinkers, and heard voices crying in the wilderness, pointing out the right way, but the plain man seemed blind and deaf. Now, at last, there is really an army opening their eyes and listening and asking to be led. Let our statesmen be the leaders.[1]

It would not be possible to get the whole matter more wrong than this. The final invocation to 'our leaders' in its acceptance of our subordination and of the legitimacy of our leaders' will to power is of the very essence of the cause of war. The voices 'crying in the wilderness' were the voices of such people as Aristophanes, Aristotle, Thucydides, Herodotus, Virgil, Cicero, St. Augustine, Dante, Erasmus, More, Grotius, Sully, the Abbé de St. Pierre, Rousseau, Kant, Goethe, Mazzini, Marx. In every case war is denounced as evil and injurious in its consequences, but also in every case, as Melian Stawell herself is aware, the institution of war, the right to make war in certain ill-defined but allegedly appropriate circumstances, is stoutly defended. What is given with one hand is taken back with the other. Limits of space permit me to do no more than illustrate this. Aristotle should perhaps head the list with his celebrated 'we make war for the sake of peace'. Thucydides, one of the world's greatest historians and most lucid prose writers, certainly understood the essence of the nature of the State, as is evident from the above quotation (p. ix) and from the following reflections on the nature of revolution:

> The causes of all these evils was the love of power, originating in avarice and ambition, and the party-spirit which is engendered by them when men are fairly embarked in a contest. For the leaders on either side used specious names, the one party professing to uphold the constitutional equality of the many, the other the wisdom of an aristocracy, while they made the

---

[1] F. Melian Stawell, op. cit., p. 246.

public interests, to which in name they were devoted, in reality their prize. Striving in every way to overcome each other, they committed the most monstrous crimes . . .[1]

But even Thucydides did not dream of renouncing the right to go to war in defence of the national interest. Quite the contrary! And it is the same with Augustine. Augustine shows himself in a justly celebrated passage to be intolerant of the customary double standard which denounces as a crime an act on the part of the subject which is defended as just and necessary when carried out by the 'legitimate' ruler:

> . . . for elegant and excellent was that pirate's answer to the great Macedonian Alexander, who had taken him; the king asking him how he durst molest the seas so, he replied with a free spirit, 'How darest thou molest the whole world? But because I do it with a little ship only, I am called a thief: thou doing it with a great navy, art called an emperor.'[2]

But St. Augustine, so far from questioning the basis of legitimacy of secular rule, held that as a general rule men ought to obey the government and especially so in matters pertaining to war and peace.

Passing to the Renaissance, Erasmus is another who, as we have seen, spoke valiantly for peace. Indeed at one point it really does begin to look as though he meant business when he proposes that those killed in battle should be prohibited burial in consecrated ground. 'Such a prohibition would certainly have an effect on warmongers.' It would indeed, so much so that Erasmus immediately backtracks:

> Of course I am speaking of those wars that Christians conduct among themselves. It is not our intention to condemn those who undertake legitimate war to repel barbarous invasions or defend the common good.[3]

Of course! But infinitely more notorious than Erasmus's humanist genuflections in the direction of peace are those of Martin Luther, the living symbol of the Reformation of a corrupt Christendom. Luther wrote with his customary vigour and clarity and on this occasion impeccably:

> As concerns yourself, you would abide by the Gospel and govern yourself according to Christ's word, gladly turning the other cheek and

---

[1] *Thucydides*, op. cit., Vol. I, p. 243.

[2] St. Augustine, *The City of God*, translated by John Healey, introduction by Ernest Barker, London 1931, Part One, p. 169.

[3] *The Essential Erasmus*, op. cit., p. 195.

letting the mantle go with the coat, when the matter concerned you and your cause.[1]

But on another occasion he wrote that in a just war:

> . . . it is a Christian act and an act of love confidently to kill, rob, and pillage the enemy, and to do everything that can injure him until one has conquered him according to the methods of war. Only, one must beware of sin, not violate wives and virgins.[2]

But when it comes to pure blasphemy, it may well be thought that Goethe should receive the first prize for the verses he bequeathed among his literary remains:

> The angels fought for us and the Right
> They were defeated in every fight;
> . . .
>
> Now it fell out that we beseeched through prayer
> And God was moved to look into the affair.
>
> Spoke the Word of God Incarnate, to whom till now
> The thing has been clear from eternity:
> You ought in no way to deny yourselves,
> You too must behave as the Devil behaves,
> Through every means till victory is won
> Then sing a *Te Deum* thereupon.[3]

Voices such as these cried in no wilderness. They served only to confuse still further the moral conscience of mankind and thus make men more pliable and more submissive to the requirements of those wielding power over them. It would have been a great mercy had the plain man been 'blind and deaf' to these voices. Unfortunately time and again he was, despite a persistent and saving scepticism, deceived by them to turn his hand against his fellows. What does emerge from 'the perspective of history' is an enormously pervasive and deep-seated resistance to the idea that the precept 'Resist not evil' is to be taken seriously.

With virtual unanimity all the great thinkers of the Western world from the classical Greeks right down to our own immediate contemporaries, although claiming to be seriously concerned about war

---

[1] *Martin Luther: Selections from his Writings*, edited by John Dillenberger, New York 1961, p. 375.

[2] Ibid., p. 398.

[3] *Goethe's Werke*, Weimar 1893, Vol. 5 (Erste Abtheilung), *Nachlass*, p. 139.

and its cause, do not appear to consider their own ignoring or rejection of the principle that it is wrong to *resist* evil to be at all relevant. Why is this? Why, since no one can refute this principle, should people not concede that it is both true and crucially important, and then go on to analyse as realistically as they wish the actual behaviour of errant men? Why can people not be morally honest and at least preserve their intellectual self-respect? The reason is that the injunction to *resist not evil* cuts the ground away from under the legitimacy of the human will to power. So much so that anyone wishing to discuss the principle, *resist not evil*, seriously is at best relegated to the monastic cloister, metaphorically speaking. Such a person, it is implied, cannot on that account alone have anything responsible to offer to men of responsible judgement who have to take the affairs of the real world seriously. Religion is all very fine; but politics have to go on, and they cannot be left to purists who lack judgement. This is of course a convenient dichotomy; but it is not one that we should be prepared to concede. Because my position is a religious position, that does not mean that I am willing to acquiesce in my excommunication from the realm of political analysis and criticism. There are not two separate realms wherein dwell politicians, soldiers, men of affairs on the one hand, and on the other the *réligieux*, the moralists, the pietists, the monastics. There is one realm only—the one in which we all perforce must dwell, and where every single individual's contribution adds to the true welfare of men or inflicts injury on that welfare, according to his values and the direction of his striving.

The way in which the idea is disseminated that the absolutist moral position incapacitates a man for responsible discussion of public affairs is so subtle that it is scarcely even noticed. For two millennia and more men have discussed political theory as a subject of profound human concern—which it is. But the definition of the central subject matter is rarely, if ever, questioned. It is assumed that this is the problem of the nature of political obligation, or why and under what circumstances men ought to obey the law of the State. From this central definition which is unchallenged from Plato to Marx there then follow a large number of questions concerning the nature and limits of freedom, the basis of legitimacy of power according to theories of authority, contract, utility, consent, and in our time, with the positivists riding high, the further epistemological question as to whether this entire historic debate has in truth ever had any objective rational basis. What is scarcely ever made clear is that this choice and definition of subject matter flows from certain assumptions, which are far from self-evident, about the relative importance attaching to human problems.

Merely to suggest that it is important to study the problem of what conditions render political obedience legitimate has already set the stage and pointed the way towards a certain kind of discussion. This definition of the subject implies that it is important to discover the conditions the absence of which might leave us with an inadequate sense of political obligation. The unstated basis of the entire discussion is man's need for the protection of law enforcement which organized sovereign States alone make possible. From this way of defining priorities, we might reasonably infer that the greatest danger confronting mankind is the condition of anarchy or absence of government and a system of law enforcement. Yet, when we look around us, we find that so far from this being a great and pressing danger, nowhere on earth are men allowed to live or to try to live in this way. It would no doubt be retorted that this is because men everywhere are determined to prevent such an occurrence because the consequences would be catastrophic to everyone. Nevertheless, whatever the truth of this reasoning, the fact is that this alleged danger of men not living in States—of men without a country, in fact—is not an actual danger; it is at worst but a hypothetical danger, since nowhere does it actually exist. Indeed, if even a handful of men try to conduct their own affairs on a non-coercive basis even on a submerged coral reef which they have themselves reclaimed from the South Pacific—to quote a recent example—the attempt is immediately forcibly extinguished.

So it would appear that the traditional manner of defining the central subject matter of political theory reflects a curious choice of priorities. It is not as if we were short of actual problems that we can afford the luxury of devoting so much effort to purely hypothetical problems.

We have and always have had on our hands one very big problem, one that is not at all hypothetical, and one, moreover, that now threatens the life of mankind itself. I refer to the problem of war. So it seemed to me important that I should begin my subject by defining its point of reference or sheet-anchor, not as the problem of political obligation but as the problem of what causes war. The subject matter is still political theory, but defined in such a way as to shift the main axis of enquiry and the focal point of interest. We then find that we are no longer preoccupied with what *might* happen if we did not have order secured by law enforcement, but with what has happened and is happening to cause men to slaughter one another by the million. The centre of such an enquiry is still the nature of political power, but power now appears in a rather different light, one not of beneficence but of ominous menace.

Political theory as traditionally oriented in terms of the problem of political obligation leads straight to all the great names mentioned above, who, whatever they have to say about why we should obey the laws of the State, are at one in returning ambiguous or self-contradictory answers to the question of man's right to resort to violence. Political theory, oriented (as I have suggested) in the light not of man's hypothetical dangers but in the light of his actual and urgently pressing danger in the shape of war, leads straight to one thinker, who dwarfs all others by the clarity and cogency of his wholly unambiguous reasoning. I refer to Tolstoy, who says quite simply: 'Resist not evil under all circumstances, come what may.' His great strength derives partly from the impregnability of the ground on which he takes his stand, but also from the immensity of the inner struggle he has had to undergo in order to reach his final ground. For no one was more of the world, flesh of its flesh, bone of its bone than Tolstoy. No one has ever rivalled him in his capacity for accurate description of every facet of our actual lives mirrored in history, in the struggle for power, in diplomacy and war, in family conflict, in human passion, in conflict with Nature herself. Tolstoy, I repeat, was of the world, one of the world's natural princes. He was no ascetic. But all his life he pursued with extraordinary tenacity and single-mindedness one aim which possessed him as nothing else possessed him, the desire to find the Truth. Given the nature of the man, this quest led, as it could only lead, to a titanic conflict of the spirit which shook Tolstoy and nearly struck him down at the age of fifty. He emerged finally tranquil and unscathed with a capacity to write and apply what he had learnt with unexampled strength and lucidity.

My purpose in this book is with political theory in the particular context of war and its cause. To this end I have sought (*a*) to trace the seeds of Tolstoy's conflict concerning the nature and role of power in human affairs and in particular as it manifests itself in *War and Peace*, and (*b*) to examine the sources in European thought out of which Tolstoy emerged or rather out of which Tolstoy's unique contribution to our understanding of the cause of war emerged. Tolstoy emerged slowly and painfully not only out of his own inner conflict but also out of a slowly developing tradition of European thought which was already there and which would have continued to develop had Tolstoy never lived. Tolstoy inherited this tradition, assimilated it, shaped it anew and bequeathed it to us stamped with the authority of his invincible integrity. The central message itself, as he himself insisted over and over again, is simply the injunction of Christ of the Gospels—resist not evil, return good for evil. But it comes to us afresh with all the force of life newly discovered, because it is born out of and based upon an exhaustive description and ruthlessly penetrating analysis of our existing culture. Tolstoy is a supreme realist—the greatest of all the empiricists: that is why he is overwhelmingly convincing to any genuinely open mind. The moral absolutism of such a man is no paradox, still less a contradiction. The absolutism flows naturally from the nature of the preceding account of our politico-historical reality. The absolute nature of the moral imperative to resist not Power and to obey it not, formulates itself spontaneously as a result of the historical portrait of Power, unrivalled in its wealth of significant detail, combined with a rigorous theoretical analysis of the nature of Power. Power, Tolstoy's evidence and reasoning compel the conclusion, is incontrovertibly the great source of evil, from which men can only free themselves by not being deceived by it and by overcoming the impulse to it within themselves.

In my view Tolstoy is supreme in his role as moral and political thinker when he is expositing and arguing his case in such works as *The Kingdom of God Is Within You*, *What Then Must We Do?*, *What Is Art?*, and in innumerable short essays and pamphlets. But through his art he reaches a much wider audience than cogent argument alone can ever hope to reach. Moreover, in his art he possesses himself of a weapon which he can when he chooses use with the devastation of a sledge-hammer to demolish a false argument. I will confine myself to a single instance. Although hardly in vogue today, an argument which achieved widespread currency in the nineteenth century was that which emphasized the poetry of warfare.[1] Proudhon for example argued that

[1] For an example of the false romanticization of warfare, see Prosper Mérimée's celebrated short story of the taking of the Shevardino Redoubt from the Russians by the French. The horror of the carnage and the futile torture and suffering are heavily muted, all the emphasis falling on the glory of the heroic sacrifice. After the attack, so heavy have been the casualties that the Colonel hands over the command to the Lieutenant, newly arrived from his Fontainebleau cadet college. 'You are severely wounded, then, Colonel?' 'Done for, dear fellow, but the redoubt is taken!' (*Nouvelles Complètes*, Édition Gallimard 1964, Vol. I, p. 48.)

it was the necessary basis of every epic and of all great Art from Homer onwards. Life, it was implied, would be the poorer without the romance, the glory, the poetry of war. In Tolstoy's *Hadji Murad*, Butler, a young officer in Circassian costume on active service in the Caucasus, is very much taken up with the poetry of warfare; he responds with his every nerve tingling to the invigorating air of the mountains, the excitement of the forays, the splendour of the uniforms, the conviviality of his comrades in arms in wine and song, the emotions aroused in him by Marya Dmitrievna's kindly gaze and shapely figure. Hadji Murad himself had especially impressed Butler with the nobility of his simple dignity, his reserve, his instinctive courtliness of manner, his fearless intrepidity as a warrior. Then quite suddenly, the reader being as wholly unprepared for the event as is Butler himself, a Cossack rides up, dismounts, takes a sack out of his saddle-bag, and in the light of the moon lifts up a man's head:

> It was a shaven head with salient brows, black short-cut beard and moustaches, one eye open and the other half-closed. The shaven skull was cleft, but not right through, and there was congealed blood in the nose. The neck was wrapped in a blood-stained towel. Notwithstanding the many wounds on the head, the blue lips still bore a kindly child-like expression.[1]

It was the head of Hadji Murad, whom so recently Butler had responded to with warmth and admiration. Marya Dmitrievna, who was also present, turned quickly away; and Butler could on this occasion find no reassurance for his uneasiness of soul in her company.

> 'War? War, indeed! . . . Cut-throats and nothing else. A dead body should be given back to the earth, and they're grinning at it there! . . . Cut-throats, really', she repeated, . . .[2]

Tolstoy's total rejection of war of any kind sprang from his intimate knowledge of it based on first-hand experience; and his rejection rested upon an entire metaphysic which revealed very clearly the antithesis between the forces of love and of power. This book concerns itself with how Tolstoy came finally after great inward turmoil to a conscious realization of this truth. But it is also concerned to trace the genesis of Tolstoy's understanding of the moral universe, oriented in particular in his understanding of the true significance of the

---

[1] Tolstoy, *Ivan Ilych and Hadji Murad*, World's Classics 1951 ed., p. 372.
[2] Ibid., p. 374.

phenomenon of war. The latter qualification is important, since a literary attempt to disentangle the different sources of influence on Tolstoy's total thought would involve an enterprise of vastly greater proportion than is contemplated here. It would involve an extensive study of Rousseau, to begin with, an enquiry into Rousseau's debt to Richardson; it would involve a study of Voltaire's influence also; of Sterne and Schiller, of Pushkin and Gogol; of Schopenhauer, too, although Tolstoy ultimately found his deterministic pessimism profoundly repugnant. It would involve above all an extensive study of Russian pan-Slavism and of innumerable religious sects actively animating Russian peasant life, with their roots deep in the Russian and wider Slavonic past. The subject of this book is not how Tolstoy came to be possible, fascinating though such a study would be. It is more limited in that it concerns itself with one aspect of Tolstoy's thought, although a fundamental one. But this more limited aspect represents a basic problem for the whole of mankind—the problem of war and its causation.

I have confined myself to a study of four of Tolstoy's predecessors—de Maistre, Stendhal, Herzen and Proudhon. I went to them originally because I learned from Tolstoy's biography and his own acknowledgements that he must have been to some degree influenced by these writers, all of them very different from him and in the case of de Maistre at the opposite pole of the moral and political spectrum. In fairness to them I should point out that it is not my intention to present a balanced study of those writers' thought in its totality; I have striven only to show that from the specific standpoint of the problem of war and its cause, there emerges through the writings of these men a new and vitally important tradition in European thought, one, moreover, which has not hitherto been adequately appreciated, if it has been appreciated at all. I am not of course suggesting that together they constitute a literary school or even a political tradition. With the exception of Proudhon, all the above-mentioned writers found de Maistre deeply repugnant, but de Maistre is important if only in provoking this reaction. Proudhon reacted to de Maistre ostensibly with great respect, but the conclusions that emerged from the intellectual ferment started by de Maistre were the antithesis of de Maistre's own. I know of no evidence that Herzen reacted in any way to Stendhal; Proudhon, who openly expressed his contempt for all fiction as a vehicle for serious thought, is very unlikely even to have read him. Proudhon, the Franche-Comté peasant and artisan, was a comparatively close friend of the Russian aristocrat in exile, Herzen; but despite their strong political sympathies, Herzen found Proudhon's bleak and austere worship of an abstract Justice ultimately repellent. Tolstoy alone lived at a time which enabled him to know the work of all these writers (although, it might be noted in passing that Herzen lived just long enough to be able to read *War and Peace*, to which he did not warm). Tolstoy found de Maistre's religious and political philosophy basically inimical; he greatly admired Stendhal's art as expressed in his two best-known works, but found Stendhal's unrepentant libertinism and its philosophic implications deeply repugnant; he admired both Herzen and Proudhon, but rejected Herzen's sybaritism and socialism and Proudhon's anti-Chrisian deification of Justice.

In short, there are great and important differences in the lives and values of all these men. But when all this has been said, they represent a new tradition of ruthless and honest analysis of our common culture; one by one they strip it of layer after layer of the humbug and the accretions of falsehood of generations, until finally with Tolstoy, after seismographic spiritual convulsions, there emerges an entirely new and original radical force in European and indeed world culture. For Tolstoy is more truly a world figure than any of the others, even Stendhal and Proudhon.

As is shown in the following chapters, the events of 1812 in particular assumed large proportions in subsequent generations; and this is reflected in the lives and writings of all the authors I shall discuss. Just as in our time six years of warfare culminated in a new dimension of horror at Hiroshima, so the years of intermittent campaigning under Napoleon culminated in the slaughter of Borodino, something on a scale larger and more intense than anything that had preceded it. Men slowly began to think more profoundly about the moral significance and human implications of warfare; and with the passage of the years, as war continued to wreak its havoc and technology made its ever more sinister contribution, the sense of deep foreboding grew among the more sensitive spirits.

De Maistre, it is true, professes to see nothing wrong in warfare, which he sees as a necessary instrument of Providence. He would have endorsed every word of Luther's opinion that war 'is in itself Godlike, and as natural and necessary to the world as eating and drinking'. But his observations on the paradoxical nature of humanity's reactions to the roles of the executioner and of the soldier respectively inevitably arouse criticism of the military function as such, even though de

Maistre disavows such an intention. Again, although he sees sovereign power as of divine origin, he also observes that sovereign power is impotent in the face of a hostile public opinion; and also that military power in particular is peculiarly dependent on the morale of the fighting man in the ranks.

This picture is unequivocally confirmed by Stendhal, who adds a totally new dimension by the ruthlessness of his probing and dissecting the world of political power both at the provincial and national levels. Moreover, he shrewdly discerns that the only genuine threat to the power world is to be found in the lonely individual, who spurns the defences of the organized party man, and who is correspondingly free to honour the Word, as revealed to him through a conscientious love of the truth.

If Herzen concerns himself less directly with the issue of war, he is unrivalled in the mastery with which he lays bare the morbidity of inequality. In the Russia of his portrait all human relations are twisted and ultimately sacrificed on the altar of social status or official position. Existing institutions are symptoms of this pathology even in the West, masks which proffer a façade of apparent choice and rational consent, but which conceal a reality of the monopoly of power by a corrupt and exploitative ruling minority. Herzen's writing is generally pessimistic in tone and heavy with the gloom of insight into his long-term prognosis of Western culture. On the other hand, his ear is never quite deaf to the spirit of love elusive of the controls of all secular power, but which for Herzen is a nostalgic yearning for the past embodied in the spirit of the *Quartier Latin* of the Middle Ages and of the Christ of the Gospels whom he knew as a child. To the future he looks for socialism but without real conviction.

With Proudhon the phenomenon of war returns to the centre of the stage. With immense energy Proudhon touches life at every point, but he sees quite clearly that the duality of war and peace is at the heart of man's interpretation of his world. Ostensibly because of its terrible destructive power due to the emergence of modern weaponry, Proudhon is anxious to put an end to war. But he is impatient of those who fail to understand that our whole existing way of life is itself a form of war, and that therefore war cannot and will not be abolished by those who remain irretrievably wedded to our inegalitarian culture, however sincerely they profess their attachment to the cause of peace. Proudhon develops the insights of de Maistre (whom he greatly respects) to illustrate the illusory nature of political power which derives its sole reality from the sovereign force generated by the dependence of so many individuals for their identity on their membership of a collective group such as the nation. In order to abolish it, it will prove necessary not only to abolish the widespread and very ancient popular belief in the right of conquest, that is to say, the moral right of force, it will also be necessary to liberate the individual from dependence upon the collectivity for his identity so that he becomes able to say 'No' to Power.

The fusion of all these separate strands of thought in the Tolstoyan synthesis is the central subject matter of this book; and nothing would be served by anticipating it here. Suffice it to say that Tolstoy's total, radical rejection of war, when it emerges from the profound inner spiritual crisis of his middle years, would not have been possible nor would it have taken the course it did if Tolstoy had been solely a religious thinker. Tolstoy's stand against war, the basis of his entire ideological position is, it is true, religious. It is Tolstoy's central contention that no other position is possible for a rational man—for Tolstoy is in this sense purely rationalist. No one is less of a mystic or more impatient with mysticism than he. But he only arrives at his rational, religious conclusion as a result of an analysis of the nature of power as it operates in our culture far more penetrating than that of either Herzen or Proudhon, and more richly illustrated in historical and sociological terms than even Stendhal had furnished. Tolstoy arrives at last at the Kingdom of God within us only after the long and anguished struggle laid bare implicitly in *War and Peace* and summarized explicitly in his *Confession*.

If we are to abolish war—and there can no longer be any *if* about it, we have got to do so—then Tolstoy's heroic stand, which led directly and inevitably to the final agony of his flight into the unknown, must be our starting point.

The Discovery of Peace

I

Introduction

My subject is peace and the discovery of peace or, to express the same thing negatively, my subject is war and the cause of war. The pity of war, the terror of war, the horror of war—these things have by now been vividly brought home to men, although even now not all men understand these things. Nightmare has been piled on nightmare in an ever-growing crescendo of horror. The vast majority of mankind loathe and condemn war. That this however is not enough is evidenced by the continuance of war and the unabated preparations on a world-wide scale for yet another war which would inevitably dwarf even previous cataclysms. In order to put an end to war it is necessary to face up to the central cause of war without flinching, and this men are very reluctant indeed to do—notwithstanding their genuine fear and detestation of war and its consequences. They are reluctant to do so because the cause of war is intimately and vitally related to the conduct of peace. Indeed war is the natural fruit of the way in which communities conduct their normal lives in a state of what is called peace, by which is meant no more than the present and temporary absence of war. War and peace are bound together in a seemingly remorseless, unbreakable dialectic, exercising a perennially sinister hold over and fascination for the minds of men.

So, in order to study why we do war, we must study also how we do peace. But we are so deeply attached to the way we customarily do peace, so inherently wedded to our traditional ways of doing things that we do not extend a ready welcome to those who would disturb our complacency by probing critically into deeply rooted existing habits. Some, it is true, driven by dire forebodings, try to arouse their fellows to a sense of the urgency of the situation. Yet the paradox remains that although war is the most ancient of man's enemies and although it now bids fair to exterminate civilization itself, among the hosts of books appearing annually on every conceivable subject, there are hardly any books which attempt to take an honest look at the causes of war.

To all genuinely responsible people living today in the aftermath of two world wars and under the shadow of the continuing arms race, consuming the world's resources at the rate of over $159,000 million a year, it is a matter of inescapable importance to consider the connection between peace and war. In the comparative dearth of literature in this crucial field, one title immediately comes to mind, and it is called *War and Peace*. It is a book that happens to be generally acclaimed as the world's greatest novel. It would be odd indeed if a book on such a theme by a man of Tolstoy's stature were not directly relevant. In fact, what Tolstoy has to say on the issue—and he has a great deal to say— he himself believed to be the heart of his vast masterpiece and his principal reason for undertaking the task. Yet from the moment the book made its appearance more than a century ago, critics and commentators, while acclaiming the book as a literary masterpeice, have all alike either ignored entirely Tolstoy's contribution to the philosophy of history, that determines the shape, structure and arrangement of the book as well as being its *leitmotiv*, or else they have deplored the fact that Tolstoy chose to meddle in matters which he allegedly did not understand instead of sticking to his *métier*. Sir Isaiah Berlin in *The Hedgehog and the Fox* went out of his way to draw attention to this singular fact and documented it with a considerable number of examples from Flaubert and Turgenev onwards. One might have thought that Berlin's purpose in doing this would be to remedy the anomaly by devoting to Tolstoy's contribution to a problem so crucial as the cause of war (and of peace) the serious critical attention which it demands. Not a bit of it! Having drawn our attention to the world's peculiar silence in the presence of Tolstoy's message, Berlin himself maintains the tradition intact. Indeed, he states this as his intention at the outset. His essay, he tells us, 'is an attempt to take Tolstoy's attitude to history as seriously as he himself meant his readers to take it, although for a somewhat different reason—for the light it casts on a single man of genius rather than on the fate of all mankind'.[1] The 'somewhat different reason' is of course crucial. I do not wish to suggest that there was a conscious *intention* to disparage or patronize, but it is impossible to avoid that *effect* if we announce that we are prepared to take seriously a man's contribution to a very grave problem for the light it allegedly throws on the author but not for the light it was the author's intention to throw upon the problem itself.

Of comparable significance to the refusal to consider seriously Tolstoy's contribution to thought is the parallel neglect of the book

[1] Isaiah Berlin, *The Hedgehog and the Fox*, London 1967 ed., p. 4.

which almost certainly inspired Tolstoy's own choice of title and quite certainly contributed to the philosophy informing the novel. I refer of course to Proudhon's *La Guerre et la Paix*, which appeared in 1861, the year in which Tolstoy had met Proudhon in Brussels, and the year before Tolstoy embarked upon his own *War and Peace*. Berlin disposes of Proudhon's *La Guerre et la Paix* in a footnote,[1] since he is avowedly not interested in Tolstoy's contribution to our understanding of 'the fate of all mankind', only in Tolstoy himself. The impression made by Proudhon's own book has been such that no one has ever bothered even to translate the work into English. And this again is surely not without significance when we consider the vital importance of the subject under discussion, the relative dearth of useful contributions, and the widely appreciated knowledge of the originality, depth and power of penetration of Proudhon's intellect.

When Tolstoy visited Proudhon in Brussels, he did so with an introduction from a friend of Proudhon, Alexander Herzen, the Russian exile living in London, at whose house in Wimbledon Tolstoy himself had been a visitor during his fortnight's stay in England prior to journeying to Belgium. While Tolstoy and Herzen had a considerable mutual respect for one another, there is little ground for suggesting that Tolstoy was seriously influenced by the older man. Herzen lived long enough to read Tolstoy's *War and Peace*, and his comments were somewhat acid, while Tolstoy disapproved strongly, as might be expected, of Herzen's sybaritic way of life. Although on other occasions he expressed his appreciation of Herzen's great qualities as a writer, in his essay, *The First Step* (1892), Tolstoy has this to say of Ogaryev and Herzen:

> I knew Ogaryev and Herzen themselves, and others of that stamp, and men educated in the same traditions. There was a remarkable absence of consistency in the lives of all these men. Together with a sincere and ardent wish for good there was an utter looseness of personal desire, which they thought could not hinder the living of a good life nor the performance of good and even great deeds. They put unkneaded loaves into a cold oven and believed that bread would be baked. And then, when with advancing years they began to notice that the bread did not bake— i.e. that no good came of their lives—they saw in this something peculiarly tragic. And the tragedy of such lives is indeed terrible. . . . The majority of men of the present day, like Ogaryev, Herzen and others fifty years ago,

---

[1] '. . . it is difficult to find anything specifically Proudhonist in Tolstoy's *War and Peace*, besides the title.' Ibid., p. 59n.

are persuaded that to lead an effeminate life, to eat sweet and rich foods, to delight themselves in every way and satisfy all their desires, does not hinder them from living a good life. But as it is evident that a good life in their case does not result, they give themselves up to pessimism, and say, 'Such is the tragedy of human life.'[1]

This criticism of Herzen, if astringent, is nevertheless just, although we should not forget the courage and great sacrifice made by Herzen when, no more than a student, he incurred the displeasure of the Tsar. At the same time, Herzen was a writer of very unusual literary gifts and possessed of exceptional insight into the human condition. He too has something to contribute to our insight into the problem of war and its cause, and I shall consider the evidence in due course.

If Tolstoy is on occasion capable of being less than warm to Herzen, there is one in particular to whom he acknowledged his indebtedness with genuine enthusiasm, and this in the very matter of his knowledge of war. I refer to Stendhal. In a conversation with Paul Boyer, Professor of Russian in the University of Paris, on 30 July 1901 at Yasnaya Polyana[2] Tolstoy stated that he knew what he owed to others: 'I know it and I say it; to others, to two in particular: Rousseau and Stendhal.' The subject that they were discussing was French literature in the nineteenth century and the role of literary criticism. After expressing his admiration for Stendhal, Balzac, Flaubert, Zola (before *Dr Pascal*, of which Tolstoy disapproved) and the Journal of the Goncourts, Tolstoy went on to castigate the type of literary criticism which traces a kind of literary genetic succession in which Flaubert derives from Balzac, Balzac from Stendhal and so on. 'Geniuses', he observed, 'do not proceed one from another: geniuses are born independent, always.' None of which, he hastened to add, meant that he himself was unaware of or reluctant to acknowledge his own literary debts. Of Stendhal he had this to say:

Stendhal? I want to see in him only the author of the *Chartreuse de Parme* and of *Le Rouge et le Noir*; we have there two incomparable masterpieces. And to him more than any other I am indebted: to him I owe it that I learnt to understand war. Read over again in *La Chartreuse de Parme* the account of the battle of Waterloo. Who before him had described war like

---

1 Leo Tolstoy, *Recollections and Essays*, World's Classics 1952 ed., pp. 105–106.

2 Recorded by Boyer in his *Chez Tolstoi: Entretiens à Iasnaia Poliana*, Paris 1950, pp. 39–40.

that, that is to say, as it really is? Do you remember Fabrice crossing the battle-field without understanding 'anything at all' and how smartly the hussars whisk him (*le font passer*) over the croup of his horse, of his handsome 'general's horse'? Later, in the Caucasus, my brother, an officer before me, confirmed for me the truth of those descriptions of Stendhal; he adored war, but was not one of those naïve people who believe in the bridge of Arcola. 'All that,' he told me, 'is braggadoccio (*panache*)! And there is no bravado in war.' A very short time later, in the Crimea, I had only to look to see with my own eyes. But, I repeat, for all that I know of war, my first master is Stendhal.

And it is thus, comments Boyer, that speaks the man who wrote *War and Peace*!

Rousseau's influence on Tolstoy in his formative years was very great; he himself tells us he made a positive cult of Rousseau, even going so far as to wear a medallion of Jean Jacques round his neck at the age of fifteen. Parts of Rousseau, particularly of the Confession of the Savoyard vicar, it is hard to believe did not proceed from Tolstoy's own pen. Nevertheless, despite Rousseau's own far-sighted preoccupation with the menace of war, his admiration for the Abbé de Saint Pierre's *Project of Perpetual Peace*, his influence on Kant's own *Perpetual Peace*, his realization of the futility of approaching existing governments with proposals for the rational conduct of international relations, his predilection for popular control and federalist organization, despite all these things Rousseau is still not of our time in the sense that the other writers to whom I have referred are. He is a great precursor; he is certainly relevant; but he does not speak directly to our problem of war in our own language in a way that the others do. The reason is, I think, that like Kant, he is eighteenth-century, that is to say, pre-Napoleonic. For the Corsican general changed the face of Europe disastrously—and enduringly. The essential laws of war may not change, but to be recognizably of our time, to be of the idiom, the appropriate dimension, one must have experienced the effects of universal military conscription in the service of rampant nationalism.

If therefore we leave Rousseau out of the reckoning, we have yet one other writer of the first order of importance to our study to introduce, and that one at first sight the last to be anticipated in the context of Rousseau and Tolstoy. I refer to Joseph de Maistre, the arch-reactionary of the European aristocracy in the first two decades of the nineteenth century. He was widely read and widely influential; he is referred to frequently in the writings of Stendhal, Proudhon and

Tolstoy himself. During his work on *War and Peace*, Tolstoy wrote[1] while in Moscow on 7 December 1864 to Peter Ivanovich Bartenev, historian and founder of the journal, *Russian Archives*, which he edited down to his death in 1912, asking him to send copies of the *Archives* for that year, which were directly relevant to 1812 and also for de Maistre's *Correspondance diplomatique* (1811–1817) and *Les Soirées de St. Petersbourg*.

It will be noted that all the writers mentioned above, with the single exception of Proudhon, have an emotionally significant connection with 1812. For Tolstoy it was the climax to his own greatest work of art. For Herzen, it was the scene and time of his birth, when he was left behind in the blazing city of the Muscovites as a new-born babe, and was extremely lucky not to have perished of starvation, if not at the hands of marauding troops. Stendhal was an officer serving in the *Grande Armée* and, sharing in the hardships of Napoleon's catastrophic campaign, found himself wintering in Moscow in 1812. De Maistre was not actually in Moscow, but as plenipotentiary of the King of Sardinia at the court of Tsar Alexander he spent 1812 and the years immediately following in St. Petersburg, thus enjoying a grandstand view of the diplomatic and military manœuvres taking place at the highest level behind the scenes in the conduct of the war.

1812 is after all perhaps the single most fitting symbol of the entry upon a new and terrible epoch. 1789 symbolized the fall of feudalism and the admission of all men to the status of citizenship. It heralded however neither liberty nor fraternity nor in the end equality for the simple reason that the principle of universal civic responsibility made possible for the first time universal military conscription. This in itself unleashed hitherto undreamed-of reservoirs of military and therefore political power. Henceforward, quite literally, whole nations would be harnessed to more and more unlimited struggles for power with ever-increasing carnage. The revolution inaugurated by Rousseau's novel theory of sovereignty ended in spawning the monster Napoleon, and the year 1812 inaugurated the era of genuinely national warfare. Increasingly, a military context involving personal skill, initiative, speed and courage was to be replaced by the logistics of organization and the capacity to mobilize at a given place and time the greatest quantities of death-dealing machinery, operated by men whose own function was increasingly that of fodder for the cannon. The battle of

[1] Tolstoy, *Polnoe Sobranie Sochinenii (Complete Collected Works)*, Russian Jubilee Edition, Moscow 1953, Vol. 61, p. 61.

Borodino which immediately preceded the occupation of Moscow by the French in September 1812 was the scene of previously unparalleled slaughter. 'The most terrible of all my battles' Napoleon himself called it. In a single day the French suffered some 30,000 casualties and the Russians 43,000. The most terrifying of all the scenes through which Tolstoy presents the kaleidoscope of Borodino is that in which Prince Andrew Bolkonski waits inactively, helplessly hour after hour in the bombardment zone before finally receiving his mortal wound. Tolstoy describes this new-style warfare as follows:

> All their rushing and galloping at one another did little harm, the harm of disablement and death was caused by the balls and bullets that flew over the fields on which these men were floundering about. As soon as they left the place where the balls and bullets were flying about, their superiors, located in the background, re-formed them and brought them under discipline, and under the influence of that discipline led them back to the zone of fire, where under the influence of fear of death they lost their discipline and rushed about according to the chance promptings of the throng.[1]

As such an era of mechanized slaughter was inaugurated and symbolized by the charnel house of Borodino, it was inevitable that sooner or later men's attitudes towards the previously hallowed and ancient institution of war would begin to show some signs of modification. A re-evaluation of war is a slow but vital development of the nineteenth century in Europe. If the greatest of Russian poets proved altogether too sanguine, it is nevertheless an important augury of new stirrings of the human conscience that already in 1821 Pushkin looked forward to an era when war would be no more.

> It is impossible that in time people would not come to recognize the ridiculous cruelty of war, in the same way as they have come to recognize the true nature of slavery, of Tsarist power, etc. They will realize that our destiny is to eat, drink and be free.

And again:

> Since a constitution is already a great step in human consciousness and since this step will not be the only one, it is bound to arouse a desire for a decrease in the numbers of armies in states, for the principle of armed force is directly opposed to any constitutional idea. It is therefore possible that in less than a hundred years from now there will be no more regular armies.[2]

---

[1] Tolstoy, *War and Peace*, London 1943 ed., pp. 885–6.
[2] David Magarshak, *Pushkin*, London 1967, pp. 120–1.

2

Joseph de Maistre
'plus papist que le pape'

It would not be easy to think of a writer likely to inspire greater distaste in Tolstoy than de Maistre; yet there is a structural resemblance between de Maistre's belief in a divine Providence guiding the general direction of historical events irrespective of the will of individual protagonists whom men regard as all-powerful, and the philosophy of history which Tolstoy espoused at the time of writing *War and Peace*. De Maistre in religious, philosophical and political outlook was everything which Tolstoy was not. More than any other modern writer he evokes the image of Machiavelli whom he resembled in the single-minded determination with which he pursued diplomatic office. From this vantage point he could observe at first hand the negotiations and intrigues inseparable from political and military power without himself being directly involved at the level of those bearing primary responsibility. As Machiavelli was Secretary to the Council of Ten at Florence for fourteen years from 1498 to 1512, the Comte de Maistre held office at St. Petersburg as ambassador at the court of Alexander for thirteen years from 1803 (appointed 1802) to 1815, when he returned to Savoy. Both share that rare quality of being able and willing to describe truthfully those aspects of reality which by their squalor, degradation, cruelty or horror do not commonly invite close or honest scrutiny except by those anxious to expose the conditions in order to abolish them. Reformers, radicals or revolutionaries, we expect to draw attention to and depict realistically the world's ills; conservatives and defenders of the *status quo* are not commonly quite so eager to draw attention to the abscesses suppurating in the body politic. Yet both Machiavelli and de Maistre do just this.

Machiavelli in particular does it so effectively, laying bare the bone with the precision of a surgeon and with the destructive quality of vitriol, that critics like Rousseau have concluded that he must be considered essentially as a satirist. Similar emotions and doubts arise in us in reading some of the passages in which de Maistre describes for example the phenomenon of war and speculates as to why men do it. But in his case as in that of Machiavelli, the intent is not at all satirical—we are not being invited to the pillory to execrate our morbid pathology—quite the contrary! The acid realism of the description is an antecedent not to denunciation but to approval. What radicals lament and revile, what the majority, busily minding their own business, avoid looking at, the Machiavellis and de Maistres zestfully expose to view in order unabashed to teach us to accept and even revere.

Although de Maistre himself attached great importance to blood and lineage, having exalted notions of his own descent from a Languedoc line, the facts suggest a steady ascent from humble and obscure origins: muleteers, then millers, then drapers, then Joseph's grandfather studied law at Turin and aspired to the magistracy, a coat of arms and a family crest, while Joseph's father rose from membership of the Savoy Senate at Chambéry to the Presidency of that august body, and was finally made a Count. He was described as 'rather surly', a man who 'did not laugh, not even with his children'. Joseph himself described his own childhood approvingly as one that was 'reared in all the ancient severity, immersed from the cradle in serious studies'. The critical note which is markedly absent in the son's account of the father's regimen appears however in a revealing comment by the grandson concerning his father's childhood. 'When the time for study marked the end of recreation, [he] appeared on the step of the garden gate without saying a word and he took pleasure in seeing the toys fall from his son's hands, without allowing him even one last throw of the ball or shuttlecock.'[1]

In short, Joseph's father enjoyed his magisterial role, a role he did not confine to the public courts. He was a man who inspired fear in others and in children in particular. Joseph's mother, who was all the more important to him in view of his father's severity, died while still young. A pious woman, who learnt to school her emotions so as not to reveal her feelings, entirely given up to the care of her family, she is said to have evinced for 'Joson', her eldest child, an 'especial friendship', which was reciprocated by Joson in pathetically but understandably hyperbolic terms. Joseph spoke of his 'sublime mother' as 'an angel to whom God had lent a body'. The boy's outstanding characteristic as a child brought up in a severely authoritarian atmosphere was one of obedience, or as his son, Rodolphe, expressed it, 'a

[1] Robert Triomphe, *Joseph de Maistre: Étude sur la Vie et sur la Doctrine d'un Matérialiste Mystique*, Geneva 1968, p. 40.

loving submission to his parents'. In their absence as well as when they were present, at all times, 'their slightest desire was a law absolutely binding for him'. He cites as a concrete illustration the way in which he remained in parental leading-strings even when departure from home for his education gave him at least physical freedom from the parental yoke. 'During the entire time that the young Joseph spent at Turin following the law course at the University, he never allowed himself to read a book without having written to his father or mother at Chambéry to obtain authorization.'[1]

As a young man we find him under his father's eye delivering speeches of rotund pomposity and unction in praise of the antiquity and grandeur of the judiciary in the presence of the assembled judicature. But although de Maistre was subsequently to express great sympathy for the Jesuits (with whom he was eventually expelled from St. Petersburg for his proselytizing activities), the major influence under which he came in the Savoyard Senate was that of the Jansenists in the writings of De la Rochefoucauld and Pascal. Jansenism (called after Bishop Jansenius, 1558–1638) continued to uphold the Augustinian position in the famous Pelagian controversy, asserting the sufficiency of divine grace as against the belief in salvation by works. It was a religious tradition within the Catholic fold as austere, as pessimistic and as committed to a theology of predestination as the Calvinist sector within Protestantism. The year the French Revolution broke out saw the death of de Maistre senior, and the son inherited his father's fortune and recently acquired hereditary title. Thus worldly self-interest coincided with his ultramontanist, authoritarian upbringing and severe, not to say gloomy religious nurture to produce the Revolution's proudest and most fanatical foe, defender of tradition, of feudal privilege, of wealth, of the authority of Church and Crown.

There remains however a curious paradox in the man's beliefs and action. Not surprisingly in the light of his religious background, de Maistre attached immense importance to the family as a social institution. His ideological regard for its status is akin to Hegel's notion of the State. He believed it to be a unique moral entity, transcending the individual's responsibility, and shaping a man more decisively than any other agency apart from the nation to which he belonged. Yet he himself of his own free will chose at the age of fifty to abandon his wife and two children in Savoy for twelve years while he occupied his diplomatic post at the Petersburg court. Perhaps, on

[1] Robert Triomphe, p. 66.

the principle that the visitation of the sins of the fathers upon the children is a basic illustration of the primacy of the family over the individual, he felt that he was in his own peculiar way paying homage to the sanctity of the *lares et penates* of the domestic hearth.

The majority of men, endowed with conscience as they are, nevertheless seem to experience little difficulty in persuading themselves that the world sanctions a 'healthy' concern for one's own interests. There is, however, ceaseless tension between conscience and self-interest. Thus most men find themselves pulled in opposite directions, with a resultant ambivalence and confused uncertainty in their moral pronouncements. In these circumstances, any man who for whatever reason is not afraid to or is impelled to adopt an evil premise on the basis of which he may reason logically and clearly, free from the temptation to soften in any way the harsh outlines of reality, is in a position to exert great influence over the weak and morally confused. De Maistre was such a man. He reasons vigorously, lucidly, logically in limpid prose; he describes reality truthfully without illusions, but all to evil purpose. He is perverted because of his whole-hearted acceptance of the monstrous proposition that war is divine. Given this premise, offensive to the sensitivities even of the naturally aggressive, he can afford to diagnose its cause quite accurately in a way embarrassing to conservatives, who are not at all anxious to look candidly at the causes of a phenomenon which both common sense and an instinct for what is politic forbid them to label 'divine'. Hence the interest which still attaches to what de Maistre has to say on this vitally important subject, notwithstanding the pernicious content of his advocacy.

What pacifist, for instance, could express as well as de Maistre, in his dialogue between the senator and the knight in the *Soirées de Saint-Petersbourg*, the extraordinariness of the fact that men should with such zest slaughter their own kind?

There is, however in man, despite his immense degradation, an element of love which draws him towards his own kind: compassion is as natural to him as breathing. By what inscrutable sorcery is he always ready, at the first sound of the drum, to divest himself of this sacred character, to go without resisting, often even with a certain excitement, which also has its peculiar character, to cut to pieces on the battle-field his brother who has never injured him, and who advances on his side to make him suffer the same fate, if he can.[1]

---

[1] De Maistre, *Les Soirées de Saint-Petersbourg*, Paris, 2 vols, 1821, Vol. II, pp. 4–5.

This strange phenomenon, de Maistre quite rightly insists, cries out for an explanation. But before embarking upon possible explanations, there is another strangely paradoxical element associated with the phenomenon of war, to which he draws our attention in striking fashion.

Suppose, he says, a visitor from outer space came to earth to be told that the human vices and corruption of which he was the spectator necessitated the killing of man by man. Killing is accordingly not accounted a crime by human beings, provided that this 'necessity' is undertaken either by the soldier or the executioner. The executioner, he is told, dispenses death only to those found guilty after judicial conviction and sentence; and there are relatively so few thus convicted and sentenced that one public executioner per province is normally adequate to the demand for his services. The soldier on the other hand is always in short supply, and there are never enough of them, because there is no limit to the numbers they are required to kill, and so far from their victims being confined to the ranks of the guilty, the contrary is true; they are permitted to kill only honest people. The man from Mars is further told that of these two professional killers, one is and always has been honoured among all nations, while the other is as universally execrated. He is then asked to guess on whom the anathema falls. He would not hesitate a moment, suggests de Maistre. The soldier, of course. For the executioner is the extirpator of crime, 'a sublime being', the main pillar of order, 'the corner-stone of society', whereas the soldier, on the other hand, is the instrument of injustice and a minister of cruelty. 'Would that not be the rational reply?' he asks; and yet the Martian would be quite wrong, for we esteem them in quite the reverse order.

How then are we to explain this extraordinary paradox? Why does war occur? Or in the striking phrase which de Maistre puts into the mouth of the Senator: 'Explain why it is that what is most honourable in the world, in the judgement of the whole of humanity without exception, is the right to shed in innocence innocent blood.[1]

Perhaps the explanation is that rulers decide on war for their own purposes, and the subjects blindly obey. This explanation de Maistre rejects as false, the reasons for which I will return to later in view of the crucial nature of the discussion. Perhaps wars are caused by nationalism. This hypothesis rather surprisingly is dismissed as not worth discussing. 'How many national wars are there?' he asks rhetorically;

[1] De Maistre, p. 14.

and answers: 'One in a thousand years perhaps.' Perhaps the desire for glory explains it all. But this is rejected (*a*) because the glory goes only to the commanders and (*b*) because this explanation begs the essential question which consists precisely of why human beings should ever have associated glory with anything so bestial as the carnage of war.

In effect de Maistre gives no rational explanation for this extraordinary and dreadful phenomenon. Instead he leans very heavily on its ubiquity both in Nature and in human affairs. It requires no explanation, he seems to believe, because it is a fact of nature, a fact of life, universal, eternal, a rule from which there is no escaping. The argument from Nature relies heavily on rhetoric, of which the following is only a sample. There is, he says, manifest throughout Nature 'a kind of prescribed rage', 'a decree of violent death'.

Already, in the vegetable kingdom, you begin to experience the law: from the immense catalpa down to the humblest *graminée*, how many plants *die*, and how many are *killed*! but as soon as you enter the animal kingdom, the law is suddenly terribly in evidence. . . . In each great division of the animal species, it [a hidden force] has selected a certain number of animals charged with the task of devouring the others: thus, there are insects of prey, reptiles of prey, birds of prey, fish of prey, and quadrupeds of prey. There is not a moment when a living creature is not being devoured by another. Above these numerous animal species is placed man, whose destructive hand spares nothing of all that lives. He kills to feed himself, he kills to clothe himself, he kills to ward off others, he kills to attack, he kills to defend himself, he kills to teach himself, he kills to amuse himself, he kills to kill. Superb and terrible king, he has need of everything and nothing resists him. He knows how many barrels of oil the head of the shark or whale will furnish him with; his sharp pin pricks . . . the elegant butterfly . . .; he stuffs the crocodile, he embalms the humming bird . . . Man demands all at one and the same time: of the lamb its entrails to make the harp sound, of the whale its bones to support the young girl's corset; of the wolf its most murderous fang to polish light works of art; of the elephant its defences to fashion the toy of a child: his tables are covered with corpses.[1]

It is a graphic picture. To a sensitive man it is a horrifying picture. De Maistre did not find it so. It was enough for him that it was so. And logic compels him to ask: 'Is there any reason to suppose that this law so evident in nature and in man will stop at man?' Why should it? Why indeed? 'Which being will exterminate that which

[1] Ibid., pp. 30–2.

exterminates them all?' And the answer is as remorseless as it is
obvious. 'He himself. It is man who is charged with slaughtering man.'
Thus the original question with which we started out, 'how man is
capable of waging war on his fellows, is neatly stood on its head. Man,
it appears, is required by Nature's law to slaughter his fellows. The
problem that then presents itself is how, given the fact that man is a
moral and compassionate being, who weeps over the calamities of
others as over his own, how is such a being to overcome his natural
sensibilities in order to fulfil what Nature requires of him? War alone
makes this possible. The earth whose thirst for blood is unsated by the
slaughter of beasts and of the guilty demands also the slaughter of the
innocent. For this, war is indispensable. This and this alone explains
the enigma of men, contrary to their nature, advancing on the battle-
field without the slightest understanding of why or to what end,
doing that which inspires in them a natural horror.

> Have you never noticed that on the field of death, man never dis-
> obeys? He can massacre easily enough a Nerva or Henry IV. But on the
> battle-field the most abominable tyrant, the most insolent butcher of
> human flesh will never hear: 'We are no longer willing to serve you.' A
> revolt there, an agreement to embrace one another in repudiation of a
> tyrant, is a phenomenon outside my recollection.[1]

Moreover, if we look at the actual history of mankind, we find that
this *a priori* law of violent destruction is empirically fulfilled. History
demonstrates that war is the normal condition of mankind, that peace
is no more than a respite, that blood is always flowing somewhere or
other. He casts a rapid illustrative eye over his own century in confir-
mation of his claim, and concludes that France alone has been at war for
forty out of the ninety-six years under scrutiny, and if some nations
have been more fortunate, others have been less so.

> The century which is ending started for France with a bloody war which
> ended only in 1714 with the Treaty of Rastadt. In 1719, France declared
> war on Spain; the Treaty of Paris put an end to it in 1727. The election
> to the Polish throne rekindled war in 1733; peace came in 1736. Four
> years later, the terrible war of the Austrian Succession broke out and
> lasted without break until 1748. Eight years of peace started to heal the
> wounds of eight years of war, when English ambition forced France to
> take up arms. The Seven Years' War is only too well known. After fifteen
> years' respite, the American Revolution dragged France once more into

---

[1] De Maistre, pp. 33–4.

a war whose consequences no human wisdom could have foreseen. Peace was signed in 1782; seven years later, the Revolution started; it has lasted to this day and has so far cost France three million men.[1]

War, he concludes, is a chronic, constant attribute of the human condition, 'a persistent fever marked by terrifying crises'. Sometimes the shedding of blood is sporadic over a wide area, at other times more narrowly confined but more intensive, and at yet other periods the spilling of blood reaches frenzied proportions, as for example in the Punic Wars, the period of the Triumvirates, Caesar's wars, the barbarian invasions, the Crusades, the wars of religion, the war of the Spanish Succession, the French Revolution. Meterologists draw up weather charts to enable us to forecast the direction from which the next squall or hurricane is expected to blow up. Is it not time we had parallel war charts? 'If tables of massacre were available like meteorological tables, who knows if some law might not be discovered after centuries of observation?'[2]

As we read the highly relevant evidence, marshalled so vividly and compellingly by de Maistre, we naturally feel profoundly disturbed as we wonder where this is all leading to. The author occasionally concedes that the picture he is delineating is 'unfortunate'; at other times the conviction seems irresistible that the author's intent must be ironic. But no! The purpose is to demonstrate not merely that violent destruction is not in general 'as great an evil as is believed', but that war is above all divinely ordained. He succeeds in finding ten or more reasons for this perverted conclusion.

It is 'divine' because it represents a law of the world. It has supernatural consequences in that it is a great privilege to die in battle, and the dead may never be said to have died in vain.[3] There is universally attached to war a glory which has an inexplicable fascination for us. Its divinity is manifest in the protection it affords the great captains in the face of all hazards, preserving their lives at least until their renown has been fully accomplished. Its divinity is seen in the way in which its declaration is the result of silent, remorseless forces which

[1] *Considerations on France*, translated by Jack Lively in *The Works of Joseph de Maistre*, London 1965, p. 61.

[2] Ibid., p. 62.

[3] I myself have noticed that those bereaved by war are not infrequently among those most painfully agitated by the efforts of pacifists to abolish war. Unconsciously they feel that a threat to war as a legitimate institution threatens the heroic or sacrificial status of the loved one whose memory they cherish.

over-ride the petty wills of the sovereigns who ostensibly declare it. The results of war transcend human reasoning powers, degrading some nations, exalting others, irrespectively of which side is the conqueror and which the conquered. Success in battle is itself determined by an indefinable force, which is entirely independent of the size of the respective battalions. Humanity may be likened unto a tree that is constantly being pruned by an invisible hand. Loss of resilience and indolence, the successes of civilization, eat like gangrene into the human spirit, which can be retempered only in blood.

So far from the arts and sciences flourishing as a result of peace, together with other great human enterprises, noble ideas and manly virtues, they take their rise from war. Supreme genius and the pinnacles of civilization are manured in the blood spilled in war. The apex of Greek civilization was coterminous with the terrible Peloponnesian war, the Age of Augustus followed hard upon the civil war and the proscriptions, the peculiar glory of the French genius itself was nurtured in the wars of the League and brought to maturity in the wars of the Fronde. The great ages of civilization, the epochs of Alexander, Pericles, Augustus, Leo X and Francis I, Louis XIV and Queen Anne were not in the least peaceful. Finally, let it not be objected that war is cruel and unjust. For the principle that the innocent must suffer for the benefit of the guilty is a universal dogma which has moreover been consecrated by Christianity itself.

In short, de Maistre's 'God', so far from being the God of the Evangel, is Mars, the god of war, of Jehovah and the Old Testament, in whose honour he celebrates a veritable hymn of praise to carnage.

> The entire earth, continually soaked in blood, is only an immense altar where everything that lives must be immolated without end, without limit, without relaxation, until the consummation of things, until the extinction of evil, until the death of death.[1]

Horrible and blasphemous as all this is, it has not in any way tarnished de Maistre's reputation. He is not only a highly respected figure in the history of European thought, he was one of the authors most widely read in the intellectual circles of his day, and he has continued to exert considerable influence. It is not fashionable to express overtly and so unambiguously what de Maistre has to say on the subject of war, but that does not mean that his dicta do not correspond to very widely held and correspondingly powerful beliefs. They do not of course

[1] *Les Soirées de Saint-Petersbourg*, op. cit., p. 34.

exhaust the content of popular belief, which is highly ambivalent, but they represent an important element, which it is salutary to bring out into the open and not repress.

War, then, and the causes of war, are according to de Maistre, natural, inevitable and 'divine'. There remain to discuss two other important topics in the context of his view of war: firstly, his theory as to how battles are won and lost; secondly, and related to this, his view of the nature of sovereign power.

De Maistre is concerned to refute the well-known saying that 'God is always on the side of the big battalions'. He makes the obvious point that numbers are not everything: that armies in a physical ratio to one another of two to three may well stand in a very different ratio in matters of courage, experience and discipline, so that a simple prediction of who will vanquish whom on the basis of that purely physical ratio may very well be falsified in the event. Moreover, he believes that so far as the physical ratio is concerned, rival forces will normally be fairly evenly balanced, for if this were not so, war would be unlikely to break out in the first instance. De Maistre, like other balance-of-power theorists, who believe in a natural equilibrium which always reasserts itself, never succeeds in explaining a central contradiction in the theory. In one context, we are assured that no small power would ever be so foolish as to take on a great power, since that would be to invite its own destruction. Yet the best way apparently to insure against the threat of war from the ambitions of great powers is to balance their power with an effective counter-power. In fact, both sets of circumstances have time and time again served as the circumstances out of which war has emerged; as, for instance, (a) Austria swallowing the Serbs in 1908; and (b) World War I erupting in August 1914 at a time when the balance of power had never before reached such a peak of perfection.

However, to be fair to de Maistre, he is theorizing not in order to prevent war, since it is a 'divine' phenomenon. His point is that there is a natural tendency for the equilibrium of power forces always to reassert itself in the sphere of international relations. If an over-mighty power threatens the balance of forces, sometimes the giant cuts his own throat, and at other times a much weaker power initially throws itself into the path of the giant and gradually and mysteriously grows until it constitutes itself an insurmountable obstacle. Thus the equilibrium, which is divinely sustained, is restored. The equilibrium depends for its maintenance not on human prudence or skill. Divine

Providence may use as its instrument even geese to save the capitol. In short, extra-human, supernatural forces are at work which effectively remove ultimate human destinies out of merely human hands, ensuring that wars always and regularly take place, that they are normally between physically well-matched contenders, and that the ultimate outcome is determined by the divine wisdom, expressed sometimes through the seemingly trivial instruments of geese or hares, but more commonly through the factor of the *morale* and courage displayed by the soldiers on either side. Battles are the least predictable of phenomena; nowhere is the hand of Providence—de Maistre suggests that a special department of Providence must be necessitated—more in evidence. 'Never is he warned more frequently and more sharply than in war of his own nullity and of the inevitable power which rules everything. It is opinion which loses battles, and it is opinion which wins them.'[1] Hence the anxiety displayed by all 'great' commanders to prevent their ranks being weakened or decimated by fear or panic.

De Maistre relates how he asked an eminent military figure to tell him what is 'a battle lost', and received the candid reply that he did not know. To which was added after further reflection that a battle lost is a battle believed to be lost. 'To conquer is to advance' is Frederick II's aphorism, but what determines who does it? De Maistre speaks significantly of 'that solemn moment when, without knowing why, an army feels itself carried forward, as if it were slipping on an inclined plane'. 'And the soldier who *slips forward*,' he asks rhetorically, 'has he counted the dead?' Everything depends upon the moral factor. The same physical events are construed quite differently by the contending sides. If A's force comes between two of B's forces, A will claim: 'I have cut him off. He is lost.' While B will claim: 'He has placed himself between two lines of fire. He is lost.' The one who in fact loses is the one who first loses his nerve, capitulates to fear and feels himself to be defeated.

In view of the fame subsequently to be achieved by Stendhal's description of the battle of Waterloo in *The Charterhouse of Parma* (*La Chartreuse de Parme*), to which Tolstoy particularly expressed his indebtedness, it is worth quoting verbatim de Maistre's description in 1821 of the nature of a battlefield. After observing that frequently no one knows who won and who lost until several days after the battle is over, he goes on to correct the popular notion of what a battle looks like.

[1] *Les Soirées de Saint-Petersbourg*, op. cit., p. 43.

People talk a lot about battles in society without knowing what one is. People are particularly prone to consider them as points, whereas they cover two or three leagues of country. People say to you in all seriousness: How is it that you don't know what took place in this battle, since you were there? Whereas often enough it is precisely the opposite that could be said. Does he who is on the right know what is happening on the left? Does he even know what is happening two paces from him? I easily imagine to myself one of those terrible scenes: on a vast landscape, covered with all the preparations for the slaughter, which seems to shake under the feet of men and horses; amidst fire and whirlwinds of smoke, dazed, carried away by the resounding din of firearms and military machines and voices which command, shout or die away; surrounded by dead and dying and mutilated corpses; possessed in turn by fear, by hope, by rage, by five or six different forms of intoxication, what becomes of a man? What does he see? What does he know after a few hours? What is his power over himself and over the others? Among this crowd of fighting men who have fought all day, there is often not a single man, not even the general, who knows where is the victor.[1]

Both Stendhal and Tolstoy had more first-hand knowledge of warfare than de Maistre—Stendhal at Borodino, Moscow and Bautzen, Tolstoy in the Caucasus and in the Crimea—each could depict it unforgettably in detail and depth in fiction, but the stage directions in a nutshell for their battle-scenes are contained completely in the graphic passage just quoted from the *Soirées de Saint-Petersbourg.*

If, as we have seen, de Maistre believed that wars occur and are won or lost as a result of the decrees of divine Providence, this belief has obvious implications for the significance of what men see fit to refer to as State sovereignty. If history is shaped by Providence, what is the real nature of the power of those earthly sovereigns who, men at any rate imagine, command the obedience of their subjects? On the field of battle, as we saw, de Maistre asserts that he knows of no instance of men disobeying their sovereign commanders by refusing to bear arms and to kill. At the same time, however, he acknowledges that the outcome of a battle has little or nothing to do with the will of the commander. How about the decision to embark upon war in the first place, since this is an even more significant event historically speaking for humanity at large than is the issue of victory or defeat for any particular side? However devoutly we may believe A rather than B to be on the side of the angels, the fact of their warring against one

[1] Ibid., pp. 47-8.

another is of much greater significance for humanity, since whoever wins, the battle for peace has certainly been lost. Here again de Maistre is consistent. Whether we are destined to have war or peace is determined not by sovereign rulers but by Providence, an invisible hand remorselessly shaping the destiny of whole nations. The power which a Napoleon or Alexander wields in reality is illusory—although de Maistre is of course not so lost to all sense of political discretion as to cite examples so near to hand. De Maistre was after all a professional diplomat; the subject is one of some delicacy: he strikes a light, almost jocular note in introducing it, by recalling the popular joke about a nation which enjoyed an academy of sciences, an astronomer royal and Observatory, and at the same time a false calendar. The implication is made explicit. There are occasions when the most powerful of sovereigns is impotent against the forces of conservatism and prejudice. Even a Peter the Great had to bring his whole invincible might to bear in order to cut off men's beards and shorten their suits. 'Sovereigns effectively command on a stable basis', he wrote, 'only within the circle of things admitted by opinion; and it is not they who trace this circle.'[1]

There is a slight element of ambiguity here, since in the case of the great autocrats whom de Maistre admires, like Peter the Great, he insists that when it comes to raising and leading their legions into war, even into defeat, their unquestioned authority is matched only by the submissiveness of their subjects. When he tells us that 'God has warned us that he has reserved the formation of sovereignties to himself by never entrusting the choice of their masters to the masses',[2] his intent is to emphasize 'the divinity that doth hedge a king', not to stress that the authority of the sovereign dissolves in the presence of firmly antagonistic opinion.

De Maistre tends to confuse two different propositions: (i) 'sovereigns' are powerless to defy firmly entrenched opinion or prejudice, and (ii) the power of sovereigns is illusory because it is directed by a superior supernatural power of divine Providence. More commonly he means the latter, especially when construing the French Revolution, the events of which he sees as a divine punishment for the sins of men, quite independently of the wills or designs of the actual 'villains' who appear to be directing events.

---

[1] *Les Soirées de Saint-Petersbourg*, op. cit., p. 3.
[2] *Considerations on France*, op. cit., p. 87.

The very villains, who appear to guide the Revolution take part in it only as simple instruments; and as soon as they aspire to dominate it, they fall ingloriously. Those who established the Republic did so without wishing it and without realizing what they were creating; they have been led by events: no plan has achieved its intended end. . . . It cannot be too often repeated that men do not at all guide the Revolution; it is the Revolution that uses men.[1]

It is interesting to compare and contrast with this reactionary theological view of the Revolution the radical republican view of Michelet, who is similarly convinced that the power of the leaders is an illusory power, but who sees the limits to this power arising not from the invisible hand of Providence, but from the force of public opinion—a view towards which de Maistre is sometimes sympathetically inclined but never where the opinion in question is radical or stemming from the masses. Michelet, the historian of the French Revolution, has this to say in his Introduction to that massive work:

Another thing which this History will clearly establish and which holds true in every connection is that the people were usually more important than the leaders. The deeper I have excavated, the more surely I have satisfied myself that the best was underneath, in the obscure depths. And I have realized that it is quite wrong to take these brilliant and powerful talkers who expressed the thought of the masses, for the sole actors in the drama. They were given the impulse by others much more than they gave it themselves. The principal actor is the people. To find the people again and put it back in its proper role, I have been obliged to reduce to their proportions the ambitious marionettes whose strings it manipulated and in whom hitherto we have looked for and thought to see the secret play of history.[2]

Tolstoy certainly read and admired Michelet, although I know of no evidence that he knew this particular work; but the above passage expresses powerfully and unambiguously the spirit which animated the author of *War and Peace* in the creation and direction of the novel. In Michelet as in Tolstoy the emphasis falls on the 'marionette' status of the ostensible leaders as contrasted with the substantive role exercised by the ordinary people. In de Maistre, on the other hand, the emphasis is on the passive and submissive role of the people to their sovereign ruler, himself subject to the will of Providence but not to the will of the people. The mass of men in de Maistre's universe play

---

[1] Ibid., pp. 49-50.
[2] J. Michelet, *La Révolution Française*, Vol. I, Preface of 1847, p. 44.

no part in political events, and this is as it should be. The people know only two words: submission and belief. Let there be no talk of scrutiny, choice, discussion. The people get the government they deserve.[1] 'In politics, we *know* that it is necessary to respect those powers established we know not how or by whom.'[2]

In so far as the people may be said to participate directly in the historical process at all, we must have recourse to such metaphors as 'wood and rope used by a workman' to give a real idea of the subordinate, not to say passive nature of their contribution, according to de Maistre. But the power of the leaders themselves only appears to be such to the inexperienced eye. In reality, the tyrant is usually himself subject to the will of a still more powerful tyrant, and if we approach close to the tyrant who is lord over all and would learn the secret of his Sphinx-like soul, we would find that he is as ignorant as the rest of us as to the source of his mysterious power. He simply does not know how it came to descend upon him. For 'circumstances he was unable either to foresee or bring about have done everything for him and without him.[3]'

To conclude this summary of de Maistre's contribution, it can be said that for all his obscurantist theology and acceptance of things and conditions that are morally indefensible, he brought a new and vividly incisive element of realism into the discussion of the nature of power in the context of modern warfare. If the reasoning is often confused, if he lapses into rhetoric, if his conclusions are sometimes pernicious, he nevertheless throws light into dark places, even when he least intended it. De Maistre has only contempt for the projects of eternal peace which emanated from the most humane of the figures of the eighteenth-century Enlightenment, the Abbé de St. Pierre, Rousseau, Condorcet, Kant. These men sincerely struggled to promote and strengthen the prospects for peace among men. De Maistre certainly did not. If in one passage he says that we must still thunder against war, it is only to denounce in the next sentence the naïveté of the would-be abolitionists. For all that, de Maistre is more helpful to a realistic abolitionist of today than the precursors of League of Nations projects for the simple reason that he is not deceived by the illusion that sovereign nations in command of big battalions will ever voluntarily

[1] 'Every nation has the government suited to it, and none has chosen it.' *Study on Sovereignty, The Works of Joseph de Maistre*, op. cit., p. 104.

[2] Ibid., p. 110.

[3] *Considerations on France*, op. cit., p. 88.

yield their sovereignty to any international tribunal not capable of enforcing its will. Free from this illusion, notwithstanding his ultimate contempt for humanity, he has much to say that is highly relevant to the student of power, with all its dire consequences for those who strive to preserve or rather to discover and create the conditions necessary for peace.

3

Stendhal
Neither Scarlet nor Black

In the course of a single novel, *Scarlet and Black* (*Le Rouge et Le Noir*), Stendhal makes no less than five separate references to the writing or work of de Maistre. The allusions are all tinctured with hostility, veiled or explicit, but it is clear that de Maistre exercised a powerful fascination for Stendhal. Balzac, the only distinguished contemporary of Stendhal besides Goethe to appreciate his genius, said of *The Charterhouse of Parma* (*La Chartreuse de Parme*) that it was the novel which Machiavelli would have written had he lived in the nineteenth century in exile from Italy. Although Stendhal is profoundly radical, sceptical, anti-clerical (and bitterly hostile to the Jesuits)—the first authentic 'anarchist' of genius in the realm of literature[1]—it is important to recognize the strength of the Machiavellian–Maistrean temper in his soul. It was part of his strength; it was the source of his weakness—an extraordinarily rare love of the truth, marred by moral confusion. I have already spoken of Tolstoy's generous and unequivocal acknowledgement of his own indebtedness to Stendhal; but he had in fact major reservations with regard to Stendhal's quality as a writer. In 1883, writing to his wife, he says:

> I am reading Stendhal . . . *Rouge et Noir*. I read it some forty years ago, but remembered nothing except my relation to the author: sympathy with his boldness and a feeling of kinship—but yet an unsatisfied feeling. And curiously enough I feel the same now, but with a clear consciousness of why and wherefore. . . .[2]

He does not say why his admiration is shadowed by a feeling of dissatisfaction, but it is not difficult to guess why in one who was in his every judgment on all matters of human concern first and last a moralist.

---

[1] He was Shelley's senior by nine years.
[2] Letter, dated 13 November 1883, L. N. Tolstoy, *Polnoe Sobranie Sochinenii*, Moscow 1938, Vol. 83, p. 410.

Men are not commonly habituated to truthful description of the day-to-day practices of those set in authority over them; rather do they blur the edges, resort to euphemism, and generally deceive themselves. They do this partly because these well-established practices conform to some degree with their own expectations and sometimes their own practices, and also because they are fearful of giving offence to the powerful. Of course, this self-deception is wounding to the self-esteem; but the common remedy for that is to retreat into further doses of self-deception. It is the authentic hallmark of the Machiavellian–Maistrean realists that they are intolerant of this widespread type of self-deception about the nature and practices of government. They want the truth about the facts and practices of government. Their self-respect will not permit of the kind of subterfuge to which the moral squeamishness of the multitude compels them to resort. They do not share in this moral squeamishness, not because they are anxious to expose the anomalies prior to abolishing them, but because they do not disapprove of them. De la Rochefoucauld observed that hypocrisy is the lip service that vice pays to virtue. Machiavelli and de Maistre do not even feel the need to pay lip service and are thus free from hypocrisy. Morally speaking, the common man undoubtedly has his being on a higher moral plane for all his hypocrisy; but, nevertheless, the *empirical* truthfulness of the de Maistres frequently casts light into dark places. The love of empirical truth is however ultimately spurious because it rests on a profound self-hatred and an abiding contempt for man. In Machiavelli's case, this chronic malaise of the soul was rendered bearable by a seemingly genuine detestation of the political instability of the Italian city-states and the resultant frequency of foreign invasions. He was something of an Italian patriot over three centuries before the *Risorgimento*. De Maistre's twisted moral values were buttressed by a kind of religious mysticism. What sustained both men was the single-minded passion for power, the consuming need to exercise a measure of real personal ascendancy over others, which lay at the heart of their identity as individuals.

Stendhal had one important quality in common with the Machiavelli -Maistrean realists: a suspicion of sentiment if it were to come between the observer and the reality he claimed to be describing. Stendhal was anti-Romantic, naturalistic, clinical, detached, scientific, determined to get the record straight, to present human beings in action as they really are, laconically, matter of fact, without any touching up. He had a horror of fine writing. The hero of *Scarlet and Black*, Julien Sorel, on trial for his life, expressed satisfaction with his legal Counsel's cool, collected manner. ' "No fine phrases," he said to him under his breath.' But in life the division between intellect and emotion, between fact and value is neither desirable nor possible. The suspicion of emotion as a factor liable to distort the capacity for objective reportage of what actually is, is itself an emotion and a very powerful one—namely, a love of truth, or at any rate that aspect of truth, felt to be threatened by loss of objectivity arising out of strong feeling. Indeed, it is the purity and *rationality* of the emotions which predominate in a man's soul and thus suffuse his writing, his *style*, with the stamp of his unique individuality, which constitutes the peculiar interest aroused by any author in his reader. Nor is this wholly absent, nor could it be, even in the most arid or severely business-like, descriptive, technological or scientific writing. Even where the author of a purely neutral report or set of instructions flatters himself that in the interests of impartial, scientific analysis he has succeeded in eliminating the slightest flavour of his own personal idiosyncrasies or values, there is left the inescapable fact that the author is devoting his time and energy to selecting a particular subject or set of facts as distinct from a myriad of others which he might have selected, and is thereby lending his authority to the view that this particular subject or set of facts is of particular interest. He is raising certain questions which thereby tacitly exclude the raising of different questions, and he is obliged therefore tacitly to draw on his own criteria of what constitutes relative significance or importance.

With de Maistre or Machiavelli what distinguishes the author's style of allegedly objective reporting is the presence never far beneath the surface of the repressed emotions of self-hatred and contempt. The result is that neither writer ever wholly succeeds in 'setting down naught in malice'. Human nature is set down as something inescapably bent and puckered, twisted, irremediably cancerous; but these 'facts' are not presented free from all accompanying expression of emotion. The emotion that shows through in the author's style is not one of sorrow that men should be thus foredoomed to failure in their moral aspiration (according to them); the emotion that colours their style is frequently one of *schadenfreude*, of bogus sorrow concealing a malicious, if suppressed pleasure.

In Stendhal we find a similar determination to mirror the world accurately without illusion; but the human nature presented by Stendhal, although no less corrupt than that of Machiavelli, is generally and consistently condemned as something that is far from incorrigible, as something that we ourselves have made and should begin to unmake. The crippling of human nature by violence, hypocrisy, bribes and threats is one of the principal themes of Stendhal's novels. Men are, in Stendhal's view, in deep trouble because they are in the grip of false-hood; men deceive themselves because they want to; their eyes are put out either by stupidity or greed or fear or other powerful emo-tions. What is necessary is for men to return to the truth; and he for his part will have no part of the world of illusion and falsehood. In a passage vividly anticipatory of Freud's impatience with those who seek consolation in illusion, Stendhal is quoted (by Paul Hazard) as soliloquizing:

> But I am not of those that are deceived. I have no need of consolation, or of hope. It is enough for me to observe the facts, stripped and bare, to be happy. Error is never sweet; truth is always beautiful, my passion is to follow the play of human sentiments to the depth of their souls; my ambition is to rank among the number of the wise; among the number of the strong who put their delight in the knowledge of the real . . .[1]

Such an ideal is as rare as it is praiseworthy. And as Stendhal himself acknowledges in an incompleted page (quoted by Martineau), it is not an ideal easy to maintain.

> It is not for nothing that one has won a first prize in rhetoric. I will admit it; it is still with pleasure that I lie sometimes. I am a poet then and a poet who improvises. But honour suffers from this pleasure and I try to lie as little as possible.[2]

Among the most celebrated examples of Stendhal's art of 'lying as little as possible' is his deromanticizing of war in his drily realistic account of Waterloo, so keenly appreciated by Tolstoy, as evidenced in the above-quoted (pp. 4–5) interview with Professor Boyer. Stend-hal, as a serving officer in Napoleon's armies, knew war at first hand, of course. Although not himself in action at the battle of Borodino, he was close at hand on that occasion; he was a spectator at the battle of Marengo, he was present at the battle of Bautzen, and he also witnessed the burning of Moscow. He was also well acquainted with the writings of de Maistre, who, it will be recalled, wrote: 'People say to you in all seriousness: how is it that you don't know what took place in this battle, since you were there? Whereas often enough it is precisely the

[1] Paul Hazard, *Le Vie de Stendhal*, Paris 1927, ed., p. 52.
[2] Henri Martineau, *Le Cœur de Stendhal*, Paris 1952, Vol. II, p. 177.

opposite that could be said.' Stendhal, in an economical, strictly matter-of-fact style in a series of short but fast-moving vignettes shows us the battlefield through the eyes of a naïve and very raw recruit. So confused is Fabrice, so sharply is his experience at variance with what he had been led to expect, that after it is all over his principal preoccupation is how he can verify whether or not he really had been present at the battle of Waterloo.

The picture of war on which we were once brought up was one of soldiers, gleaming in bright uniforms, drawn up in lines of strict battle order, helmets gleaming, swords polished, muskets at the ready, awaiting the signal to advance in step, from a plumed general on a nearby hillock, while even the dead lie gracefully and gallantly postured as befits a frieze of symbols of moral sacrifice. At this mythology Stendhal struck a powerful blow. His Waterloo is a world far removed from such a scene—a vast landscape, often empty but broken by episodic, confused and highly bewildering movement, a platoon of infantry emerging from a clump of bushes here—a posse of cavalry suddenly racing into view only to disappear just as rapidly for reasons apparent to no one, least of all to themselves—and all to the constant booming of the deadly barrage of the cannon. The impression overwhelmingly created is one of chaos and confusion in which the rank and file soldiery have no conception of what is happening, in which the high command are distinguished only by a knowledge of what they thought was supposed to happen and a consequent need to pretend that they grasp the meaning of what is in fact as bewildering to them as to everyone else. And through the smoke, the noise, the confusion, the mutilation and slaughter, a pattern of reality gradually emerges from the actual courage and fear, the self-respect and soldiering toughness of old campaigners with their resilience and versatility expressed in a host of chance encounters with an enemy displaying like qualities in their soldiers when the opportunity presents itself. The individuals are largely concerned with preserving their own lives with a minimum of hardship in circumstances frequently unendurably cruel and at best exhausting and futile. Eventually a victory is claimed for one side or the other, and another battle vanishes in the mists of history's roll of honour—or is it dishonour?

Stendhal makes no comment, of course. His hero, Fabrice, is immensely pleased and exhilarated with his blooding in war—at least once he has finally recovered from his wounds. But Stendhal does not need to comment. War as an institution has been debunked with deadly efficacy—certainly more effectively than by any previous writer. Fabrice is initiated into the mysteries of a traditional and highly organized ritual of mutual slaughter through the gruff, motherly tutelage of a veteran *vivandière*, a Napoleonic Mother Courage, to whom Brecht may have been not a little indebted. Her prosaic, strictly commercial *savoir-vivre* conceals an honesty and warmth of humanity which contrasts effectively with the arbitrary, mechanized violence striking at random at all unfortunate enough to fall within its radius. Stendhal nowhere indicts war; his drily prosaic style is nevertheless unforgettable in its impact. Among the books which Stendhal had, like Rousseau, read appreciatively in his youth was *Le Philosophe anglais, ou histoire de M. Cleveland* by the distinguished author of *Manon Lescaut*, l'abbé Prévost. M. Cleveland therein observes: 'War has always filled me with horror. It is the shame of reason and of humanity. In the principles of my morality, a military hero is but an infamous monster.'[1]

After the cannonade of Bautzen, a quarter of a century before he set out to describe Waterloo, Stendhal with his razor-sharp capacity for observing truthfully and describing how he reacted thereto, commented ironically:

> We see very well, from midday to three o'clock, all that can be seen of a battle, that is to say, nothing. The pleasure consists in the fact that one is a little awed by the feeling of certainty one has that there is being enacted there a thing that one knows to be terrible.[2]

Stendhal knew war at first hand; here as elsewhere his primary concern is not to allow established myth to prevent his using his eyes for the purpose they were given him. We have seen how incomparably he conveyed the 'rien' that he perceived for three hours at Bautzen in his re-enactment of Waterloo. But how about the aspect that is terrible? How does Stendhal with his almost morbid fear of sentiment convey that? For he does convey it in his slightly mocking fashion. If the *vivandière* had not existed, it would have been necessary to invent her; she was indispensable to mediate Stendhal's tightly repressed emotion. Like Tolstoy he witnessed a public execution in his youth— an ex-priest, Jomard. He was 'so close that after the execution he *saw* the drops of blood form along the knife before falling'. The horror

[1] Quoted by Fernand Rude in *Stendhal et la Pensée Sociale de son Temps*, Paris 1967, p. 47.

[2] Martineau, op. cit., Vol. 1, p. 300.

that this spectacle aroused in him produced no polemic, still less a campaign against capital punishment, but he did not forget it, and at the end of *Scarlet and Black* when Julien awaits execution, Stendhal permits him to hope that before very long 'some wise, far-seeing legislator' will have secured the abolition of the death penalty. The following passage from the Waterloo battle-scene is purely descriptive, but it evokes the long-remembered sense of the 'terrible' that he had experienced at Bautzen and no doubt elsewhere.

> The kindly cantinière, anxious to break her novice pupil in to the facts of violent death as painlessly and swiftly as possible, urges Fabrice to dismount and inspect a corpse.
>
> A bullet, entering on one side of the nose, had come out by the opposite temple, and disfigured the corpse in a hideous fashion, leaving it with one eye still open.
>
> 'Get off your horse then, lad,' said the cantinière, 'and give him a shake of the hand, and see if he'll return it.'
>
> Without hesitating, although almost ready to give up the ghost from disgust, Fabrice flung himself off his horse and taking the hand of the corpse gave it a vigorous shake. Then he stood still as though no life was left in him. . . . What most particularly horrified him was that still open eye.[1]

The horror of war is effectively conveyed without comment—as effectively as Maupassant, for instance, conveys without comment the profoundly moving qualities of courage in his laconic, unemotional description of two fishermen accepting immediate death rather than betray their compatriots by revealing the password to their beleaguered city. Yet in the above-quoted passage one dimension is significantly missing. There is no compassion. Disgust, horror are there—they need no expression; they are implicit in the physical details selected for description; but compassion is not felt. Stendhal may have felt it, but he feared to give rein to it. When Julien Sorel is present at M. Valenod's dinner for his fellow officials and members of the Liberal party, Julien evinces indignation at the silencing by his host of the pathetic singing of the inmates of the poor-house, audible next door. In spite of his sedulous imitation of those he deemed to be successful in life and his assiduous apprenticeship to the art of hypocrisy, Julien 'felt a big tear stealing down his cheek'. Stendhal then takes the unusual step of interjecting an aside on the part of the author: 'I must say

[1] *The Charterhouse of Parma*, translated by Margaret R. B. Shaw, Penguin Classics 1967 ed., p. 54.

the weakness Julien gives proof of in this soliloquy gives me a poor opinion of him. He would be a worthy colleague of those kid-glove conspirators who aspire to change all the ways and habits of a great country while not wishing to bewail the least little scratch.'[1] His hero for a brief moment deserts his customary attitude of cultivated calculation to give vent to an impulse of honest indignation at brutal insensitivity and oppression, and his creator hastens to disassociate himself from his hero.

Stendhal himself is nowhere better described than in a short passage characterizing Roizand in an unfinished fragment, entitled *Une Position sociale*: 'Of a character in appearance the most volatile, a single word would sometimes reduce him to tears. At other times, ironic, hard through fear of being moved and then of despising himself as weak . . . His pride would have been in despair at allowing his feelings to be guessed.'[2] And this is the essence of the paradox that lies at the heart of Stendhal. He aspires, he tells us, only to mirror the facts of life as he journeys down life's highway—accurately and without emotion. But the facts that he truthfully observes, selects and with penetrating discernment sets before us are facts that men are generally anxious to keep decently veiled, facts that men of action do not want uncovered, and that writers, who wish to please their cultivated contemporaries, are not usually impatient to reveal. Stendhal selects these social and psychological facts for display because they not only offend his reason, but they outrage his moral sentiments, that is to say, his sharp love of truth and detestation of injustice. But to express such sentiments openly, to probe with his scalpel into the vulnerable areas of the body politic would have meant declared war between Stendhal and society, and would have been highly dangerous. As it was, Stendhal had to pay a high price in terms of security and income in his profession, and the even higher price for an artist of being largely ignored and unappreciated in his own day. Stendhal himself was very far from being a coldly calculating, practising hypocrite like Julien Sorel. On the other hand, he consciously displayed prudence, since he was far also from being of the stuff of which martyrs are made. While Stendhal observed remorselessly things about his fellow creatures which aroused his contempt, he was himself not entirely free from those self-same vices. He sought powerful patrons; he felt resentful at his exclusion from preferment

---

[1] *Scarlet and Black*, translated by Margaret R. B. Shaw, Penguin Classics 1967 ed., p. 156.
[2] Quoted by Martineau, op. cit., Vol. II, p. 247.

after his part in the Russian campaign; he was even capable of the pathetic pretension of putting a prefix before his name, de Beyle; he tried after the palace revolution of 1830 to obtain an interview with Guizot in order to secure for himself a prefectship; he enjoyed wearing his consul's uniform bedecked with the insignia of office.

These must have been things unbearably painful to acknowledge to himself—as painful as the wounds to his tenderest emotions as a child, orphaned of his beloved mother at the age of seven and left to the mercies of a father he cordially, if somewhat unjustly, detested. In order to achieve some degree of stability out of disunities so precarious Henri Beyle wore the mask of Stendhal—a mask of worldly-wise, Machiavellian-like observation of the facts of power in order the more skilfully to exploit them for his own advantage. This advantage was defined in the light of a hedonistic utilitarian philosophy to which was added a dash of insouciant, devil-may-care admiration of the will to action, of bravado for its own sake, compounded of the sabre of Cyrano de Bergerac and the perfumed philtres of Casanova, especially these last. But this mask, which is universally associated with the name of Stendhal, concealed a quite different moralist—a passionate individualist, who understood more accurately than any of his predecessors the havoc wrought by the love of power in the individual soul, and the consequent chaos and savagery which result from the concentrations of power at the collective level of sovereign states. And having understood this, Stendhal rejected power utterly as the basic ingredient of privilege, injustice, cruelty, poverty and war. But Beyle continued not very happily as French consul at Civitavecchia.

A superficial reading of *Scarlet and Black* might well leave the impression that it is essentially a novel of social manners by a man most sharply impressed by the facts of class conflict in a society where great gulfs stretched between the privileged sector and the poor. *Scarlet and Black* is the kind of book we would expect from the author of the observation: 'In England, thirteen million people wear themselves out with work, while seven to eight hundred families possess riches of of which we on the continent have no conception.'[1] Julien Sorel is the son of a grasping but poor provincial peasant, the owner of a saw-mill; he is exceptional in that his literary aptitudes combined with a limited classical education have nurtured within him the desire for and the means towards realizing social ambitions. Cost what it may, Julien is determined to get to the top. But the road to his advancement is beset

[1] Quoted by Rude, op. cit., p. 167.

by people whose principal characteristic is consciousness of the distinctions of wealth and power. Consequently he suffers from an ultimately ungovernable pride, born of his preternatural sensitivity to his own social inferiority; and this pride brings about his downfall. Finally, when he has lost all worldly ambitions, he feels free to tear aside the mask of prudent falsehood that he has been wearing; and throws his life away by a passionate indictment from the box of the accused of judge and jury as instruments of class rule designed to keep men of his class in unjust subjection. After worshipping military glory on the Bonapartist model, he rejected this model of success for that of ecclesiastical preferment as one more appropriate to the time of the Restoration in France. After assiduously practising the hypocrisy necessary to make his way in a world governed not by moral standards but by wealth, intrigue, patronage and lack of scruple, Julien achieves dazzling success, only to throw it all away when wounded in his pride; and finally reveals himself as a true, class-conscious warrior, a Jacobin, at heart.

Such a reading would be perfectly just—it fits the essential facts, it strains none of the evidence, it clearly corresponds to the main essentials of the plot. It does, however, leave entirely out of account all that which makes the novel and its author of unique interest to us. For Stendhal belongs by right not to the political tradition of class struggle but to the anarchist tradition which appeals against the brutal oppression and coarse vulgarity of secular power not to allegedly counter-middle class or proletarian power but to the truth acknowledged by and made manifest in the solitary human heart, pure and free, untrammelled by any compromising loyalties to party, sect, faction or drawing room of either a political or a religious character.

The contemporary power world is presented in *Scarlet and Black* at two levels: at the provincial level as exemplified in the official life of Verrières and in the political life of the capital epitomized in the drawing room of the de la Moles. The life of the people who run Verrières, the de Renals, Valenods and Maugirons, is one in which respect is determined by wealth, where human relations are perverted by preoccupation with petty financial interests and the quest for dishonest profits. The men who rule the community have no convictions other than obedience to laws which derive from their own blind adherence to the struggle for social prestige. Insensible themselves to everything except money, precedence, decorations, they set the tone for public opinion, which they at one and the same time shape and fear. While the leaders exemplify false values and blind bigotry, the public, made up of small tradesmen and peasants, fear the power of those set over them but are too ignorant to recognize that their own pecuniary greed is the basis of their exploitation by the bigger fish above them. De Renal, the mayor, is a hollow man because he acts not out of genuine desire or impulse but in obedience to social fetish and his intuitive fears of public opinion. He marries Louise de Renal not because he loves her, but because by her breeding she represents for him a major social acquisition. He buys and develops property not for his own comfort or aesthetic taste but because he believes the public are impressed by the number of walls he erects. He employs Julien as a domestic tutor not because he is concerned about his children's real needs, still less out of interest in Julien, but because it is the best riposte he can think of to M. Valenod's recently acquired Norman carriage horses. As a direct fruit of his own spiritual emptiness, before long he finds himself cuckolded by the tutor; but characteristically the loss of his wife's affections is not what disturbs him. The crisis of his life is the imminence of the scandal becoming a matter of common knowledge and public gossip. It is public opinion which he fears, for public opinion ultimately determines his social position and public standing, the matter which he cares most about. When he has finally to face this real crisis of his personal life, the irony is not simply that he has no one to turn to for advice, consolation or moral support, but that his two most intimate friends are those whom he fears most.

Parallel with the small world of provincial power is the arena of central power represented by the drawing room of the Hôtel de la Mole in Paris. In essentials it is the same world as Verrières, but because everything is on a grander scale, the entire milieu being one of gilded opulence and the consciousness of the possession of great power, it is a world in which corruption goes deeper. The petty coarseness of provincial greed is replaced by the languid elegance of Parisian *noblesse oblige*, but the stench of moral decay is much stronger. Nobody attends the de la Mole's drawing room for disinterested reasons; therefore the real reasons for the rigorous attendance cannot of course be alluded to. This fundamental and universally understood ground for tacit censorship gradually extends to and lays its blight upon every other subject of potentially genuine interest. The consequence is that all serious conversation is taboo, boredom is enthroned, and the substance of such conversation as is left is made up almost entirely of snobbery and sycophancy. Advancement in precedence in the drawing room rests not on merit—which when present by error, so to speak, as in the case of the exiled Altomira, is not understood, still less appreciated—but on skilful manœuvring in what is termed service to all the parties or by the possession of great masses of shamefully acquired wealth. One man's wealth, for example, was made by lending money to kings to make war on the common people. People animated by such perverted values are ruthless in persecuting those who might threaten them, and especially the artist, courageous and eloquent enough to expose them. Béranger, the leading poet, who openly scorned the sinecures and decorations by which lesser men are bought, was accordingly imprisoned, so that he could be slandered with impunity in the drawing rooms.

The world of the Hôtel de la Mole is, in short, a squalid world, inhabited by intriguers, snobs, placemen, fops, people who either take wealth for granted or seek out the means to such favour. Its elegance, grace and boredom mask cruelty and oppression behind the façade. Its chief redeeming feature seems to be found in the Marquis himself, the presiding genius of undisputed mastery over his court, who, although himself ambitious to be a Minister and a Duke, and passionately desirous that his daughter should be a Duchess, had at least through his experience of the harshness of exile as an émigré in '93 been saved from the degradation of the canker of gold.

So much for the world created by those who worship power. What of the world of those whose role is to obey the decrees of those set in authority over them? Why do they submit dutifully to men whose lives are as corrupt as those of the de la Moles and the de Renals? They do so, says Stendhal, because they are themselves as corrupt but lacking sufficient aggressiveness to overcome either the harshness of their inherited circumstances or their inborn servility. Our picture of the ruled is drawn from the peasants of the Franche-Comté who constitute the body of the students in the seminary attended by Julien in Besançon. They have been reared in economic circumstances, both harsh and precarious, where the day's toil in winter frequently offers no guarantee even of bread, potatoes or chestnuts in the evening. For such as them, the ecclesiastical calling is neither more nor less than a passport to a good dinner in perpetuity. And whosoever has power to imperil their modest ambition is treated circumspectly and with deference. The very idea of standing up for their rights, if necessary of contesting them when challenged in the courts, would strike them as the height of folly. Nothing is ever to be gained by crossing swords with the wealthy, is their first maxim. 'Big pots is the expression reserved for them.' So, comments Stendhal, '. . . you can judge of their respect for the wealthiest concern of all—the Government! In the eyes of these peasants of Franche-Comté, failure to smile respectfully at the mere mention of the Prefect's name passes for rashness; . . .'[1] When Julien is made an assistant tutor in the Old and New Testament, when the Bishop himself bestows upon him a signal mark of his favour, and when into the bargain he receives from his friend Fouqué a gift of a boar and a stag, Julien's fellow students immediately reverse their attitudes towards him. Envy was replaced by deference, insolence by cordiality. More than that, they 'almost seemed as if they might complain because he had not warned them that his family was rich and had thus made them run the risk of failing to show respect for money'.[2]

We have then only to observe the world of rulers and ruled, as Stendhal sees them, to deduce without difficulty the author's view of the nature of political power and its relation to morality. But the author is not content to leave it to our inference; he spells it out quite explicitly. The real, as distinct from, the nominal ruler of Verrières, is M. Valenod by virtue of his energy complete unscrupulousness and his open-handedness with his loot. But Valenod could not govern alone:

> M. de Valenod had, as it were, said to the grocers of the district: 'Pick me out the two stupidest men among you'—to the lawyers: 'Point me out your two greatest dunces'—to the medical officers of health: 'Tell me who are your two greatest quacks.' When he had collected the most shameless members of every calling, he said to them: 'Now let's govern together.'[3]

Again one of the chapters is headed by a quotation attributed to Arthur Young: 'All those whom I see rising to success have an independence and a harshness of heart I do not find in myself.'[4] When Julien gets his first major break in his struggle to rise in the world through the patronage of M. de la Mole on the recommendation of Father Pirard, the reaction of his old friend, Fouqué, who has Julien's true welfare genuinely at heart, is one of gloomy foreboding.

> It'll all end up for you . . . with a government post where you'll be forced to do something for which the newspapers will slang you. I shall have

---

[1] *Scarlet and Black*, op. cit., p. 196.
[2] Ibid., p. 212. [3] Ibid., p. 161. [4] Ibid., Pt I, Ch. 26.

news of you by seeing you shamed. Mind you, it's better, even from a money point of view, to earn a hundred louis in a sound timber business, where one is one's own master, than to get five thousand francs from any government, even if it were that of King Solomon himself.[1]

Julien, excited as he stood, as he imagined, on the threshold of the world's great arena, dismissed such advice as provincial small-mindedness. Finally, when Julien awaits the Paris mail coach to take him on his great adventure, he overhears a conversation between two travellers, one of whom speculating on the distant future, says:

There'll still be a king wishing to extend his prerogatives, still people ambitious to become Deputies . . . Extremists on the Right will still be possessed by a longing to become peers or gentlemen in waiting. Everyone will want to have a hand on the tiller of the Ship of State, for it's a paying job. Will there never then be even a tiny, humble place for a simple passenger?[2]

The world of political power, of the eternal preoccupation with wealth and place, painted over with a top coat of social hypocrisy, is paralleled by a similar picture of ecclesiastical power, ranging from the Cardinal who addresses the meeting of the Ultras to the Abbé de Frilair and the sycophantic Jesuit, Father Castanède of the Besançon seminary. Madame de Fervaques, obsessed by pathetic pretensions to rank and social superiority, derives her entire satisfaction from the dispensation of ecclesiastical patronage. These powerful ecclesiastics inhabit a world consistent in the pettiness of its concerns and the egoism of its motives. But set over against these are two very different figures, Father Chélan and Father Pirard. Father Chélan is a humble and selfless parish priest in Verrières, who is deprived of his living because of his compassion and faithful love of the truth. As Julien's first mentor, he acted as unwisely by Julien, says Stendhal, as he did in his own case. For he taught Julien how to reason correctly and not to be satisfied with meaningless words, while at the same time neglecting to tell him that such a habit is regarded by society, to whom all competent reasoning gives offence, as a crime. It is Chélan too who spells out in the clearest fashion the nature of the price that will inevitably be exacted from those who seek, as courtesans of power, the rewards of the world.

If you are thinking of paying court to those in authority then your everlasting damnation is assured. You may get on in the world, but you'll

---

[1] Ibid., pp. 226–7.   [2] Ibid., p. 243.

have to do things which will harm the poor and needy. You'll have to flatter the sub-prefect, the Mayor, and, in short, any man of importance, and make yourself the servant of his passions.[1]

And Chélan's prophecy is fulfilled. Julien, encouraged in his taste for the pleasure of dispensing patronage, is permitted by M. de la Mole to exercise a whim. Julien accordingly appoints out of sheer perversity an 'old idiot' as keeper of the lottery bureau in his native town, only to discover that by so doing he has deprived of his just deserts the one honest man in town, a mathematician and a Jacobin, who out of his poverty had been subsidizing the previous incumbent. Julien stifles his misgivings by the reflection that 'I'll have to bring myself to commit many other acts of injustice if I want to get on, and know how to cover them up, moreover, with fine sentimental phrases.'[2]

The other good cleric, the Jansenist Father Pirard, a man of simple austerity, while understanding the corruption of power, nevertheless serves loyally the Marquis de la Mole and advances Julien in his worldly career. What is significant about Pirard is that notwithstanding the sincerity of his other-worldliness, such is the hard-bitten cynicism of the ecclesiastical world in which he moves that everyone flatters himself that he is not taken in by the Rector's absurd 'pretensions'. They were incapable of believing in his sincerity, for to them it was inconceivable that a man should fail to use a post with so many lucrative possibilities to his own advantage and then resign it voluntarily. When he takes leave of them, he states with admirable bluntness the twofold choice that confronts every man.

Do you wish for worldly honours, for every social advantage, for the pleasure of being in authority, of defying law and order and being rude with impunity to all men? Or, do you desire your eternal salvation?[3]

The only reaction that this address provoked among the seminarists was the comment that the Rector must be suffering from 'sour grapes' as a result of resentment at his 'dismissal'.

This then is the world which Julien step by step discovers for himself as he proceeds along the ladder of ascent from the saw-mill peasant's much-cudgelled son to the much-decorated son-in-law of the Marquis de la Mole himself. A man of boundless energy, capable of great daring and impulsive courage, driven by the sacred inner fires of his own restless ambition, asserting himself scornfully against every

[1] *Scarlet and Black*, op. cit., p. 63.   [2] Ibid., p. 292.
[3] Ibid., p. 222.

obstacle that appears in his path, determined to out-Herod Herod in the art of universal hypocrisy, he brushes aside every moral imperative as a mere attempted restriction put on the strong by the weak in order to bridle them. Accordingly he carries everything before him, and he is the object of universal admiration or envy. His is the single-minded will to power, which will not be deflected from its goal even by his own finer feelings, dismissed as sentimentalism. And the origin of this ravening hunger is diagnosed clearly as the loveless condition, in which he was vulnerable to the violence of his father and brothers, where he was 'despised by everyone as a weakling'. His faintly hypocritical air was itself adopted originally to ward off anticipated blows. At the core of his being is an immense sense of his own inferiority and weakness. He despises himself and fears above all else ridicule. Consequently when he arouses in women emotions of genuine tenderness and affection, as he does in the starved soul of the Mayor's wife, he is able to return it only with a spurious love. It is in reality but another expression of his single consuming desire, namely, to rid himself of and to avenge himself for his feelings of social inferiority and resentment at the patronization he suffers at the hands of the nobility. When Mme de Renal bestows upon him the first unmistakable sign of her favour, and takes his hand, his thoughts are of triumph, not of sentiment.

> He could have wished to have as witnesses all those proud nobles who had stared at him at dinner with such patronizing smiles as he sat at the bottom end of the table with the children.[1]

And this is even more true when he succeeds later in subjugating the haughty pride of Mathilde de la Mole. The principal emotion he experiences is that of gratified ambition that the poor carpenter from the Jura should have gained the day over so distinguished a social figure as the Marquis du Croisenois. When the de la Mole daughter despite her captive emotions continues to treat him as a social inferior, she is the one who is reduced to suing as a humble supplicant to be taken back into favour. For Julien will bend all his diplomacy and persistence, sacrificing even his powerful lust in the service of the pride, which is his ultimate master. But it is this pride, combined with the fact that his intelligence observes the world truthfully so that his hypocrisy does not come natural to him as to others and thus has constantly to be calculated and struggled for, that proves his undoing.

[1] Ibid., pp. 95–6.

M. Faguet, the distinguished French critic of the early part of this century, considered that *Scarlet and Black* was a brilliant novel—brilliant in its powers of characterization and psychological subtlety—marred by the absurdity of the melodramatic conclusion. As soon as Mme de Renal despatches to the Marquis de la Mole her letter denouncing Julien as a cold-blooded seducer, animated by worldly ambition, everyone, and in particular Julien himself, begins to behave absurdly and out of character, according to Faguet.[1] All that Julien had to do, it is suggested, was to lie low until the storm blew itself out, since all the key pieces were in his possession, and the Marquis, after his initial rage had expended itself, would have been compelled to submit. But this analysis ignores the real nature of Julien's spiritual vulnerability. Julien's dilemma is that of any man who is unable to blind himself to the pervasiveness of deception and sham, who despises class distinctions, riches and sycophancy and obsession with rank, and yet at the same time is himself still in thrall to such false values. For such a man is of all men least able to endure self-contempt, and yet is held fast in the grip of passions he most despises. If anyone or anything should bring his conflict, ever smouldering below the surface, to the point of eruption, the resultant explosion is bound to be sharp indeed.

What Julien can under no circumstances endure is patronization or any form of condescension which at once reminds him of the inferiority of his birth and status, which he cannot entirely rid himself from feeling. When a young man in a café in the Rue St. Honoré, like Amanda's lover in the Besançon brasserie, stares at him—the insolence has to be inferred, it is not stated—the effect on Julien is on both occasions electric. To his humiliation he is thrown into a state of intense agitation, even 'dripping with sweat', so great is his excitement. 'How can I rid myself of this humiliating sensibility?' he reflected. And conversely, any mark of recognition flattering to his self-esteem, acts as an immediate balm to his insecurely poised identity and enables him to relax in a measure of self-confidence. After sending Julien on what purported to be a diplomatic mission to England, de la Mole rewards Julien with a Cross or some such insignia. 'This Cross set Julien's pride at its ease; he talked much more freely. He less frequently felt himself insulted . . .'[2] His subjugation of the pride of Mathilde when he

[1] Emile Faguet, *Politicians and Moralists of the Nineteenth Century*, London 1928, pp. 60-2.

[2] *Scarlet and Black*, op. cit., p. 291. Ironically, it is the conferring of this mark of favour to which Julien owes the visit of Valenod, about to replace de Renal as

discovers that she is unable through passion to return his scorn, has a similar effect: '. . . his face no longer bore the hard imprint of a pride turned inwards on itself by a constant sense of inferiority.'[1]

It is therefore not difficult to understand the intensity of Julien's reaction when he is charged with making a catspaw of the Marquis's daughter in order to gain ascendancy over the Marquis himself, the seat of power. It is sufficiently close to the truth to make even more intolerable the fact that the accusation is unjust. It is unjust because Julien above all despises those who sacrifice human relations, genuine affections to the degraded values of status seeking. For example, he not only felt a real affection that was fully reciprocated for Mme de Renal's children, but he noted the instantaneous chilling effect on the children's spirits of the arrival of their father whose egoism and worldly preoccupations had long since driven out all possible affection. At the same time, although the charge of hypocrisy against Julien is untrue, it reminds him of the world's evident refusal to forget his humble status that he seeks so desperately to escape, and also of the fact that this unconscious preoccupation acts as a blight upon his ability to love. He was powerfully attracted, it is true, to Mme de Renal, but he had rewarded her disinterested tenderness by abandoning her without a qualm to her peculiarly loveless marriage. The case with Mathilde is even worse. In a battle of aristocratic pride with the pride of ambition, it is his pride that wins the day. There is no real love. But there was as much love as he was capable of, and he respected the Marquis to whom he was genuinely grateful; and he scorned those who trafficked in human feelings for the sake of worldly advancement.

Julien is also in a condition of ever-increasing strain because of the double role that he is compelled to play. Throughout his life he has to hold himself severely in check in order by calculation to evince the response of artificiality, pretence and hypocrisy that is necessary for the social advancement he yearns for. It does not come naturally to him. By dint of great and ceaselessly renewed effort he can achieve the duplicity necessary to deceive others; but himself he cannot deceive. His Achillean heel, ultimately more fatal to his ambitions even than his consuming pride, is his love of truth. 'I have loved truth . . . where

---

mayor of Verrières, and anxious to consolidate his position still further. Julien, close to the source of patronage, thus helps Valenod into a prefectship, from which position Valenod felt strong enough to defy the ecclesiastical patronage of the Abbé de Frilair at the end by bringing in a verdict of guilty against Julien from the jury box in his trial for attempted murder.   [1] Ibid., p. 316.

can I find it?' he avows to himself when very close to the end. 'Every-where I see hypocrisy, or at least charlatanism, even among the most virtuous, even among the greatest men.'[1] He had to act a part because his innate truthfulness, if given free rein, would result in his being shunned by polite society. 'How immensely difficult it is, he went on thinking, to play the part of hypocrite every minute—it's enough to make the labours of Hercules pale beside it.'[2] There is no greater emotional strain than to live in a situation, be it of one's own or others' making, where one is not free to be oneself. Julien aspired to a brilliant and secure place in the world, where no one would so much as suspect that he was the poor son of a brutal Jura carpenter. But from the stand-point of his aspirations he had made the fatal mistake of learning to reason correctly and to respect truth at the hands of the good priest, his first tutor, M. Chélan, whose own virtue proved sufficient to cost him his own humble post.

Julien's divided soul can best be seen in his reaction to the pealing of the church bells in Besançon, especially if we contrast his state of mind with that of Fabrice del Dongo at prayer in the cathedral in *The Charterhouse of Parma*, '. . . Julien's spirit, borne upwards on the rich, bass tones of the bell, was wandering through worlds upon worlds of the imagination. . . . Natures yielding to emotion like this are good at most to make artists only.'[3] This was the natural, spontaneous ex-pression of Julien's self, but his ambition was to be a successful ad-ministrator, a man of power and position; and to this end his natural reactions were not well adjusted. He would accordingly have to act the part; to pretend to a nature not his own, one baser than his own.

> The deeply sonorous tones of this bell should not have awakened any-thing in Julien but the thought of twenty men working for fifty centimes apiece, aided, perhaps, by fifteen or twenty pious worshippers. He should have thought of the wear and tear on the bell-ropes and the wooden framework, of the risk to the bell itself which comes tumbling down every two hundred years. He should have reflected on some way of reducing the wages of these bell-ringers . . .[4]

In short, Julien's natural emotions and responses are at war with his consuming ambition that sets goals for him to which he is ill fitted by nature. The world's values do not come to him naturally. This psycho-logical situation, which was Stendhal's own, is high-lighted by the

[1] *Scarlet and Black*, op. cit., p. 501.
[2] Ibid., p. 194. [3] Ibid., p. 207. [4] Ibid., p. 206.

reverse situation described in an episode in *The Charterhouse of Parma* where Fabrice confesses his sins in order to obtain pardon. Fabrice gives way to emotions that are perfectly genuine for him, although his sincerity is dependent upon his ability to remain oblivious to certain evident facts of his situation.

> Fabrizio asked pardon of God for many things, but what is indeed remarkable is that it never entered his head to number among his sins the plan of becoming Archbishop simply and solely because Count Mosca was Prime Minister and considered that office and all the social distinction it conferred to be suitable for the Duchessa's nephew. He had desired it without passion, it is true, . . . It had never occurred to him to think that his conscience might be concerned in this project of the Duchessa's.[1]

In order to succeed in the world it is necessary that the moral sensibilities be spontaneously and naturally blunted. It will not do merely to simulate them. Simulated hypocrisy leaves people unconvinced and uneasy as well as imposing a strain on the actor greater than the labours of Hercules. The hypocrisy must be natural so that it in effect ceases to be hypocrisy.

Fabrice knew by heart the list of sins printed in the Latin rendering of *Preparation for the Sacrament of Penitence*, and when he came to the article, *Murder*, he acknowledged his offence, but sought exoneration on the grounds of self-defence. But when he came to the sins of Simony he passed them by oblivious. For while he would have recoiled with horror at the suggestion that he should buy ecclesiastical office for cash, it simply did not enter his head that the employment of influential political interest on his behalf was a form of Simony. This ability, comments Stendhal, he owed to a Jesuitical education which has the double merit of depriving a man of the courage to reflect in the face of habit and of forming the habit of ignoring things plainer than daylight.

> A Frenchman, brought up among the characteristic self-interest and irony of Paris might, without being deliberately unfair, have accused Fabrizio of hypocrisy at the very moment when our hero was opening his heart to God with the utmost sincerity and the very deepest emotion.[2]

It was the lack of this facility, an inherent inability to deceive himself and a scrupulous regard for the truth within his own mind that was Julien Sorel's 'undoing', in that it doomed him in his ambitious

---

[1] *The Charterhouse of Parma*, op. cit., p. 209. [2] Ibid., pp. 209–10.

enterprise. Julien brilliantly mirrors the conflict that divided Stendhal's soul. Stendhal's love of the truth operated as a fatal bar to his ambitions. But he could not root out ambition from his soul; it required the violence of impending execution to root it out of Julien's. 'One after the other, all the hopes ambition had planted had to be rooted up out of his heart by the fatal words: "I am to die."'[1] Ambition, be it noted, not pride or vanity.

The picture of Stendhal with which the world is most familiar is that of the secularist and sybarite, a man who worshipped action, even violence, dynamic heroism to redeem the boredom of a life whose only meaning was to be found in the act of living itself. Faced with the mystery of human existence in relation to the universe and eternity, Stendhal gave us the graphic metaphor of the ant-hill disturbed by the hunter's boot—'The most philosophical among the ants will never be able to understand . . .' If there is any meaning to life which transcends life itself, it is not given to men to understand it—we are no more equipped to understand such mysteries than the mayfly born in the morning and destined to die in the afternoon could grasp the concept of night. Therefore, it behoves a rational man, in the great encircling night of non-existence, to draw on his resources of fierce energy, to seize to the full the passing minute, to live for the day without thought of the morrow, to intoxicate himself with the delights and joys of life and action, of ambition and love. Dynamic action, heroic intensity are to be admired; pale insipidity, actionless morally inhibited lives are to be despised. He admires the man of passion, the Bonaparte, the Casanova, the man who does not allow his ambitions or lusts to be trammelled by the snaffle and bit that restrain men of common clay. He respects the man who follows his bent in contempt of conventional religion and morality.

This side of Stendhal—and it is assuredly there—is the one that is best known. It found its lasting monument in the character of Julien, fighting his way up by the secret fire animating him, from a position of obscurity among the most despised classes of society, via a tutorship, seminarist, abbé, marquis's secretary, to become himself a powerful minister and noble. But this is only one side of Stendhal.[2] If that had been all, we should not have remembered him. At war with this element was a quite different one.

[1] *Scarlet and Black*, op. cit., p. 456.
[2] 'Man, in truth, he [Julien] reflected, has two separate beings inside himself. Who the devil hit upon that malicious idea?' Ibid., p. 488.

If the Marquis de la Mole noticed that Julien's pride and inability to endure contempt made him vulnerable to his power, there was another and mysterious quality in Julien, which he sensed without being able to define, and which justifiably alarmed him. It required the perceptive insight of his daughter, Julien's lover, to enlighten him as to the real nature of this highly significant quality. 'My daughter expressed it to me very aptly—"Julien doesn't belong to any drawing-room or any particular set." He has not provided himself with any backing against me, not the least resource if I throw him over . . .'[1] This is so contrary to all the rules of common sense, to the entire logic of power which dominates all their lives, that the Marquis is at a loss to understand it. He tries to reassure himself that Julien might behave in this manner through 'ignorance of the present state of society'. Yet this stratagem does not succeed in allaying his fears. And the Marquis's instincts are quite correct, although he is incapable of articulating the ground of his fear consciously to himself. For Julien's apparent vulnerability, his neglect of the most obvious forms of prudence and self-defence, his freedom from the demands of allegiance of party or faction constitutes the essence of a free spirit that cannot be tamed. His non-membership denied his adversaries any hold on which they could obtain a purchase. He cannot be bought or intimidated by the blandishments or threats which so easily work their way with normal organized men.

This free, anarchic spirit, untamable by virtue of its very defence-lessness is, moreover, not the dupe of the tinsel of imperial power and heroic action, over-riding the scruples of morality. It sees through the bombastic fraudulence of Napoleonic empire and its overweening ambition to the spiritual sepulchre it conceals. At the end Julien himself concludes by echoing Saint-Giraud's earlier verdict on Napoleon: 'What with his chamberlains, his pomp, and his receptions at the Tuileries, he produced a new edition of all the senseless follies of monarchy.'[2] Julien's own verdict is: 'Napoleon at St. Helena! . . . Pure charlatanism, . . .'[3] 'Less and less fooled by appearances, he comes gradually to see behind the façade into the reality within men's hearts. He is no longer gulled. When the Public Prosecutor appeals to natural law, he dismisses it as ancient humbug wherewith the rich, whose ancestors owed their wealth to the property confiscations of Louis XIV, justify their present depredations and persecutions of the poor. 'No,' he reflects, 'the men whom people honour are only rogues who have the good fortune not to be caught red-handed.'[4]

[1] Ibid., p. 446.   [2] Ibid., p. 246.   [3] Ibid., p. 501.   [4] Ibid., p. 500.

But how is he who sees through the world's protective defences himself to avoid contamination? Hardness of heart, contempt for one's fellows, cynicism will bring a man lower than will hypocrisy. Julien is saved by his essential purity of heart and by the genuine love which he had aroused in the breast of Louise de Renal. When he learned in prison that she had not after all died of his bullet, his heart melted with remorse and relief, and sinking to his knees, he wept hot tears.

> In this supreme moment he believed in God. What matter the hypocrisies of the priests? Can they detract in any way from the truth and sublime majesty of God?[1]

He returns more than once to this theme, namely, that the bitter anti-clericalism which he directed against the Maslons, the Frilairs, the Castanèdes, arose from the pain he felt at witnessing the behaviour of those who debased and perverted the example and teaching of him in whose name they professed to act. He contrasts the God of the Christians with the God of Fénelon. The former he fears as 'a tyrant'. He is 'full of ideas of vengance, his Bible speaks of nothing but horrible punishments. I have never loved him. . . . He is without pity.' But the God of Fénelon is altogether different. 'He will say to me perhaps: "Much shall be forgiven thee, for thou hast loved much" . . .' And Voltaire's God too was 'just, kind and infinite'. The difficulty is caused, he reflects, not by the great name of God, but by 'the frightful abuse that our priests make of it'. Why should we, however, allow them a monopoly of our linguistic inheritance, merely because they contaminate and debase it? If only priests were true exponents of Christianity, poor men like the first apostles! But in the self-same breath he is unable to silence the corroding suspicion that even St. Paul was not free from the taint of egoism, if only in the satisfaction he must have experienced as a law-giver and in hearing himself praised. The pendulum still swings right to the end between the will to worship goodness and an ineradicable cynicism springing from a wounded vanity. And yet Stendhal's last word in this truly magnificent novel is a paean of praise to Duty, not Duty as the stern daughter of the Puritans, but of Pascal, of Rousseau, who found its voice most clear in the melting of the human heart. As Julien reflects about what we can know here on earth, it is the truths which spring from the heart, not the truths of science which he finds of supreme value. 'We know nothing about the source of the Nile,' he thought; and what, it is implied, does it matter, one

[1] *Scarlet and Black*, p. 458.

way or the other? For 'I have a heart that is easily moved; the most commonplace things, when uttered with an accent of truth, can make my voice tremble with emotion and even bring tears to my eyes. How many times have stony hearts not despised me for this weakness!' And because he had a heart, and is a man among men, he dwells not in isolation, but known fellowship. Ultimately he is not alone, because the sense of duty that comes from the God that speaks through the heart is always with him as his constant stay and support, even if he is not infallible in interpreting that voice.

> I always had the compelling thought of duty with me. That duty, that, rightly or wrongly, I had prescribed for myself, has been like the solid trunk of a tree against which I could lean during the storm. I swayed to and fro, I was shaken. After all, I was only a man . . . but I was not carried away.[1]

Before taking leave of Stendhal, there is one other point to be noted of considerable significance for the student of Tolstoy as well as of Stendhal. Every reader will readily recall the dark omen by which the final tragedy of Anna Karenina herself is foretold when, at the beginning of the story, on Anna's arrival in Moscow, a railway worker is run over by the wheels of the train. The device is taken straight out of Stendhal. At the end of the fifth chapter of *Scarlet and Black*, Julien sees on a pew in church a scrap of paper concerning the last moments of a man executed in Becançon. He notices that the name has the same ending as his own and finally by a trick of light he receives the impression that he sees blood near the holy water stoup. The device is repeated in *The Charterhouse of Parma*—less artistically because it takes the form of an explicit prophecy put into the mouth of Father Blanès, but it enables Stendhal to develop his own feelings through the reactions of Fabrice. Father Blanès warns Fabrice that he is destined to be immured in a prison, more painful, more terrible than the one he had briefly experienced on his pilgrimage to Waterloo, but that he will be enabled to escape by the crime of another person. We are made aware of Stendhal's acceptance of the status of science, his distrust of the attempt to assimilate its capacity to predict to the affairs of humanity, and his uneasy belief in the controlling hand of what he suspects or rather desires to believe is the will of Providence. 'Every foretelling of the future is a breach of the rules,' he comments, 'and contains this danger, that it may alter the events; in which case the

[1] Ibid., p. 502.

whole science falls to the ground, as in one of those games that children play with cards or bricks.'[1] This single objection is seen as fatal to the pretensions of those who would project a science of history.

Fabrice mirrors his creator's antipathies and is little concerned with the empirical curiosity of those who seek to penetrate by experiment the relations of effects and causes or how to adapt themselves to the laws of universal order. 'He was far from employing his time in a patient examination of the actual character of things in order to discover their causes. Reality still seemed to him dull and sordid.' Instead, he was animated by what he was reluctant to acknowledge as a religious belief in the authentic significance of omens in presaging the truth of an underlying metaphysical reality, to which men are far too ready to close their eyes.

> Thus it was that, although not lacking in intelligence, Fabrizio could not manage to see that his half-belief in omens was for him a religion, a deep impression received on his entry into life. To think of this belief was to feel, it was a happiness. Yet he persisted doggedly in an attempt to discover how this could be *proved* a real science, in the same category as geometry, for example: . . .[2]

When Julien Sorel heard Father Pirard offer him a curacy and half the income from his living if things did not turn out well for him at the Hôtel de la Mole, Julien, conscious of the contrast between the hatred felt for him by his own father and the kindness shown to him by this fatherly priest, felt the tears welling up in his eyes. 'I'll never rail at chance any more . . .' he says, only to be gently rebuked by Father Pirard, 'You must never speak of chance, my son, but always of Providence.'

By the manner of his dying, if not always of his living, Stendhal set the seal on the faith he ascribed so feelingly to Fabrice, of whom he wrote: 'And he would have felt an insuperable repugnance towards the person who denied the value of omens especially if he had resorted to irony.' Writing this time in his own person—of Henri Beyle—he later wrote: 'I find that there is nothing ridiculous in dying in the street when one does not do it on purpose.' Twelve months afterwards, on the evening of 22 March 1842, he fell to the Paris pavement from a stroke from which he did not regain consciousness.

---

[1] *The Charterhouse of Parma*, op. cit., p. 168.
[2] Ibid., p. 164.

4

Alexander Herzen:
The Wheel in the Squirrel's Cage

Tolstoy greatly admired Herzen's writings in general, although he strongly disapproved of Herzen's teaching on sexual ethics. Sergei, Tolstoy's eldest son, wrote of his father: 'He used to say of Herzen's personal tragedy that it was partly brought about by the fact that the men of those days, Herzen included, were light-hearted about betraying their wives with housemaids or prostitutes, whereas the women took such matters very much more seriously.'[1] After leaving Herzen in London (1861) Tolstoy wrote to him from Brussels in cordial and enthusiastic terms concerning his writings, and humbly asked Herzen's opinion about his project of writing a novel around the subject of a Decembrist family returned from exile in the mid-fifties. Nearly half a century later when in 1905 an edition of Herzen's works appeared in Russia—it was the occasion of the first Russian publication of *From the Other Shore*—Tolstoy, after reading this work, noted in his diary that it was excellent and that it was so far above the heads of the present-day Russian intelligentsia that it would still have to await an audience capable of understanding it in the future. He was right. Since

[1] Sergei Tolstoy wrote: 'In the fifties Father had formed a preconceived hostile opinion of Herzen, but after 1861, when he actually met him in London, he changed his mind. They were photographed together on the momentous day of the proclamation of the emancipation of the serfs. . . . They shared a hatred of Nicholas I and Father was often to quote Herzen's words on tyrants in general: "Chenghiz-Khan was no doubt a menace and difficult to fight again [sic]. But how much more terrible it is when at the disposal of such a figure there can be guns, railways, telegraphs and telephones and all the other achievements of modern science. Nobody can fight against that." . . . Later on he came to appreciate Herzen more and more. He said that the banning of Herzen's writings in Russia left Russian society unaware of an important trend in Russian letters and that this caused a distortion in Russian thought. He approved of Herzen's opinion of the slavophiles, who wished to remind the people of something they really wanted to forget: orthodoxy and autocracy. Sergei Tolstoy, *Tolstoy Remembered*, translated by Moura Budberg from the Russian edition (1949), London 1961, pp. 67–8.

then another half-century has passed, and Herzen is still awaiting an audience willing to understand him.

In Martin Malia's intensive study devoted to Herzen as a thinker and forerunner of Russian socialism, Herzen's intellectual evolution is carefully traced. We are taken through his youthful enthusiasms, divided between Hegelian idealism and his addiction to explanations of causality consistent with the metaphysic of scientific materialism, to his full maturity as leader of the Russian revolution in exile after his fleeing to the West and briefly participating in the abortive Paris revolution of 1848. Professor Malia, surveying in retrospect Herzen's contributions to political thought in the years of his creative maturity, has this to say:

> . . . the utopian form in which Herzen's ideals, no less than Bakunin's, were expressed is alien and even disturbing to the empirical, pragmatic Anglo-Saxon mind. It is only too easy for the insular or transatlantic critic of continental ideologies to demonstrate that in a literal sense such utopian extravagances are unreal or untrue; and the present book in particular has not neglected this enterprise of 'de-mythologizing' and of ideological deflation. Nonetheless, the world is moved as much by visions as by reasoned reflection on reality. To be sure, grandiose schemes such as Herzen's never are, or can be, applied literally. Yet, just as surely, utopias are 'over-ideologized', or inflated, statements of possible solutions to real problems, statements that are inflated in response to the pressure of staggering obstacles to action; and the more refractory these problems are to reasonable resolution, the more exaggerated the utopia becomes. In short, utopias arise in situations where, in order to make a point at all, it is necessary to overstate it. Indeed only in this way can the psychic energy be generated that permits the beginning of action under oppressive conditions; for utopias are effective not as pondered social blueprints, but as dramatizations of nascent ideals and catalysts of new values.[1]

Malia, in this somewhat laboured passage, clearly feels himself to be on the defensive in asking readers in the Anglo-Saxon milieu to take Herzen seriously at all. So credulous is the prevailing climate of opinion of the normative status of whatever actually is—its sheer ubiquitous pervasiveness appears to carry its own justification—that people wear an apologetic air at best when they approach a writer like Herzen. For Herzen does not for a moment permit a reality deranged by other people's practice to cloud or otherwise get in the way of the

[1] Martin Malia, *Alexander Herzen and the Birth of Russian Socialism 1812–1855* Cambridge Mass. 1961, p. 419.

clarity of his intellectual conscience. What others call his vision, his unreality, his utopias is in fact simply his truthful reporting of the findings of his mind and heart—'conscience'—concerning the truth of how we ought to live and how we do in fact live.

Herzen spent the last twenty years of his life in London; yet he is not very widely read in the English-speaking world. He died in 1870, an exact contemporary of Dickens (1812–1870), and the 1911 edition of the Encyclopaedia Britannica contains only a brief entry on him. Judging by the frequency with which it is quoted, he is perhaps best known for his own description of his reaction to the news of the death in 1855 of the Tsar, Nicholas I, of whom the historian, Alison Phillips, wrote: 'The emperor was a kind husband and father, and his domestic life was very happy.'[1]

> On the morning of the fourth of March I went as usual at eight o'clock into my study, opened the *Times*, read a dozen times and did not under-stand, did not dare to understand, the grammatical sense of the words at the head of the news column: *The death of the Emperor of Russia.* Hardly knowing what I was doing, I rushed with the *Times* in my hands into the dining-room; I looked for the children and the servants to tell them the great news, and with tears of joy in my eyes gave them the newspaper . . . I felt as though several years had rolled off my shoulders. It was im-possible to stay in doors. . . . I ordered champagne . . . In the streets, on the Exchange, in the restaurants, people were talking of nothing but the death of Nicholas; I did not see one man who did not breathe more easily from knowing that that sore was taken out of the eye of humanity, and did not rejoice that that oppressive tyrant in the big boots had at last re-turned to clay.[2]

The sheer exuberance and force of the writing makes the passage a difficult one to forget. It is writing inspired by deep emotions of a kind: 'tears of joy', 'champagne', 'the great news'—the language of a cele-bration, a great festive occasion. But what is the occasion? The death of a man. 'Not a man', we can imagine Herzen replying, 'the death of Impernickel, the death of Nicholas the Stick, of "White Straps", of a sore in the eye of humanity.' Nevertheless, the death of a man also; and while we sympathize with Herzen and are on his side, something in us recoils from the living, unforgiving hatred of the words. Herzen

---

[1] Tolstoy gives us a shuddering glimpse of Nicholas's 'very happy' domestic life in *Hahji Murad*.

[2] *My Past and Thoughts: The Memoirs of Alexander Herzen*, translated by Constance Garnett, London 1924, Vol. III, pp. 311–12.

of course knew this. Not only were his own instincts of the gentlest. He had been brought up on the Gospels from his early childhood, and they remained with him throughout life as a steadfast support of the gentler side of his nature. Speaking of his childhood, he writes:

> . . . I used to read the Gospel a great deal and with love, both in the Slavonic and in the Lutheran translation. I read it without any guidance, and, though I did not understand everything, I felt a deep and genuine respect for what I read. In my early youth I was often influenced by Voltairianism, and was fond of irony and mockery,[1] but I do not remember that I ever took the Gospel in my hand with a cold feeling; and it has been the same with me all my life; at all ages and under various circumstances. I have gone back to reading the Gospel, and every time its words have brought peace and gentleness to my soul.[1]

And the central message of the Gospel is, of course, that we should love even our enemies, do good to them that injure us, persecute us and despitefully use us, forgiving them even unto seventy times seven. All this Herzen knew, understood and valued—it brought 'peace and gentleness' to his soul. Yet he deliberately goes out of his way to reject these sentiments in the plainest possible way. The passage on Nicholas's death, it seems to me, has great significance. The full depths of the wounds in Herzen's soul are here laid bare. That he has hated Nicholas, that he still hates him now for all his dreadful crimes—that is one thing, but what Herzen cannot forgive either Nicholas or himself is precisely that the cruelty and suffocation of his reign have stifled in Herzen himself and in the best of his generation the ability to believe the truth of Christ that in their inmost souls they most wanted to believe. There are some crimes, says Herzen, that it is impossible to forgive; and it is this knowledge that spiritually disfigures and deforms us, for spiritual truth requires of us that we should forgive; that if we do not, if we carry the hatred around with us, it is we ourselves who are mutilated, who are the sufferers. Herzen knew this, but was impotent to struggle against his hatred of Nicholas; and this knowledge yet further embittered him. He had been insulted and injured

---

[1] *My Past and Thoughts: The Memoirs of Alexander Herzen*, Vol. I, p. 53: Compare with this his keen insight into the nature of irony expressed elsewhere. 'Really virtuous men are devoid of irony . . . Irony springs from the coldness of the soul—Voltaire, or from hatred of mankind—Shakespeare, Byron. It is a retort to humiliations undergone, a reply to insult, it is the reply of pride, not of the Christian.' Quoted by E. H. Carr, *The Romantic Exiles*, Penguin 1949 ed., p. 14.

imprisoned and exiled; these he could have forgiven; what he cannot forgive is that he has been robbed of the power to forgive.

My Past and Thoughts is an essential source-book—the best we have for the climate of thought that shaped and was shaped by the generation of the 1840s in Russia. But it lives and will continue to live in the realm of literature because indirectly it is an astonishingly vivid self-portrait of a man remarkable for his integrity and truthfulness. It is, moreover, still the best study in literature of the atmosphere and social effects, the suffocating futility and pointless cruelties of tyranny.

There were at the time a handful of students, who tried not so much to resist—such was not possible—as simply to speak. The only visible consequence was a sudden empty space in a lecture hall. 'X's place was no longer occupied; 'X' had disappeared—spirited away at night; later his papers and belongings were taken away. Those who had known him were told no longer to speak of him, and there the matter ended. Months passed; other classmates were seized in the night; they too vanished without trace. When however the victim was a member of a well-known family, it was impossible to suppress the truth entirely, and the facts leaked out and were gradually pieced together. Sungorov, for example: Herzen gives a brief account of this young man's sufferings in captivity before he died at Nertchinsk. Sungorov was a man of property. His estates at Bronnitsky and Arzamas were confiscated to pay for his keep and that of his comrades while awaiting trial. Having thus ruined his family, 'the first care of the authorities, however, was to diminish it'. This, the authorities accomplished by imprisoning his wife and two children for six months in the Pretchistensky prison, where her baby died. Herzen's comment is brief but just: 'May the rule of Nicholas be damned for ever and ever! Amen!'

Herzen himself was more fortunate—at the age of twenty-two he was imprisoned for nine months and then exiled for more than three years, first in Vyatka, a provincial town half-way to the Urals, and later in Vladimir, closer to Moscow. But then he was still virtually a student; his punishment conferred on him the dignity of one who had had the courage to offend the Autocracy; his exile proved compatible with romance in Vyatka and marriage in Vladmir after an illicit nocturnal visit to Moscow in order to rescue his bride from a threatened marriage by eloping with her. What embittered Herzen much more than these early trials, severe as they were, was the personal and petty humiliation he suffered at the hands of the Tsar at the age of twenty-eight. Employed through his father's influence in the Ministry of the Interior in

St. Petersburg, a married man with a growing family, he suddenly found himself dismissed from his post and sentenced to twelve months' exile in Novgorod, his 'offence' consisting of a casual reference in a letter to a friend to some six murders which had taken place near a well-known Petersburg landmark, in which he rashly permitted himself the luxury of remarking: 'So you may judge what sort of police we have here.'

Herzen had the best of reasons for understanding the significance of the spoken word in Russia. Everywhere truth has a peculiar power of its own, so that its statement in a world where it is not accustomed to frequent frank avowal does not go unnoticed. But in Russia under autocrats like Nicholas I and Joseph Stalin the truthfully spoken and, even more so, the written word achieved a special, almost holy status. As Herzen himself expressed it in his celebrated *Letter to Michelet* defending the Russian people: 'The terrible consequences of speech in Russia inevitably give it a peculiar force. A free utterance is listened to with love and reverence, because among us it is only uttered by those who have something to say. One does not so easily put one's thoughts into print when at the end of every page one has a vision of a gendarme, a troika, and, on the far horizon, Tobolsk or Irkutsk.'

Certainly Herzen's own words were effective in evoking the atmosphere of fear and suspense in the rigidly centralized police state administered by Nicholas and his gendarmes. If members of the ruling *élite* who stepped out of line by so much as a suspicion of a step, were dealt with so harshly and humiliatingly, it can be imagined what was the fate of the defenceless peasantry, the serfs. Herzen however does not leave it to our imagination. He gives chapter and verse to illustrate the only too justified terror of the peasants not so much of the arbitrariness of their masters, bad as that was, but from the processes of 'justice' itself. The victims, says Herzen, actually look forward to exile in Siberia, since what they have to endure at the hands of the authorities while awaiting trial is far worse. Torture, he underlines significantly, was abolished by Peter III, Catherine II and Alexander I, much as successive American administrations abolished jobbing and corruption in the Civil Service or successive British administrations abolished the slums and intolerable housing conditions. Many instances of official brutality and persecution, sometimes of whole villages, are given. The directing hand at the apex of the pyramid, the hand that governed all Russia, the Tsar's chief gendarme, was Araktcheyev, of whom Tolstoy was to write in *War and Peace*, where he compares his role *vis-à-vis* the Tsar with that of Davout *vis-à-vis* Napoleon: 'In the organism of States such men are necessary, as wolves are necessary in the organism of Nature, and they always exist, always appear and hold their own, however incongruous their presence and their proximity to the head of the government may be.'[1]

Herzen illustrates his view of Russia's rulers under Nicholas with an account of Araktcheyev's conduct of the investigation of the murder of his mistress, a serf girl in Novgorod. One of those investigated, although entirely innocent, was ordered to be flogged. The police captain, hardened as he was, could not bring himself to flog a pregnant woman and broke down. But it made no difference. The woman was duly tortured and killed. With such examples set by those at the apex of power, what could be expected at the hands of a host of petty despots with powers of life and death over their serfs throughout Russia? Again, a single episode briefly alluded to by Herzen, although less spine-chilling than countless atrocities, conveys unmistakably something of the atmosphere in which it was possible for human beings, even children, to be so basely degraded. A servant in the family of a police colonel at Penza spilt a kettle of boiling water as a result of being bumped into by his mistress's child. The child was in consequence scalded. The mistress, determined that the punishment should fit the 'crime', ordered the servants' child to be summoned and duly scalded the child's hand from the samovar.

Living in a land where such things were possible, it is not surprising that Herzen was of the opinion that 'Man is cruel and only prolonged suffering softens him.' Nevertheless, there are degrees of cruelty and pathology; and life in Russia under Nicholas excited the revulsion of the world. Even Queen Victoria, who acted as hostess to the Most High, Father of all the Russians, felt it necessary to find excuses for having this particular crowned head beneath her roof. Herzen's loathing was simply more intense than most; he was exceptionally sensitive to injustice, and he had suffered in person. But Herzen was much too intelligent to suppose that the responsibility for the peculiar suffering of his countrymen could all be laid at the door of a single royal drill sergeant and his blood-stained henchmen. Herzen attempts a diagnosis and it is remarkably shrewd.

His analysis of the nature of the relations between aristocrats, peasants, house-serfs and children is interesting because it rests on the

[1] *War and Peace*, translated by Louise and Aylmer Maude, London 1943 ed., p. 678.

unstated assumption that all men (including children) are in every-thing that is *humanly* essential equals. He believes that the sadness of their behaviour results from the way in which that equality is violated by their life situation in a rigidly class-structured culture. For example, the house-serf spends his leisure drinking in the restaurant in order to attempt to restore his dignity outraged by the long hours of servility, waiting around below stairs or in the hall to obey any whim or caprice of his masters. In the restaurant for a moment the roles are reversed, and he too can savour the pleasure of giving orders and finding himself obeyed. The moral depravity of serfdom as an institution is illustrated in the lives of Alexey, his father's cook, and Tolotchanov, the feldsher, whose lives were ruined by the peculiar humiliations of serfdom. The cook saved assiduously in order to buy his freedom, the achievement of which for him constituted the great goal, indeed the meaning of his life. He succeeded at last only to find that his master refused to allow him to buy it. He gradually sank into drink and despair; his life was irretrievably wrecked. Tolotchanov led a prosperous, useful life until the day that his wife discovered that he was a serf. She was so appalled that in the anguish of her disappointed social aspirations she drove the feldsher to suicide. Good, valuable, honest lives totally ruined and for no purpose! Such is Herzen's reckoning with serfdom; and again the basis of the analysis is of course the assumption known to each one of us that, whatever the institutions under which we live, all men are equal. This same realization underlies his peculiarly shrewd analysis of the mutual attraction he observed frequently to obtain between servants and children under serfdom. He himself as a child often used to take refuge from his loneliness below stairs where he was welcomed by and spent many long hours with the house-serfs. 'Children hate the aristocratic ideas of the grown-ups and their benevolently condescend-ing manners, because they are clever and understand that in the eyes of grown-up people they are children, while in the eyes of servants they are people.'[1] This is true—and brilliantly observed.

Herzen sees perfectly clearly that the cause of the pathology in the system is the denial of equality in human relations at every point from top to bottom of the pyramid. And in the absence of the recognition of that which is most distinctively human, the system in its inhumanity requires the labelling of people, so that each will know how to behave to another according to his badge of rank. For human relations are substituted insolence and servility, in which each seeks to take turn and

[1] *My Past and Thoughts*, op. cit., Vol. I, p. 33.

turn about in order to avenge on others weaker than himself the humiliations he has had to undergo at the hands of those more powerful than himself. The characteristic phrases of intercourse so based *de haut en bas* are 'Hold your tongue; I won't put up with your answering me!' or (turning pale with anger) 'You forget yourself; do you know to whom you are speaking?' When these ejaculated imperatives are the emanations of petty tyrannical egos throughout the land, the voices of landowners to serfs, of departmental heads to clerks, of officials to members of the public at large, it is inevitable that the entire collective is headed by a drill sergeant-in-chief ready to imprison men in the Peter Paul Fortress or to exile them to Siberia for the uttering of a thoughtless word, the expression of an opinion or the writing of a poem. If Russia groans under the knout, it is not because there happens by chance to be a bad man at the apex of the hierarchical pyramid. For, comments Herzen, all the rulers together, landowner, bureaucrat, Tsar, despots all, 'are readier to forgive stealing and bribe-taking, murder and robbery, than the impudence of human dignity and the insolence of an independent word'.

Herzen, himself an aristocrat to his finger-tips, ascribes the arrogance of power in the person of the great dignitaries not to aristocratic sentiment—since the old-style grand gentleman was at any rate a genuine personality—but to the insolence of what he calls 'liveried and powdered flunkeys in great houses'—insolent to their inferiors, abject to their superiors. He gives a vivid portrait of one, Tyufyaev, the Governor of Vyatka, whom Herzen knew and suffered at first hand during the first period of his exile. An ex-copying clerk, who combined in his person a truly Byzantine servility with the total obliteration of personality required by official discipline, he meted out to his subordinates in full measure the portion of suffering which had been his own lot under the whip of the bureacracy and the aristocracy. 'A true servant of the Tsar' is Herzen's description of him, void of all will, innocent of thought, a docile instrument in the hands of authority, but savage in oppression of those beneath him in the hierarchy. These faithful servants of the throne Herzen in an apt simile likens unto the medals of the Emperor Paul, which bore the inscription: 'not to us, not to us, but to thy name'. People exist not so much as individuals as units of rank consciousness—soldiers, clerks, station superintendents, considering their claim to immunity from blows or insult or their right to administer same to derive not from personal identity, ability or courage but from the badge of office, the Anna, the Stanislav, the

Vladimir ribbon—'not for ourselves, not for ourselves . . . but for our rank!' Russia has become a gigantic regimental barracks in which individuality is replaced by the uniformity of Facelessness, of the neutrality of lifeless obedience, in which the ideal is neither to laugh nor cry, neither to rejoice nor grieve, neither to praise nor criticize, but simply to conform.

If Herzen understood quite clearly then that autocracy sprang not from the will of a single man, but was a vast network of human relations grounded in the arrogance of power and the humiliation of servility, how did he see the sociology of parliamentary democracy in the more liberal West? Essentially his view, like that of Pestel, the Decembrist martyr before him and like that of Tolstoy somewhat later, was that parliamentary democracy rested on military force no less than an Autocracy, but that the face of violence was better concealed and also less harsh in its application. Its relative ability to enforce a non-discriminatory rule of law sprang from a degree of administrative decentralization obtaining in countries like Switzerland, England and America, which contrasted sharply with the extreme centralization of Russia and to a lesser degree of the Second Empire in France. He concedes the practical benefits of centralization in the organization and maintenance of posts and telegraphs, roads and currency; but for the rest warmly endorses the Swiss and Anglo-Saxon suspicion of the centralization of power. 'Centralization may do a great deal for order and for various public undertakings, but it is incompatible with freedom. It easily brings a nation to the position of a well-tended flock, or a pack of hounds cleverly kept in order by the huntsman.'[1] To see what disastrous, soul-destroying effects it has when applied to education, for instance, we need only look to the experience of the French, who, believing that equality in intellectual development was inseparable from the principle of uniformity, proceeded to centralize education. In consequence, the French are turned out ready-made by thousands on the same pattern. All public education—and in France all education is public—is organized so as to produce a soulless uniformity. 'In every town of the empire the same thing is being taught on the same day, at the same hour, from the same books. At all examinations the same questions are asked, the same examples set; teachers who make any departure from the text, or make any change in the syllabus, are promptly removed.'[2]

[1] *My Past and Thoughts*, Vol. III, p. 105.
[2] Ibid., Vol. III, p. 73.

But if Herzen found the English suspicion of centralization to his taste, he was not at all disposed to accept the claims of parliamentary liberalism at their face value. He was deeply influenced at the most impressionable time of his youth by the trial of the Decembrists, which took place when Herzen was thirteen years of age. He described in lyrical terms the rapturous emotion with which Ogarev and he took the vow on the Sparrow Hills overlooking Moscow always to be faithful to the ideals for which the Decembrists had died. Three of the condemned men tried in vain to obtain mercy by convicting themselves and expressing penitence. Pavel Ivanovich Pestel retained his complete integrity to the end and did not forswear himself. In his interrogation in the Peter Paul Fortress concerning the source of his liberal ideas, he acknowledged his debt to the works of Destutt de Tracy (who exercised such a strong influence on Stendhal) and to the successful experience of liberal democracy in the United States, but of Anglo-French parliamentary democracy he was scornful, and gave the following reason.

> I believed that in France and England the constitutions served only as covers and did not prevent the English Cabinet and the French King from doing what they wanted. And in this respect I preferred autocracy to such a constitution, for I reasoned that in an autocratic government the unlimited power is openly seen by all; in constitutional monarchies, on the other hand, there also exists limitless power, though it acts more slowly, and because of this it cannot correct evil fast . . . It seemed to me that the main trend of this century consists in the struggle between the popular masses and aristocracies of all kinds, whether of wealth or of birth. I estimated that, as in England, these aristocracies would eventually become stronger than the monarch himself and that they were the main obstacle to the state's happiness . . .[1]

Herzen shares this complete disillusionment with Western liberal constitutionalism, which he sees as a mask to conceal the avarice of Protestant commercialism. The medieval world was possessed of a certain aristocratic dignity, symbolized in the figures of the knight and the feudal lord, whose position rested on the principle of *noblese oblige*. Even if the obligations were far from honoured in reality, the code of chivalry was understood, could be appealed to and provided a certain measure of mutual security. Catholicism even more obviously imposed clearly defined moral obligations which again, though more honoured in the breach than in the observance, set limits to natural extravagance

[1] See Marc Raeff, *The Decembrist Movement*, New Jersey 1966, pp. 54-5.

and compelled those who lapsed to seek justification. This world could not survive because its structure rested on the classification of men according to status and this evoked the resistance of free men in the shape of the Reformation and the French Revolution. The feudal world perished at the hands of a wide variety of men, knights, gentlemen, watchmaker's apprentices, army doctors, merchant's sons— Ulrich von Huttens, Voltaires, Rousseaus, Schillers, Goethes—who had in common an inability to accept the wholesale categorzation of men on a basis solely of birth. Such historical change was necessary and not in itself to be deplored. The wretched consequences of this change sprang from the fact that there was nothing human to replace it; and in the void arose the petty bourgeois culture of property worship, expressed most characteristically in the religion of the Puritan, bleak, dreary, bigoted, and in the politics of republicanism, civic, formal, artificial. In place of a medieval culture resting on ideals which were found wanting arose a culture involving no obligations, terrifying in its bankruptcy. The petty bourgeois culture is purely commercial— emancipated from absolute monarchy and serfdom, it is true—but resting on no sense of moral obligation, not even the obligation to serve in the army so long as voluntary mercenaries can be found and governments can be hired to ensure their fiscal and physical security.

> ... its only obligation is *per fas et nefas* to have property. Its gospel is brief: 'Heap up wealth, multiply thy riches till they are like the sands of the sea, use and misuse thy financial and moral capital, without ruining thyself, and in comfort and honour thou wilt attain length of years, marry thy children well, and leave an honoured memory behind thee.'[1]

This is the spirit which informs the general atmosphere of European life with the result that where its principles are to be found most highly developed in the most industrialized, wealthy, cultured part of Europe, life is there at its most stifling, oppressive and insufferable.

In such a culture all conflict is inevitably canalized into two camps, contending with each other for property and power. On the one hand are the bourgeois property owners, who stubbornly defend their privileges and monopolies, and arrayed against them are the petty bourgeois, driven on by envy and avarice, possessed of no property but desperately anxious to wrest it from the bourgeoisie, if only they had the power. A man's role in life, the position he takes up on either

[1] *My Past and Thoughts*, op. cit., Vol. III, p. 146.

side in the conflict is thus determined not by moral principle—since a conflict over possession is morally meaningless—but by the accident of birth and fortune, status or class position. These being the basic socio-economic conditions governing political conflict, the institutional political forms best suited to the working out of this spurious conflict are those of liberal parliamentary democracy. For they provide the illusion of activity when the reality is one of moral bankrupty in the void left by the collapse of catholic feudalism. Even education is fraudulent, since the culture demands that its basis shall be the inculcation of the values of business and commerce in a nation of petty *commerçants*, battling against inherited or manufacturing wealth in the persons of the big bourgeois.

> One wave of the opposition after the other triumphs—that is, attains to property or position—and passes naturally from the side of envy to the side of avarice. Nothing can be more favourable for this transition than the fruitless swing backwards and forwards of parliamentary parties— it gives movement and sets limits to it, provides an appearance of *doing something*, and an external show of public interest in order to attain their private ends.

In the light of this analysis, he is then ready to illuminate his subject, namely parliamentary government, by means of his gift, shrewdly noticed by P. V. Annenkov, 'for making on the spur of the moment, and one after another, parallels between heterogeneous things'.[1]

> Parliamentary government not as it follows from the popular foundations of the Anglo-Saxon *Common Law*, but as it has taken shape in the law of the state, is simply the wheel in a squirrel's cage, and the most colossal one in the world. Could a show of a triumphant march forward whilst remaining majestically in the same spot be possibly achieved more perfectly than it is by the two English Houses of Parliament?[2]

His contempt for parliamentary democracy is not confined to the conservatism of the English model. The system itself is fraudulent, providing an illusion of choice, of possible change, when the reality is one of greed administered by 'X' or 'Y' within the framework of the *status quo*. His analysis of Gallic republicanism on the other side of the Channel is accordingly on all fours with the scathing exposure of the Anglo-Saxon squirrel's wheel. 'Do you want political action within the present order?' he asks rhetorically. Do you really want to emulate

[1] P. V. Annenkov, *The Extraordinary Decade*, Michigan 1968, Ch. XVII.
[2] *My Past and Thoughts*, op. cit., Vol. III, p. 144.

the liberal politicians of the moment, the Marrats, the Odilon Barrots? Answering his own questions, he replies:

> You don't want this, you feel that any decent man is outside all politics, that he can't seriously concern himself with such questions as whether a republic needs or doesn't need a President, whether an Assembly may or may not send men to hard labour without trial, or, whether one should vote for Cavaignac or Louis Bonaparte? You may spend a month or a year thinking which of them is better; but you won't decide because they are, as children say, 'both worse'. All that is left for a self-respecting man is not to vote at all. Look at the other topics à l'ordre du jour, they are all the same, . . . death looms up behind them.[1]

This entire soulless order of things is so irrational that it is doomed. Waste no pity on it; Tsarist autocracy and the so-called 'freedom' of bourgeois republics are alike condemned to death; for they are incompatible with genuine freedom and the ultimate aspirations of men. And what of the people? Although from time to time Herzen hurls an anathema in their direction, and although he is utterly contemptuous of the liberals' idealization of the people, fundamentally he looks to the people eventually to sustain the individualism, the love of independent character or personality, on which he sees freedom to be necessarily based.

He laments the apathy of the common people in England, who are three centuries behindhand. Not even the Chartist agitation stirs them, this being confined to a minority of town workmen. He was also pained by the servile snobbery of the English, which he was wont to illustrate with the following anecdote: Two flunkeys, rolling out a carpet across the pavement and up the steps of a London mansion, forced the passers-by to walk in the gutter so as to avoid the carpet. Herzen, brushing the servant aside, walked onto the carpet. Before he could be checked, Herzen heard the flunkey he had pushed out of the way, call to his colleague: 'Let him pass. He is a gentleman.'

As regards the French masses, after the disillusionment of 1848, he was at first bitter. The believers in an arithmetical universal suffrage put the very existence of the infant republic into the hands of the people, only to see them use the weapon of the suffrage to crush it. 'Is anyone who respects the truth', asks Herzen sardonically, 'going to ask the opinion of the first stray man he meets? What if Columbus or Copernicus put America or the movement of the earth to the vote?'

[1] Herzen, *From the Other Shore*, translated by Moura Budberg (first German ed. 1850), London 1956, pp. 96-7.

The masses are indifferent to the issue of individual freedom, of free speech; they are still in the stage of being dazzled by the glitter and pomp of power. Hostile to privilege and the monopolies under which they suffer, they want a government to govern *for* them, not against them; but that they should govern themselves is an idea wholly foreign to them, and they look with suspicion on those individuals marked by independence and talent to stand apart, refusing to do as others do.

But there is a paradox for the individualist—one who believes in the right and duty of every man to realize his own identity and act it out with conviction or even stubborn persistence—if he also affects to despise the people, who after all are no more than a large number of separate individuals. Herzen is aware of this, and in more expansive and mellow mood, he comes to the defence of the people. He sees them as having been misunderstood and cast for an impossibly artificial and idealized role by the liberals themselves awakening from the uncritical torpor of their privileged existence. In this way he not only works off his exasperation with the liberals, the men who had persecuted his friend, Proudhon, but re-establishes his identity and solidarity with the long-suffering, if ungrateful people. The people he sees as an elemental, majestic force which shapes history; to criticize the people is akin to criticizing the ocean or an earthquake. It is necessary only to understand the people whose irresistible sweep is destined to crush everything that stands in the way of their primeval aspirations.

> The pedagogic method of our civilizing reformers is a bad one. It starts from the fundamental principle that we know everything and the peasantry knows nothing: as though we had taught the peasant his right to the land, communal ownership, organization, the artel and the mir.[1]

Tolstoy similarly was apt to apotheosize the role of the people as a primary historical force with its own culture, institutions and its own inescapable momentum. Deeply antagonistic as both Herzen and Tolstoy were to Orthodoxy and Autocracy, they yet had much in common with the Slavophiles in their belief in the historic mission of the people, in their suspicion of Western materialism and in their rejection of the doctrine of progress through science.

It is absurd to blame the people even when they destroy what is good, because they are consonant with their circumstances, past and present, which have made them what they are. The people are a force of nature, transcending moral categories; they are as much a fact of

[1] *My Past and Thoughts*, op. cit., Vol. V, p. 329.

life as an oak, a blade of grass, the harvest. As well blame these for being what they are as hold the people responsible for being a kind of historically determined tidal wave. Responsibility lies rather with the cultured minority who represent the conscious thought of the time, although they too are not really to blame. The rich and privileged are no more to blame for their splendid legacy than are the poor to be held responsible for the poverty they find in their cradle on their entry into the world. Both are alike victims of injustice, of a tragic fate, which weaves its historic web regardless of the deserts of rich or poor. The liberals are not to blame—they at any rate evinced a tardy repentance, the pang of guilt felt by the privileged, educated minority at the end of the eighteenth century, as they suddenly bethought themselves of the meaning of equality, from which the majority were hopelessly shut out both in possessions, opportunity and understanding.

> In a genuine desire to reward the people for thousands of years of humili-ation, they declared it sovereign, demanded that every peasant should suddenly become a political person, should grasp the complicated pro-visions of a half-free, half-servile code of law, abandon his work, that is, his daily bread, and that this new Cincinnatus should now concern himself with general issues. . . . It was easier for liberalism to invent the people than to study it. It told lies about it out of love, no less than others had out of hate. The liberals constructed their people *a priori*, created it out of memories of things read, dressed it up in a Roman toga or a shepherd's cloak. No one thought about the real people. It lived, laboured, suffered nearby, round the corner, and if there was anyone who knew it, it was its enemies—the priests and the legitimists. Its lot remained unchanged, but the fictitious people became the idol of the new political religion. The holy oil with which the foreheads of the Tsars had been anointed, was transferred to its swarthy forehead covered with wrinkles and bitter sweat.[1]

In this way Herzen exculpates the people from responsibility for what has gone wrong, inveighs against romanticism, repudiates his own liberal past and yet without stripping the liberals of the authentic generosity of their impulses. The liberals at any rate 'loved the people after their fashion'; they sacrificed much for their cause, and therefore much shall be forgiven them. No one is to blame. Sancho Panza is a sturdy, honest figure, unimaginative but commanding respect; and Don Quixote, if a figure of fun in the absurdity of his extravagant delusions, also commands our sympathy by the essential nobility of

---

[1] *From the Other Shore*, op. cit., pp. 93-4.

his aspirations. Both alike are victims of an inherited culture, a social system based on injustice, a historical destiny almost impossible to escape. The mood is tolerant, but it is also deeply pessimistic, resigned and without the consolation of 'religion'.

But if Herzen has been tempered by years of disappointment, exile, crushed hopes, personal tragedies, he is of course never resigned in his own person to the evils that surround him, which he ceaselessly diagnoses with a view to struggling against and urging others to do likewise. For the inequalities, injustices and persecutions which he arraigns are not the end of the matter; their periodic outcome on the larger theatre of international relations is war. And the causes of war are shrewdly diagnosed in a short and little-known fragment which Herzen wrote on the occasion of the Austro-Prussian War in 1866. His view is that it is essential to recognize it as a morbid natural phenomenon in the sense that cholera is natural, and then on the basis of the evidence proceed to a scientific diagnosis of the causes of war as such—an attitude by no means common at that time. In the presence of cholera, we do not engage in futilities of justification or finding excuses; we do what is needful: bow our heads, treat the afflicted, bury the dead; but above all we seek the causes in the hope of eliminating them. Cholera, we know, has its origin in pits, awash with putrefying filth, where the germs breed. So these pits we clean out or rather, Herzen, always truthful, adds: 'we are always on the point of cleaning them'. Thus far, the analogy with war is exact save for one crucial difference. Whereas with cholera the rottenness is at the bottom of pits, in the matter of war the offending rottenness is to be found in the summits; and it is there that it is necessary to take our preventive measures.

He then makes an assertion which contains the two basic propositions on which Tolstoy was to erect his giant edifice of *War and Peace*, namely, (*a*) the elemental fatalistic character of war as a great natural, historical phenomenon, and (*b*) the fact that this fatal *motif* rests on lack of conscious responsibility on the part of the masses and unscrupulousness on the part of their leaders. In Herzen's own words:

> For the masses War has that self-same fatalistic, unconscious character as the sea. It is only powerful through the absence of consciousness at the bottom and the absence of conscience and truth at the top.[1]

Which is not to say that there are not specific causes, 'sufficient reasons' to explain the outbreak of each particular conflict, as there are, for

[1] A. I. Herzen, *Sochineniya*, Moscow 1958, Vol. 8, p. 268.

that matter, for each particular outbreak of cholera. At the moment wars are arising out of the dissolution of old national groupings and their forcible unification in new and larger ones, in the abortive failure of revolutionary attempts from below and in the feverish instability arising out of popular hopes disappointed by the failure of revolutionary promises to materialize. But the basic law holds good without which war could not occur: mass apathy and the falsehood and irresponsibility of rulers. Only a basic re-education, almost at the biological level, could modify the endless cycle of 'again blood and more blood...' That logic, although Herzen believes it to be educable, is so endemic and universal that he describes it as 'chemical'.

Herzen allowed for the possibility of moral development and never abandoned his faith in it; but, as he grew older, he had to struggle with a growing sense of pessimism and gloom. He speaks of the 'childishness of the human brain' which is accordingly unable to accept the truth in all its simplicity, but which requires a muddled complexity, incomprehensibility and irrationality of explanation to match its own confused incoherence. Nor, he insists, is he speaking of the uncultivated masses, but of the learned, the literary, juristic, governmental and revolutionary would-be governmental people who vie with one another in 'maintaining the innate senselessness of mankind'. Injustice, irrationality, absurdity must in the nature of things always prevail over their contraries, since the contending forces are so hopelessly unequal. On the side of rationality and truth never more than a handful of scientists and doctors, two or three thinkers and poets and arrayed against them the whole world, 'from Pius IX with the Immaculate Conception to Mazzini with the Republican Iddio; from the Moscow orthodox mysteries of Slavophilism to Lieutenant-General Radowitz...; from American spiritualists who call up the dead, to English missionary colonels who preach the Word of God to Indians on horseback at the head of their soldiers'.[1] In the face of this overwhelming senselessness, religious mania, men driven out of their wits and terrified in the name of maintaining necessary social unity, what is there left for a free man? Only the solace of consciousness that he is right and, in despite of all the evidence, hope in the future. Elsewhere he writes that the truth is too terrible to bear. To look some things in the face is so bitter that one is compelled to wonder whether it is necessary to tell plainly what we see.

[1] *My Past and Thoughts*, op. cit., Vol. III, pp. 198-9.

'The truth, the bare truth and nothing but the truth!' All that is very fine;
but is the seeing of it compatible with our life? Will it not corrode it, as too
strong an acid eats away the sides of a vessel, and is not the passion for it a
terrible infirmity that bitterly punishes one who cherishes it in his heart?[1]

Herzen himself saw with piercing clarity what was wrong and
diagnosed it brilliantly. But he was less sure of himself when it came
to prescription. He had the sharp insight of one who truly understood
and valued freedom, but, an atheist to the end, he had no solid metaphysical base on which to stand, and was accordingly driven back on
to the shoals of relativism. This is also seen in the fact that, although
his warm-hearted, sustained sincerity is never in doubt, he failed
himself to live up to his own best insights. He rejects wealth and
privilege as inconsistent with equality, as the fruits of avarice or the
cause of envy and as corrosive of the simplicity of the human spirit
at its best, but he justified his own wealth on the grounds that money
is power, a weapon, and it would be stupid to throw away a weapon in
time of war. 'It would be hypocritical to affect to despise property in
our time of financial disorganization.' And as always, when we have a
bad conscience, we are not convinced by our own reasoning and we
cast around for yet further decisive reasons. So he adds that besides
all this, 'the slavery of poverty is awful'. He has seen many good men
shipwrecked through loss of all their possessions. Again, his reasoning
turned him to reject civilization, particularly bourgeois, Protestant,
capitalist culture and to find it most insufferable where it was most
truly itself, namely, in the advanced industrialized states like Britain
and France in contrast to Italy and Spain. But it is France and Britain
where he in fact prefers to live, given the necessity of his exile from
Russia. But none of this touches the truth of his portrayal of the
poverty and misconceived direction of Western culture, and his
indictment of its sacrifice of spiritual values for the values of comfort,
physical well-being, technological change and the goals of acquisitiveness. He rightly perceives that these are the values of people who are
always in a hurry, because they have no confidence in where they stand
and seek not to renovate the basis of their impoverished lives but only
to escape into distraction or forgetfulness. He finds it all a 'melan-
choly, tragic' spectacle.

I see this not only in the careworn, wrinkled faces, but also in the fear of
any serious thinking, in the turning away from any analysis of the position,

---

[1] Ibid., Vol. IV, p. 162.

in the nervous thirst to be busy, to fill up the time with external distractions . . . All are moving, rushing, flying, spending money, striving, staring and growing weary, living even more uncomfortably in order to keep up with *progress*—in what? Why, just progress.[1]

This frenetic, feverish way of life springs from inner emptiness, frightening in its sheer *ennui*. It rests on a refusal to examine the source of what is wrong or even to admit that anything is wrong; and when the emptiness becomes intolerable, the tension is relieved by war. 'And when they are sick of exhibitions, they will take to war and find distraction in the sheaves of dead—anything to avoid seeing certain *black spots* on the horizon.'

Elsewhere he excoriates our effete need for comfortable security in the context of a discussion as to why it is that those who, unable to bear Europe and its entrenched injustices, flee to the promise of the New World across the Atlantic, generally come back disillusioned. They do so, he says, because modern Europeans can no longer bear to come face to face with Nature in all its primitive majesty, untouched by the hand of man. Our true values are those of the epicurean and the aesthete who demand the kinds of comfort and graciousness in living which are inseparable from permanent habitation and efficient administration, buttressed by police, Church, Law, Army, the whole being propped up by the ignorant acquiescence of the masses whose exploited labour alone makes it possible. And for this, he expostulates bitterly: 'For the sake of this mess of pottage, *well served*, we sacrifice our share of human dignity, our share of sympathy for our neighbour, and give our *negative* support to the *régime* which is in reality hateful to us.'[2]

The difficulty with Herzen is that he has nothing to offer to the individual as to why he should make sacrifices to attempt to stand fast against such overwhelming pressures. Consciousness of being right or hoping that somehow or other things will improve in the future are reasons which do not seem entirely convincing. He has outlived the romanticism of the revolutionaries, he tells us; he has put behind him the mystic belief in progress to which he had remained wedded longer than 'other theological dogmas'. All this is admirable if a sure anchorage is found at last. But what was there left? Nothing, he confesses, except a passionate, what he calls 'religious' belief in the individual, in the human will, by which he means a confidence in himself and faith in two or three friends. What is this ultimately other than the individualism

[1] *My Past and Thoughts*, Vol. V, p. 186.
[2] Ibid., Vol. VI (1927), p. 5.

of, say, John Stuart Mill, stripped of the utilitarian rhetoric? As he himself candidly admits, there were inner contradictions in such a position, and this fundamental contradiction between absolute and relativist values he never did resolve. It is the fatal flaw, the Achilles heel in Herzen.

He is quite explicit in avowing his relativism. In answer to the question: 'Is there not an eternal morality, one and indivisible?' he answers categorically, 'No.' Such an absolute morality necessarily could have no existence outside the realm of theory and abstract thought. There are several moralities which unfold and succeed each other in historical time. The first Christians themselves, he makes bold to claim, acknowledged the relativism of all moral codes, by announcing that the heathen virtues, the values of Plato, the maxims of Cicero, the entire pantheon of the Olympic gods, had been super-seded by a new morality, that proclaimed by them, a religiously based morality which has now grown old in its turn and stands in urgent need of renovation. In default of such revivification in a new-found morality, the people, backsliding from a Christianity in which they no longer believe, are descending into the pit of a heathen patriotism, in which they have nothing better to honour than the honour of the flag. As in the days of the Caesars of old, conscience has given way to a moral void in which the people become the accomplices of their own enslavement, without regret, without remorse, approving of their own abasement. In the ensuing darkness, men pitching about rudderless, not knowing where to turn, fall into the trap of nationalism, the doctrine that in the absence of right, we might just as well respect might. In short, there is no Truth, only new values gradually forged to replace old ones which have ceased to carry conviction and are found wanting.

But at different times we find Herzen striking a different note. For instance, in a paean of praise to the Latin Quarter of the Left Bank of the Seine, he evokes the shades of the religious orders of the Middle Ages, the Carthusians or Camaldoli (a Benedictine order) whom he extols for turning away from the noise of Vanity Fair in order to preserve their faith in mercy, brotherhood and the immanence of the Kingdom of God. And this at a time when violence reigned supreme, when knights and *ritters* plundered and raped, burnt and slayed. Time passed and the longed-for brotherhood, the prophesied Second Coming did not materialize. On the contrary, new horrors have succeeded the old. '. . . Women are outraged now for pay, men are robbed in accordance with accepted rules.' The Kingdom of God is as distant as ever, but the Quartier Latin retains its faith undimmed.

> At every blow which sends the last fragments of freedom flying into dust, at every downward step of society, at every insolent step backwards, the Quartier Latin lifts up its head, . . . The Quartier Latin believes in its course and boldly draws the plan of its 'kingdom of truth', running directly counter to the 'kingdom of reality'.[1]

Here it is dolefully acknowledged that the world of reality evinces few signs of significant change for the better; but over against this is seen a vision, equally constant, unchanging, unspotted, lovingly cherished, of the contrasting Kingdom of Truth, God's kingdom. No relativism, no historical sloughing off old skins for new, no several equally subjective moralities here. Simply the Kingdom of God eternal, unchanging, diametrically opposing by love the world of burning, raping and slaying outside the walls.

Ultimately the profoundest and best side of Herzen's nature identifies quite unequivocally with the free spirit of man, capable of emancipating itself from the determining influence of appetite and environment. He believes in the ineluctable freedom to choose inherent in each and every individual. If history is determined, it is not inexorably so. The existing form of the State is doomed; nothing, he believes, can stand in the way of socialism eventually. But the forms of development will be determined in detail by the will of individuals. Progress is possible, albeit very slow. He likens it to the movement of Alpine glaciers. Every summer the ice crust melts, every autumn it begins to freeze again a little thinner. Meteorologists can reckon how many aeons of time will be needed for the summer finally to beat the winter and melt all the ice; the historians have not as yet made their parallel calculation. In fact, they could not do so, as Herzen in his non-scientific mood, well understands. For there is nothing inevitable about progress. As he himself points out, the power of evil as of good is dependent on the will and work of individuals. 'It is possible to lead astray an entire generation, to strike it blind, to drive it insane, to direct it towards a false goal. Napoleon proved this.'[2] And in our own time Hitler proved it even more decisively.

If there is freedom for evil, there is certainly freedom for good. The mistake people make lies in yielding too easily to the power of the

[1] *My Past and Thoughts*, Vol. V, pp. 271–2.
[2] Herzen, *From the Other Shore*, op. cit., p. 157.

external world; they give in without really willing it and thus find their independence, their most priceless possession, forfeit. Once we cease to rely upon ourselves, 'the fatal power of the external becomes invincible; to enter into battle with it seems madness'. To reject the sway of the temporal and material forces that seem to dominate our lives is, Herzen knows, not easy; frequently it requires long arduous trials in which a man feels himself sore beset. When dogged by misfortune he comes close to despair, and then at last when most at odds with the world, he feels confident not only that he understands it but that he understands himself; that he is no longer dependent on the world, because he knows that to struggle against it against all the odds is somehow indubitably right. There then arises in the soul the simple liberating question: 'Am I really so fettered to my environment in life and death that I have no possibility of freeing myself from it even when I have in fact lost all touch with it, when I want nothing from it and am indifferent to its bounty?'

From that moment a man is free, no longer herding together with his brethren for warmth and security, but alone, a stranger, an alien outside the gates, at war for ever with the City of Destruction, alone but standing on 'open, manly ground'. On this ground alone is nourished the inner spiritual freedom to advance humanity in defiance of the pressures of the power of autocracy above and of the masses below. Everything good comes from the individual, standing his ground, unafraid, yet humble enough to know that he is called upon to wage an unending struggle within himself as well as with a hostile, external world.

Finally, we take leave of Herzen with his individualist plea, which Tolstoy too reiterated over and over again. It is a passage which Tolstoy was fond of quoting, and which was in fact the central thesis of one of the last essays that he wrote, *The Inevitable Revolution* in 1909: 'If only people wanted to save themselves instead of saving the world, to liberate themselves instead of liberating humanity, how much they would do for the salvation of the world and the liberation of humanity.'[1]

---

[1] Herzen, *From the Other Shore*, op. cit., p. 128.

5

Pierre Joseph Proudhon
'War is divine':
'Humanity wants no more war'

Sainte-Beuve apart, some of the acutest observations we have on Proudhon we owe to his friend, Herzen. Almost exactly contemporaneous—Proudhon was three years senior—the Russian aristocrat and the Franche-Comtois peasant shared a common cause for which they each suffered imprisonment and exile. In 1855 at the height of the Crimean war, Herzen delighted Proudhon by inviting him to contribute to his first expatriate paper, *The North Star*—they had first met in Bakunin's lodgings in Paris during 1849. Proudhon replied: 'Our ideas, I believe, are the same, our causes are in solidarity, all our hopes are mingled.' Six years earlier, when Proudhon was on trial and his newspaper suppressed, Herzen had come to his rescue with 24,000 francs as a guarantee fund to start a new paper, *La Voix du Peuple*. Recalling the occasion in *My Past and Thoughts*, Herzen commented: 'I owed a great deal to Proudhon in my intellectual development, and, after a little consideration, I consented, though I knew that the fund would soon be gone.'[1]

Lamenting in biting terms the shameful and petty manner in which Proudhon had been persecuted, Herzen hailed him as 'one of the greatest thinkers of our age'—he might have added 'or of any other age'. He valued in Proudhon the earthy qualities of stubborn, blunt honesty which lifted him above the taunts of his numerous foes. What appealed to Herzen was the directness and simplicity of the challenge which Proudhon presented to Power, admirably illustrated in Proudhon's reply in the National Assembly to Thiers's rejection of his financial schemes not on economic grounds but by insinuations against his moral character. Proudhon, scorning the challenge of a duel—on one occasion he actually fought a duel—challenged Thiers instead to appear on the rostrum, and tell publicly the whole story of

1 Herzen, *My Past and Thoughts*, op. cit., Vol. III, p. 211.

his life fact by fact, as he himself would readily do. Thiers scowled, but made no answer.

As a rationalist Herzen admired Proudhon's impatience not only with the mysticism of Catholic theology but also with the sentimental, high-flown rhetoric of the Jacobinical heirs to the Revolution. Not content to exorcise heavenly phantoms, he liberated radical thought from the charge of utopianism and from litanies invoking fraternity and progress in an atmosphere of bitter sectarian squabbling. Herzen also admired Proudhon for anchoring morality in the heart of man as he deplored his resurrection of a new idol in the shape of the austerely rational, inhumanly cold abstraction of Justice. Herzen preferred to take his stand solely on Freedom, unshackled even by the demands of abstract Justice, although, as we have seen, such a position is fraught with ambiguity.

Herzen quotes Proudhon as expostulating with an English tourist, rash enough to have expressed his admiration for Proudhon's 'system': 'But I have no system.' Proudhon, he feels, is of greater significance for his method than for his results. With devastating effect he combined the method of the Hegelian dialectic and the traditional Catholic logic of controversy to forge a uniquely powerful instrument wherewith to crush the remnants of the old social, moral and intellectual culture. The importance of the method lies not in the content of the ideal which is unattainable, thought Herzen, but that in the course of working up to it, the present problem is correctly stated.

Certainly Proudhon's method needs examination before proceeding to the content of his argument, for if it was the source of his strength, the keen penetration of his destructive analysis, it was also the source of his besetting weakness. To state with equal vigour both sides of an argument is a great merit, since nothing is more calculated to convince the sceptic than a willingness to state the rejected case with the utmost force and persuasiveness of which it allows. If after this has been done the case can still be thoroughly demolished, we rightly feel that there is no more to be said. If however the writer in his enthusiasm for the dialectical method states the false side of the case in such a way as to leave the reader no alternative but to believe that that is the author's conviction, no amount of subsequent protestation that that was merely intended as a torturing of the evidence prior to the transition to the synthesis which represents the author's true belief will undo the damage. At best it will be concluded that the author is equivocal; at worst he will be held to be responsible for the dissemination of falsehood. This has to be said, since while the foregoing remarks are not generally applicable to Proudhon in his very forthright, vigorous, frequently almost denunciatory style, they do most unfortunately apply to the work with which I shall in the present context be mainly concerned, namely, *La Guerre et la Paix*.

What Proudhon has to say on the subject of war is of the first order of importance—nobody before him with the possible exception of de Maistre (Proudhon's own starting point) came anywhere near to analysing its cause and nature so perceptively as he did. The influence he exerted on Tolstoy was enormous—from the internal evidence of Tolstoy's own *War and Peace*. Moreover, Proudhon, although certainly no pacifist, was decidedly hostile to war and struggled always on the side of the political forces working in favour of peace. To cite but one example of many, he wrote of the French invasion of Piedmont to the brothers Garnier on 1 July 1859:

> We go from victory to victory. But this fortunate chance does not reconcile me to the war; I find that 50,000 Frenchmen out of action, and 60 to 70,000 Austrians, not to speak of the other costs, are a price ten times as big as the advantage of governing themselves that will have been gained for the Italians, if so much is really gained for them.
> And this is not the end. . . .[1]

Yet Proudhon's hostility to war did not prevent him from apostrophizing war in the greater part of his large book on the subject. He developed at length an argument designed to establish not the immense significance of war in determining human fortunes, which is clearly incontrovertible, but the *right* of force as an arbitrator of history. In his enthusiasm for his case, he even goes so far as to devote two pages to establishing the like *right* of rape, if perpetrated by the victor as an act of war at the expense of the women of the conquered people. The rape of the Sabine women for Proudhon in this mood was all in order. Such writing is revolting and absolutely unpardonable. It does therefore oblige us to raise at the outset the important question as to what it was that could lead Proudhon, an honest, upright, humane, courageous, consistent champion of the oppressed to write in so perverse a manner.

Emile Faguet, a distinguished literary critic at the turn of the century, considered the Hegelian method in Proudhon represented more than a technical choice; it was an instinct, an inborn turn of mind. Of the

[1] P.-J. Proudhon, *Correspondance*, 1875, Vol. IX, p. 107.

method Faguet says: 'He shows of every human institution that it is true, that it is false, and that it becomes true again when taken in a new way and cleansed of what made it false; . . .' And of the instinct, he quotes Proudhon himself as saying: 'You know that, by temperament, I rather make fun of everything, even of my beliefs, and that this constitutes the basis of my conscience.'[1] To see ourselves as others see us is admirable; to play the part of devil's advocate against our most cherished hypotheses is prudent; but Proudhon sometimes goes beyond what is permissible in appearing to trample on his own and our holy places.

Proudhon perceived more sharply and clearly than any of his predecessors, not excluding Rousseau, that the world is upside down, our values inside out, that what we admire and esteem is generally the reverse of admirable and estimable. The dialectical juxtaposition of opposites seemed to him just the weapon he was looking for wherewith to scandalize the bourgeois class out of their ugly complacency into critical reflection. Proudhon flung his antinomies out with bravado and courage, but was bitterly disappointed if they failed in effect and feared above all to be ignored. 'God, he is evil!'; 'Property is Theft'; 'War is divine'. It is Proudhon's authentic trade-mark. Sainte-Beuve likened it to a kind of 'tic'—'a sort of flourish and signature which parades itself and which leaps to the eye'.[2]

Sainte-Beuve again notices the resemblance in this respect between Proudhon and de Maistre, comparing the plebeian audacity of the one with the aristocratic insolence of the other, although the two were in every respect poles apart from one another. There is a crucial difference, however. De Maistre not only meant his paradoxes to bite; the content of their assertiveness corresponded to his own real beliefs. What is infuriating about Proudhon is that he outrages by the ferocity of his attack only to inform us by subsequent painstaking analysis that his own beliefs are in reality quite the contrary of that suggested by the original paradoxical statement. We are reminded of Rousseau's celebrated 'Man is born free; everywhere he is in chains', only to discover that Rousseau is a vigorous supporter of the State and opposed to life in a free state of nature. 'Property is theft', proclaims Proudhon to a horrified world; and it turns out that Proudhon is among the most tenacious supporters of the right of peasant proprietorship

[1] Emile Faguet, op. cit., p. 119.

[2] C. A. Sainte-Beuve, *P.-J. Proudhon: Sa Vie et Sa Correspondance*, Paris 6th ed. 1894, p. 231 n.

and implacably opposed to communism. 'War is divine', he echoes de Maistre, but with this difference, that Proudhon is deeply opposed to war. 'God, he is evil!'—this might be thought to establish at the very least Proudhon's atheism. Not at all! Compare his letter to a friend in 1856, written not for the purpose of gladiatorial display but in the intimacy of quiet reflection. Sympathizing with his friend's desolation, he urges that we should never lose sight of the principle:

> that, whatever opinion we form of the government of the Universe—be the directing Thought that of a superior nature, or diffuse and latent in all the atoms that constitute the world—in the last analysis *things have been arranged well*; that neither death, nor revolutions, nor the loss of beliefs, nor the exhaustion of loves are an evil; that it is a gain for him who knows how to understand them, who judges these things for what they are worth, who enjoys them a moment and throws them off so as himself to stay always the same, like the universe whose equilibrium is unalterable.[1] [*My italics.*]

That a man should be in conflict with himself is not surprising. But Proudhon often seems to give free rein to contrary impulses within himself, so as to leave his readers unsure of where he really does stand. We do not know a great deal of Proudhon's childhood; but we do know that there was a very marked imbalance in the relations between his father and mother. If his father was not exactly a weak man, he was also not a successful man; and it was attributable to him that the family always lived in dire poverty, a poverty which prevented Proudhon from obtaining even school books and compelled him to abandon his studies prematurely in order to contribute to the slender family budget. His father was a cooper, publican and smallholder in turn. As a tavern-keeper, he brewed excellent beer which he sold at barely more than cost price. But in fact the family's inability to make ends meet would appear to have derived not from the bread-winner's scrupulous honesty, but from the more familiar weakness of the peasant, an ill-judged passion for litigation.

The mother, on the other hand, was a powerful personality, who may have kept within the sphere of domesticity traditionally allotted the peasant's wife, but who took all the decisive steps which lay behind the education and expectations of her eldest son. The personality strength lay decisively with the mother, not with the father. While there is marked, conscious ambivalence in the son's attitude towards

---

[1] *Correspondance*, op. cit., Vol. VII, p. 134.

his father—admiration for his honesty, simplicity, courage, resentment against his ineffectiveness and impecuniousness—there is no such ambivalence expressed towards his mother. His life-long admiration expressed itself in the simple and moving testimony: 'To her I owe everything.' But that could only have been one side of the picture. True, Proudhon identified himself closely with the maternal will and admired the strength of character it represented. But a will so strong could scarcely fail also to have been productive of resentment at some level. This, it is true, is conjectural, since Proudhon gives no expression to it. But our knowledge of human character formation is sufficient to suggest that with the degree of imbalance known to exist in the respective personality power of Proudhon *mère et père*, the mother's eldest son would have had a very severe struggle to liberate himself from the power of the maternal hold upon him. Judging by the absence of any detached assessment of and the presence of a very powerful identification with his mother by Pierre Joseph, the conflict must have been almost wholly unconscious and correspondingly severe. All that we know is that the mother's hopes that her gifted first-born would redeem the family fortunes were doomed to disappointment, and that Proudhon felt this keenly. That this did not prove possible was due to his invincible integrity as a radical critic of the existing order, aggravated by his gratuitous belligerence.

But while Proudhon's vanity and deep emotions were immensely gratified by his awesome reputation as the *enfant terrible* of the bourgeoisie, the scourge of governments, there was on the other hand another Proudhon, never completely repressed, which hoped with unbelievable naïveté to be taken up by Authority as its guide, philosopher and friend. Despite his denunciations of parliamentarism and the suffrage, he himself was willing to stand in elections and serve as a deputy in the Assembly. He seems to have been glad enough to meet and discuss the political situation with Louis Napoleon himself in September 1848, regardless of the calumny to which it inevitably gave rise. In 1855 he again alarmed his friends by the frequency of his visits to the Palais Royal, and by the vigour with which he attempted to enlist the support of Jerome Bonaparte, President of the Paris Exhibition, on behalf of his scheme to use the Exhibition as a vehicle for revolution. Nobody impugns his integrity, but one is left wondering at the sources of a judgement that could seriously entertain the idea that the Bonapartes might be used by the Machiavellian Proudhon to further the radical, revolutionary cause. Again, when the Swiss canton of Vaud announced in 1860 a prize for a monograph on Taxation, Proudhon entered and was duly awarded the first prize in May 1861. To Proudhon's avowed pleasure, the jury considered his work 'eminently conservative'; and he appears to have been inordinately flattered by this recognition—absurdly pathetic when measured alongside Proudhon's real stature as an original thinker. 'M. Proudhon crowned for a work of political economy by the State council of a sovereign State!' he wrote, preening himself to a friend. So difficult was it for the great rebel to rid himself altogether of the desire to be taken back into the warm shelter of parental acceptance and approval.

But that being said, it should be remembered that a life-time of resistance to the world's follies and evils, coupled with the comparative isolation, the rebuffs, the silence, the withholding of all recognition, if not actual calumny by the dispensers of society's approval, is not easy to bear. The strongest spirits are generally apt to chafe under the burden at least occasionally. Proudhon himself put it with that force and clarity which characterize his writing at its best. His prose normally scorches with the energy of the fires that consumed him. Warned by his friend Bergmann on the occasion of his publication of the notorious *What is Property?* that if he were to continue along the path upon which he appeared to have embarked, he could look forward to nothing beyond the martyr's crown, he replied that he could not accept such a prophecy:

> You judge too harshly of the knavishness of power, of the ignorance of the public and of the tyranny exercised by the leaders of opinion. The first has an interest in letting the truth die; the second hears without understanding and looks without seeing; the others care only lest their charlatanism be exposed. No, no, I shall be neither martyred, nor disturbed, nor even read: . . .

But no sooner is the disclaimer uttered than he feels the weight of the sacrifice which he knows to be inescapable for those who strip from society the mask of its pretence that power is virtuous. He continues:

> What am I saying? I will not suffer martyrdom! Is there anything more grievous than the oppression of knaves and fools? Oh! if my heart does sometimes bleed, it is to see my zeal without result, and all the efforts of my reason expended in vain. My consolation is great, I admit: the suffrage of a few men of heart and intelligence such as yourself suffices to compensate me for everything. But is it not painful to see the patient refuse the

remedy, the blind man refuse to see the oculist, and art as well as truth become useless?[1]

Although Proudhon had always been preoccupied with the subject matter of *La Guerre et la Paix*, and indeed the bare bones of the argument of that book are to be found in his great work on *Justice*, the immediate trigger of the book was the Italian war of 1859 coming so soon as it did after Napoleon III's previous venture in the Crimea. Proudhon felt that the time was overdue for a book which made a serious attempt to come to grips with war and its causes. It is significant that Proudhon's prime coincided with Europe's first concerted peace movement; and although Proudhon was always fiercely anti-militarist, anti-adventurism and imperialism, he had no sympathy with the contemporary minority who sought to arouse opinion against war as such. The peace movement of the forties drew on the tradition of *fraternity*, to which the Revolution had given at least verbal emphasis, as well as on the humanitarianism of the later Romantic movement, and its pacific avowals emphasized especially the cruelty and horror of war. In England, Bright and the Quakers, in the USA William Lloyd Garrison and Adin Ballou, in France Raspail in his paper *Le Réformateur* attacked war as barbaric. The Americans began to raise the demand for an international arbitration tribunal, and in 1843 an international conference was held in London, attended by 300 delegates. In the eighteen-sixties a number of peace congresses were held in Switzerland.

Such strivings towards peace aroused not Proudhon's sympathy but his irony; and he rejected them as well-meaning but futile attempts by sentimentalists with no understanding of the realities underlying the phenomena of wars. He wrote in *La Guerre et La Paix*:

> It is not with subscriptions and meetings, with federations, amphictyons, congresses, as the abbé de St. Pierre believed, that peace can become serious and placed beyond all attacks. The statesmen can do no more than the philosophers: the Holy Alliance has failed; no philanthropic propaganda will achieve anything. Peace signed at the point of the swords is never more than a truce; peace elaborated in a secret meeting of economists and Quakers would make one laugh . . .[2]

Elsewhere he attacked the advocates of peace through international institutes of arbitration, supreme courts, peace congresses for their

[1] *Correspondance*, op. cit., Vol. I, pp. 211–12.

[2] *Œuvres Complètes de P.-J. Proudhon*, new edition edited by C. Bouglé and H. Moysset, *La Guerre et la Paix*, Paris 1927, p. 487.

lack of realism, a failure to realize that attachment to the State is a basic part of the identity of the individual.

> They forget only one thing, these excellent pacificators, namely, that religion, country, liberty, institutions are not things on which one budges; that the mere thought of a deal is apostasy in itself, a sign of failure in which no one can wish to take the initiative.[1]

For those who sought a remedy for war in some form of world government he reserved a still greater scorn. He rejected it on the grounds of impractical utopianism, that it would be fatal to human liberty, and that it was incompatible with the dignity and autonomy of States, on whose reciprocal influence one with another the advance of civilization depended.

> The idea of a universal sovereignty, the dream of the Middle Ages and formulated in the pact of Charlemagne, is the negation of the independence and of the autonomy of States, the negation of all human liberty . . .[2]

Nor was he any more favourably disposed towards proposals for disarmament, which he does not so much as discuss. His hostility to modern armaments rested on a revulsion from the wholesale nature of their destructiveness. Similarly, his hostility to standing professional armies rested on a fervent faith in a people's militia or national army, an institutionalized version of the Revolution's *levée en masse*.

What is necessary, first and last, he insists is to understand war as a sociological phenomenon, to come to grips with this 'extra-dialectical method' of resolving differences between nations, to find out why governments behave with such apparent irrationality as to prefer to destroy rather than to persuade each other. For he noticed, not without shame, when he attempted to reason about international affairs and foreign relations, that his reasoning lacked any basis in principle, and he was accordingly prone to purely conjectural conclusions, resting on nothing better than his own personal sympathies and antipathies.

He takes as his starting point de Maistre whom he quotes with warm approval, 'the great theosophist, a thousand times more profound in his theosophy than the so-called rationalists whom his word scandalizes'.[3] The shaft of Maistrean illumination which particularly arouses

---

[1] Quoted by Madeleine Amoudruz in *Proudhon et l'Europe*, Paris 1945, pp. 254–5.

[2] *La Guerre et la Paix*, op. cit., pp. 292–3.

[3] Ibid., p. 31.

Proudhon's admiration is the celebrated aphorism concerning the 'divinity' of war. War is divine, we are told, because it is a law of the world, because it bears along with it a mysterious glory, because it affords a remarkable protection to the great captains who achieve heroic feats of arms, because of the manner in which war is declared in consequence not of individual decision but of the overwhelming tide of events, and finally because of the stupendous consequences of war, the significance of which eludes the most sophisticated conjectures. Proudhon proceeds to develop and embroider this theme at very great length.

War, he argues, is an institution as old as man, who from the beginning of things has always conceived it as a law of the universe, symbolized in the heavens by storm and tempest, thunder and lightning, and on earth in the warring hostility of the most primitive tribes. Common to earliest tradition, the legends, epics, fables of poets, the speculations of metaphysicians, the dogmas of theologians, is the belief that Jehovah is the God of War; that war in all its terror is inseparable from the drama of life in which humanity is eternally divided against itself. Good and evil themselves are at war with one another for all time as two enemy powers, and in nature as in human life a condition of war is and will be, until the final consummation, the fate of every creature.

He quotes with no hint of disapproval the notorious passage from Hegel:

> War is indispensable to the moral development of humanity. It gives relief to our virtue and sets the seal on it; it reinvigorates the nations that peace has enervated, consolidates States, strengthens dynasties, puts races to the test, gives empire to the most worthy, communicates movement, life, fire to everything in society.[1]

Proudhon indulges in a good deal of rhetoric on his own account in his own description of war—phrases like 'the orgasm of human life', 'the fertilizer of chaos', 'a sphinx' that reason must metamorphose, a human sacrifice proportionate to the magnitude of the offence. Everything in human history presupposes it; without it, nothing of our familiar world would exist. He who knows war knows all there is to know of humanity. And much more. And all this, he assures us, is part of the necessary process of understanding war, of coming face to face with it and its real, all-pervasive significance, in order to put an

[1] Ibid., p. 51.

end to it. War cannot be abolished, it can only be metamorphosed or transformed by revolution into something else—a revolution in all aspects of life, in religion, law, politics, work, art, family and social relations.

It is clear what is wrong in all this. If Proudhon had contented himself with saying: 'To be indignant at war and to demand its abolition is not enough. It is necessary first to realize the deep-seated nature of its cause,' he would have been irreproachable. But the fact that his purpose is to understand in order to abolish war does not make any the less excusable his hymns apostrophizing the warriors' slaughter of the past. The explanation is to be found in the fact that although he was genuinely horrified by the indiscriminate nature of the slaughter of modern war, he nevertheless deeply admired the qualities of force, courage, charismatic leadership and military prowess. Like so many human beings he admires and respects at one and the same time mutually incompatible qualities, thus making it possible for him to write self-evidently absurd and contradictory statements and call them mysteries. For example, war, he tells us, is a unique mystery in which 'right, piety and murder unite in a fraternal embrace'. In short, Proudhon reveres both prophet and warrior, both Christ and Robespierre or Napoleon; and laments in anguish (or at any rate pretends to do so) that we cannot see these respective qualities united in a single person. What a leader, what a force we should then have! Now, we do not find men bitterly lamenting their fate in not having discovered square circles or how to make hot ice. And therefore, it is a matter of interest and concern when minds as original and as honest as Proudhon's are to be found writing passages such as the following: If only, he says confusedly, Robespierre had known how to bestride a horse, if Savonarola had donned instead of a Dominican cloak the cuirasse of a Bayard, if the Papacy like the Caliphate held in the same hand the sword to shed blood, as well as the power to excommunicate. He then continues:

> Ah! if the Nazarene whose word carried away the multitude had been able to supply his religion with the sanction of arms! . . . So much grandeur is not accorded to simple mortals: the same individual would not be able to unite in his own person the qualities of hero and saint, of emperor and pontiff. . . . What a scandal originally when instead of the warrior announced by the sibyls, the missionaries of the Gospel proposed for the worship of mortals their crucified Lord! Jesus, the Christ of the slaves, destitute, disarmed, nailed on a gibbet, Jesus was treated as anti-Christ.

The true Christ for the masses is Alexander, Caesar, Charlemagne, Napoleon.[1]

Proudhon sees clearly enough the vast gulf between Christ and Caesar; he also perceives (without deploring) that the masses have historically submitted out of belief, out of conviction to the sword of Caesar; he also sees that the qualities of Christ and Caesar cannot be united in the same person; but he laments this fact as though it were some kind of innate deficiency in human nature. In short, his worship of force blinds him to the fact that the qualities of love and of power are logically antithetical, and cannot, as a matter of logic, ever be reconciled to each other.

In order to abolish war, Proudhon continues his efforts to understand it in all its profound significance. There is a right of war, which derives from the fact that war is a judgement, an expression, albeit terrible in form, of Justice; and the mass of humanity understands this because it possesses the supreme sanction of force. War is the grand assize, wherein humanity finds its rights. It is this feeling or half-awareness which sustains the conscience of the soldier in hardship and peril. It is the belief that victory confers a right, resting on valour, generosity of sacrifice, contempt for death, probity and temperance, that steel the citizen to endure the discipline and regimentation inseparable from war. The army, the instrument of justice based on the right of force, is a nation's true representative in its foreign relations.

Proudhon is well aware, indeed he goes out of his way to call attention to the fact, that this realist, sociological Maistrean view of war stands in sharp contrast to that of the classical writers and his more immediate predecessors who have applied themselves to this theme. Aristotle held that the most natural war is that waged on wild beasts and on men who resemble them; Cicero held that discussion was the attribute of man in contrast to the violence of the beasts; Grotius rejected the view of war as a medieval trial by combat in favour of the view that war is the negation of justice and of judicial authority; Pufendorf held that peace is what distinguishes man from the beasts. The significance of Proudhon's different approach is that if war now appears as a principle or doctrine, an institution in its own right, it does at any rate exclude the traditional justification of war in terms of self-defence. The conventional view was that war was terrible and intrinsically immoral but justified when strictly defensive against aggression;

[1] *La Guerre et la Paix*, p. 58.

and generally speaking, it was customary for each side to claim that its own actions were justified as essentially defensive or preventative. Proudhon's view was contemptuous of this kind of sentiment and declamatory invective.

If the classical writers, philosophers, editors, commentators are all arrayed against him, the mass of the people have always seen the matter in a different light. We do not find them arguing that force can never make a right, that war is unjust in itself, says Proudhon. Originally, man knows only force, and values this supremely as indistinguishable from right and reason. Force is glorified, made into a divinity, as witnessed by Hercules, Thor, Samson. The basic division of the population into the aristocrats and the plebeians is a distinction resting on force. *Aristri*, *optimates* mean literally the strongest, and by extension, the bravest and best. *Plebs* means those who are weak, slaves, men without force, *ignavi*. The first possess rights, the latter are *ex leges*. When disputes arise among men, or injuries need to be atoned for, the issues are resolved by trial by battle, by duel or judicial combat; in short, a judgement of force. But eventually this mode of settling differences gives way to the will of the Prince, whose primary function is to protect his realm and to administer justice. The Prince is supreme or sovereign because he represents the collective force of the community, against which no man can stand; and therefore he alone can dispense justice, which he must do to prevent his followers from warring among themselves. The source of the legitimacy of his power is simply that he who has the force has the right, and he who is Prince, who wields the sword of justice, is always he who is most powerful.

All right is not synonymous with might, but might is the original source of right, and in the international sphere, where judicial combat has not been replaced by the judgement of the prince, might is still the only arbiter of justice. And this is why the masses rightly respect conquest, the prize of superior courage and force. The just war is not that conducted by the victim of aggression according to Proudhon. It is a war waged according to the most fitting conditions in which ruses and stratagems are excluded so that the issue can be resolved by the pure merits of force, uncorrupted by wile and deviousness. Proudhon sees in the multiplicity of institutions and rules and protocol attaching themselves to war, evidence in support of his view of war (as understood by the mass of mankind) as an elaborate juridical institution. How else are we to explain the conventionalization of such procedures as declarations of war, arbitration proposals, mediations, ultimatums, recall of ambassadors, national prayers and Te Deums, exchange of hostages and prisoners, rights of neutrals, refugees, the wounded, respect for bodies, rights with limits of victor and vanquished, a whole elaborate system of jurisprudence, in fact?

All legislation, all juridical relations, indeed all sovereign States, nations themselves, all originated in and derive their legitimacy from force, from war and the rights of war. It is the fact that uniquely characterizes man. Other animals resort to violence, in a sense make war, but only man aspires to make out of his physical superiority an *obligation* for others to obey. The reason why this is not admitted by the learned, the jurists and the professors is simply lack of candour on their part, or to put it more brutally, hypocrisy. But in practice, like everyone else, they bow to the *rights* of force, despite their protestations to the contrary, 'compromising with their conscience, and trying with a lot of equivocations and mental reservations, to reconcile their esoteric doctrine with the faith of the vulgar'.

Since received opinion does not officially recognize the right of force, it is quite unable to explain the existing structure of the political world, with its sovereign states, empires, kingdoms, republics or to account for the course of history which brought it all to pass. In the absence of a rational philosophy of history, based on the recognition of the legitimacy of force, they are compelled to fall back on explanation in terms of chance, fate, caprice, bad faith, violence. In short, the existing order has no intelligible base, rests on purely arbitrary forces, which can overthrow tomorrow what they have set up today. And this in fact corresponds to the instability of States, men's expectations of continued instability; and in their precarious condition they look forward hopefully, if without rational evidence, to a solution of their feverish, disordered condition in terms of a universal empire or world government. Thus we find praise lavished on the Alexanders, Caesars, Charlemagnes, Charles Vs, Philip IIs, Louis XIVs, Napoleons because they reach out through conquest towards the goal of universal monarchy, while their opponents who sought to resist their tyranny, the Mennons, Vercingetorix, Witikind, William the Silent, Gustavus Adolphus, William III, Kosciuzko, Wellington, are scorned as rebels against Providence who went down to just defeat.

The argument is strained and fails to carry conviction. Proudhon rightly sees the hypocrisy in the conventional view which purports to be shocked at the naked insistence on the rights of force while at the same time living in and approving an entire way of life whose every institution rests on that implicit principle. He also sees the resultant unreality in pious working for peace through congresses attended by the very people who live by force, and also in the vague aspirations towards greater concentration of force in the form of world empires. But his own alleged candour fails to clear up the mystery for the reader in the way Proudhon clearly hoped for, because Proudhon himself is as irretrievably wedded to a doctrine as false as that of his opponents. Proudhon was right to insist that his opponents really believed, as he himself did, in the right of force, but were afraid or too squeamish to say so. But he was wrong to believe in the right of force. It has and can have no right. And his opponents are only vulnerable to his attack, because they proclaimed without sincerity that force has no right. It was their lack of sincerity, their hypocrisy only which Proudhon should have attacked. All his analysis is excellent as a description of men's real beliefs; the confusion is caused and error is made worse confounded because Proudhon proudly proclaims that which his opponents blush to acknowledge. Yet Proudhon for all his vaunted Machiavellianism and admiration for de Maistre intends from the very first page of his work to reach a conclusion demanding an end to war as a scourge no longer tolerable to humanity. How does he resolve his paradox?

Proudhon does not deny Hobbes's argument that man enters into the great Leviathan of civil society based on a sovereign jurisdiction out of self-interest and reasons of necessity. But, he says, the Hobbist theory of law is only a half of the truth. It fails to take into account the principle of Justice which, Proudhon never wavered in insisting, is an idea and sentiment, a spiritual force animating the soul of man, immanent in his very nature. If it is not always the most energetic of our impulses, it is the most universal and the most constant. 'Justice', he wrote in *De la Justice*, 'is the supreme God, it is the living God, the all-powerful God';[1] and this truth is not an esoteric one, it belongs to everyone. It is written in all hearts. It rests on a respect for our own dignity, which arouses our deepest emotions when we behold that dignity violated in respect of any human being, be it our neighbours or ourselves. Justice then rests on the strength of the conscience of the individual. And in a community there is thus generated a collective association, the incarnation of Justice and possessed of tremendous force, by virtue both of its material and spiritual power. This force,

[1] *Œuvres Complètes de P.-J. Proudhon*, op. cit., *De la Justice Dans La Révolution et Dans l'Élgise*, Vol. I, p. 225.

Justice, a part spiritual, part material force is the true ruler of mankind. It is the basis of international relations, although here the material element is almost completely in the ascendant. Politics between nations is at bottom, he says repeatedly, only the reason of armies. Any State that sought to base its relations on anything else would rapidly commit suicide. Wars will only cease, he insists, Justice and Freedom will be established only when men recognize that Force is a matter of Right in itself. It is of course capable of abuse and corruption, and therefore the right of Force must carry with it its own limitations.

This also provides the key to domestic politics. The ballot box is no more than the most economical, least bloody means of discovering where the right of Force resides, whose interests are the majority interests. While it is felt that it is better to proceed according to the conscience of the nation rather than of a sect or minority, at the same time it is not mere opinion which commands respect, it is the sense that the majority represents the *interests*. Upstarts, despots, puny or immoral figures have time and time again commanded the sovereign power of whole communities, provided always they genuinely represented the majority interests. When they forfeit this support or try to act in defiance of it, insurrection occurs and they fall from power. For example, Charles X having lost that majority support, wished to act against it, to be right, so to speak, against Force. This is impossible, and he was rapidly deposed. So great is the prestige of Force, that where it exists, it commands the respect of the multitude, who hasten to acknowledge its authority, independently of all other values.

War, therefore, he concludes, both domestic and foreign, whether conducted by the ballot box, the sword or whole armies, is the great animating creative spirit of society. It has given both impulse and force to religion and philosophy, to the liberal arts, to all essential institutions. It is what has made our civilization, indeed the human race, what it is, without which it would not be recognizable.

At the same time he makes no attempt to conceal the hideousness of the face of war and its appalling cost in terms of human suffering and wastage of resources. 'War,' he writes, 'with its bloodstained arms and its piles of corpses, seems to us, from every point of view, atrocious.'[1] Have we any guarantee, he asks, that this judgement of force, imposed on the nations by destiny on pain of shame, bought at such terrible cost, is a constant and reliable index of the good and true? Can we have confidence in the judgements of history? It is fine to die for a great

[1] *La Guerre et la Paix*, op. cit., p. 200.

cause, he says, but the sacrifice of so many generous lives would be monstrous if humanity did not actually benefit therefrom. Does the appeal to history and experience confirm that the dead have not died in vain? Proudhon's answer to this question is indistinguishable from Hegel's own.

> The philosophic study of history reveals that human tumults, in so far as they concern the formation, fusion, decadence, dissolution and reconstitution of States, obey a general direction, whose goal is the gradual creation of harmony and freedom on the globe. The agent or minister of this high thought is war.[1]

History, according to Proudhon, consists essentially of the efficacious judgements of war in the interests of a Providential plan designed ultimately for human well-being. This sounds at first rather like the proposition, 'Whatever is, is right'; that to be on the side of the big battalions is its own justification and proof of acting as a Divine agent. This apparently is not the case, because victory does not always and necessarily go to those who command the superior force. For the outcome to be confirmed by history as a permanent providential contribution, it is necessary that victory be the fruit of a genuine trial of strength, that it be not sullied by guile, treachery, fraud, surprise, chance, corruption, incompetence. In the latter eventuality, the apparent deliverance of judgement is not truly judicial, will not coincide with Justice, and will not be sustained or confirmed by history. And this is the reason why the forms and institutions and procedures of war, of belligerent justice, are, like those of civil and criminal justice, ritualized on a conventional basis to ensure their competence, integrity and validity. A venial judge may corrupt a judicial pronouncement, but in general we have confidence in the impartiality of the judicial process, Proudhon argues. Similarly, a victory on the battlefield obtained by trickery or corruption or fraud is invalid in that it does not coincide with the conditions of conflict which alone deliver a judgement in conformity with the superior reason of Providence. Such judgements will have no permanence. On the other hand, 'the judgements of war, if in conformity to the plan of Providence, become definitive, and no power can abrogate them'.[1]

Historians, not understanding that victories achieved in defiance of the true law of force cannot endure, necessarily construe historical developments irrationally. Lacking the key of the Right of Force, we

[1] *La Guerre et la Paix*, p. 202.

necessarily find history unintelligible, and therefore fall back on such pseudo-explanations as the turn of fortune's wheel, the inconstancy of fate, chance, Providence, genius frustrated by hazard. 'The authors of war narratives have no other philosophy.'[1] He takes Bonaparte's early military career as an illustration of General Jomini's thesis that 'general causes decide the destiny of empires'.[2]

The historians write about Napoleon's military career in terms which suggest that he should have been satisfied with the gains he had already won, and that at the first sign that the wheel of Fortune had turned, should immediately have withdrawn. Napoleon himself certainly proved to be no judge of the stability of his own conquests and thought himself to be at the height of his power when he was actually at its nadir. But if the principal actors in the drama and their historical critics were mystified by the course which events took, there is no reason why we, illuminated by the law of the right of Force, should share their mystification. The law of Force is sovereign, but it requires time to work itself out. It cannot be rushed. Thiers, the Bonapartist historian, for example, prostrates himself before the victories, awed by the lightning flashes of military genius; and the reader is left as breathless reading of the succession of victories as the soldier in winning them. The mistake lies in the failure to understand that 'war, being a function of humanity, creates nothing in the twinkling of an eye, and that, like vegetation and life, it needs time to accomplish its works'.[3]

For a country like France, it would have required several generations to accomplish the task of assimilating and incorporating the provinces between the frontiers of 1790 and the Rhine. Napoleon, heir to and military arm of the Revolution, could not wait several generations. He had only one life to live and he was in a hurry. He himself, of course, thought that it was he, a new Ajax, that was making history by his brilliant victories, conquests, and administrative genius. In fact, he was the puppet being forced along the path he took by twin forces as far outside his control as they were of his understanding. On the one hand, he at first made himself the mouthpiece of the Revolutionary egalitarian spirit and later (and more congenially) found himself the embodiment of the reactionary principle inevitably generated after a long period of revolutionary agitation. On the other hand, he was the victim of the false idea of war then prevalent that glory was the essence of the clash of arms, that accordingly victory

[1] Ibid., p. 208.   [2] Ibid., p. 233.   [3] Ibid., p. 237.

was the more impressive, the more glorious in so far as it was gained with fewer men arrayed against more numerous and powerful forces.

Napoleon was thus led on not by obedience to the true law of Force but by the impetus of the Revolution and by the requirements of his own charismatic prestige and vainglory. In the course he had embarked upon after the first triumphs of Marengo and Hohenlinden, he found himself condemned to a treadmill of conquest without end from which there was no escape. The result was that he automatically roused up more and more enemies, accumulated more and more fractious and resentful subjects, over-extended his lines of communication, and increased his risks out of all proportion to his ability to consolidate his superficial gains. His downfall was thus inevitable. Whatever skills he developed and displayed, however corrupt, stupid and incompetent his foes, the day was bound to come when the whole empire would topple like a house of cards. In the Italian campaign at the beginning of his career, Bonaparte's victories resulted from his enemies' mistakes, fortunate chance, and the skill and address of the French soldiers. The conquest of Italy was therefore not founded on true superiority of Force, it was thus precarious, and led to another Italian campaign in 1800 and yet another on the Rhine. Each apparent victory was illusory since it necessitated further victories, because the military strategy was flowing not from political policy but vice versa. Even the greatest of captains cannot indefinitely win victories in complete defiance of the true principles of war grounded in the Law of Force. Napoleon ultimately was swallowed up by an avalanche that he had himself unleashed; and he left France less powerful than he found her.

A further corollary of the Law of Force is the common-sense principle of utility that one should not expend more blood and treasure on gaining a victory than the victory itself is likely to be worth. In this context as an instance of the violation of the right of war, Proudhon cites the case of the papal police setting fire to the forests of the Papal States in order to destroy the brigands living within them, the remedy being even more destructive than the disease. This episode serves, in a manner highly characteristic of Proudhon's extremely discursive style, to trigger off a discussion of the controversy over Rostopchin's alleged burning of Moscow in 1812, in the course of which the latter part of Napoleon's career is subjected to a similar analysis to that accorded to his early Italian campaigns. Napoleon, of course, thought the burning of Moscow fell outside the rights of war on the grounds that the country would have suffered less by his occupation of the capital city than by its destruction. What the Russians considered heroic self-sacrifice, Napoleon considered barbarism; although, as Proudhon says, who is to dictate to another what price he shall set on his own freedom?

Proudhon argues that in deciding to invade Russia in the first place, Napoleon was himself guilty of a fundamental violation of the rights of war. Not of course because a war of aggression is immoral. That is a judgement characterizing the tradition of 'just war' defined in moral terms—a tradition scorned as completely by Proudhon as by Machiavelli. Napoleon's offence in crossing the Niemen on 24 June 1812 consisted of two false assumptions: firstly, that he and his army could live off the country, and secondly, that the Russians would agree to fight the war on the terms chosen by Napoleon, namely, in a decisive duel consisting of one or two pitched battles.

The first and fundamental offence against the right of war is to seek victory in defiance of the true logic of the balance of force. (Proudhon is not criticizing Napoleon's waging of war according to Napoleon's own understanding of the rights of war, but according to allegedly objective standards.) In order to conquer Russia on a genuine, stable basis, it would have necessitated sufficient troops to occupy the country militarily speaking and a sufficient commissariat to maintain their supplies in hostile territory. The minimum numbers with which he should have crossed the Niemen, Proudhon accordingly calculates, would have been 1,200,000. With no more than 400,000 at his disposal, he should never have given the order to advance, no matter how grave he considered Alexander's provocation to be. As it was, marauding and pillage were a necessity for the French army, unable to subsist by its own means. Even the transport system which Napoleon tried to organize from Danzig to the Niemen was hopelessly inadequate. Moreover Napoleon had himself ordered that whatever could not be pillaged should be burnt, in order to harass and delay the enemy's movements. And Davout saw to it that this savage order was executed with exemplary force. Therefore even if it is considered that Rostopchin violated the rights of war in burning Moscow he was doing no more than respond in like fashion to Napoleon's own brutal provocation.

So far as concerns Napoleon's strategy of forcing the enemy to a major all-out military confrontation it was obviously not to the Russians' interest, a nation of 50 million people, to gamble its independence by risking everything on a single throw of the dice. To do that would have been to play Napoleon's game for him. Consequently on both counts, given the inadequacy of numbers and of supplies of the *Grande Armée*, the invasion of Russia was already doomed when the French were no more than 100 leagues (250 miles) on the other side of the Niemen. The victories of Smolensk and of the Moscowa (Borodino), the burning of Moscow, the arrival of General Winter with his merciless retribution could none of them vitally affect the issue one way or the other. It was already decided from the moment that Napoleon ordered an invasion 1,500 miles from his own capital in defiance of the Law of Force. The fact that Napoleon represented, albeit very inadequately, the principles of the Revolution as against the autocracy of Alexander, did not touch the crux of the matter, namely, that he did not possess the necessary force. This being so, Napoleon became a mere adventurer, a disturber of the peace, 'a usurper of sovereignties'.

Looking back over Napoleon's career as a whole, Proudhon concludes that were we to consider him as an outsize Prince *à la Machiavelli*, acting and judging according to reasons of State or the rights of Force, it would be necessary to condemn him as a great delinquent. But this would be false to the forces which govern history. Napoleon did not exercise the degree of responsibility that he imagined he did. For it is 'general causes', not the will of individuals, however powerful, that shape the course of history. Proudhon put it thus:

> Trace back once more the chain of causes, and at the moment you imagine that you have before you only the faults of a man, you will arrive at a current of opinions, at a spring of national energies which in accord with its directing idea, now raises up to the skies the chief of state, at the same time Generalissimo of the army, and now makes of him its first victim.[1]

The reason why in the end Proudhon, despite all his vaunted realism, comes down against war is that the institution is corrupt and becoming more so. He concedes that to some extent atrocity is inherent in war as an institution, and that this disfigures it. He cites as an example the butchery of a family of eleven Piedmontese (including an old man of sixty and a boy of fourteen) suspected of espionage by the Austrian general. Although Proudhon evinces his lack of sympathy with Cavour's denunciation of the deed on the grounds that no general dare allow himself to be taken by surprise and that even this episode was in accordance with accepted practice, he concedes that such practices

[1] *La Guerre et la Paix*, p. 287.

undermine the legitimacy of war itself. But his principal objection to war rests on the destructiveness of modern technology. There is even talk, he says, of equipping all French troops with revolvers with six rounds; he is further appalled by weapons 'loaded with shame' such as the rifled gun, Congreve rockets and the Paixhaus howitzer. They might be legitimate means of destroying brigands, pirates, slave traders. But they are not legitimate instruments of warfare, because by supplanting energy, courage, loyalty, prudence with simple extermination, they vitiate war as a justifiable instrument. The outcome of wars fought by such methods cannot prove anything, since under such conditions victory must always go to the biggest scoundrel. Vain also is the hope of those who delude themselves into believing that the sheer terror and destructiveness of modern weapons will of itself put an end to war. For wars fought by such deplorable means will inevitably lead to political and social chaos.

While these scruples are no doubt to Proudhon's credit—although here too he is careful to avoid any direct emotional appeal to reasons of humanity—it seems extraordinarily naïve to complain that while war itself is a good thing, it has been ruined by its enthusiasts carrying the logic of the conflict beyond legitimate, albeit ill-defined limits. Much the same is to be said of Proudhon's other source of dissatisfaction with war, namely, his lament that military organization is not democratic. Instead of the officers being elected, as befits a citizen army, rank, the very badge of inequality imposes on an army the relations of command and obedience which are basically incompatible with those of Justice, to serve which, according to Proudhon, war exists. In the world of the imperative, the subordinate necessarily finds himself sacrificed, and the common soldier is increasingly used simply as cannon fodder.

> The soldier, in the hand of the general, is no longer, in effect, like the peasant in his village, a human soul; he is a weapon to be hurled, a killing machine, a material thing, in short, like the cannon and the munitions, a product of the military industry, that is used sparingly because he costs money, but who for the rest is as cheap as his cartridges and his rifle.[1]

What, in Proudhon's view, is the cause of war? It is, in a word, the maldistribution of wealth, which results in what he calls 'pauperism', a great evil, to distinguish it from poverty, a great good. War is thus infamous not only by its corruption and excesses, but also by the

[1] Ibid., pp. 285–6.

nature of its inmost cause. Welfare depends not so much on the amount of material wealth available as on the equity of its distribution. The greater the inequity in distribution, the greater the luxury on the one hand and the destitution and pauperism on the other; and this condition is always highly unstable, producing the original impetus to war. The wealthiest societies are not in the least free from it. Take, for example, England. England is opulent in the sense that it is the home of the largest fortunes, but it is also the home of the most grinding poverty. 'The English people have laboured enormously; they have fasted still more.'[1] And the consequence: England, at once the most aristocratic and the most famished of peoples, the original home of pauperism, is of all nations the one which more than any other has spent its substance in invading others, living not so much by pillage as by exploitation. Britain has never produced so much industrial wealth as she does today; yet, the mass of the people are indigent. Britain is the wealthiest country, but she suffers most from maldistribution. The result is war.

> England, who interferes in the affairs of other countries only to get commercial treaties from them, who promises her support to those who buy her goods, who dreams of taking possession of China as she has taken possession of India, England, . . . who, after having devoured the Irish people and the Scottish people, cannot nourish her own; England arms her coasts, casts cannon, increases her war flotillas, exercises her volunteers, inflates her budget, raises her discount rate (doubtless by applying her theory of free exchange), and prepares to repel by fire and sword whoever would talk of touching her trade, her conquests, her monopolies.[2]

The instability, restlessness, acquisitiveness always disturbing the economic equilibrium and leading to war itself, arises from a false philosophy of life which holds that the purpose of existence consists in increasing productivity. 'To create wealth, to make money, to get rich, to surround oneself with luxury, has everywhere become a maxim of morality and government.'[3] As a result modern man spends his life amassing, accumulating, hoarding until his soul is gorged. He even persuades himself that wealth and the dissemination of comfort are themselves a means to promoting morality and virtue and diminishing violence and crime. Again Britain is singled out as the primary example, if not the actual *fons et origo* of this false philosophy,

[1] *La Guerre et la Paix*, p. 394.
[2] Ibid., p. 395.   [3] Ibid., p. 342.

which rejoices in the name of utilitarianism. 'Utilitarianism was born in England: you may say that it is in the English blood. All the philosophers, the moralists, the theologians, the novelists, the statesmen of Great Britain are penetrated by it.'[1] Men, having lost their ancient moorings, no longer believing either in God or humanity, unable to understand that wealth is not a reality but merely a relationship, seek not true welfare but are animated by greed. Produce, produce, do business, get rich, be happy, is modern man's religion. The goal of tripling or quadrupling productivity, as rational a means to happiness as the attempt to square the circle, remains a constant illusion. It is an illusion because the working day, a true yardstick of human material welfare as a reflection of both production and expenditure, is always at the mercy of contradictory forces. On the one hand, it benefits from the windfall of technology and industry, commerce and agriculture, colonization and conquest. But against these gains are always to be offset the corresponding losses from bad harvests, epidemics, revolutions and wars.

A true philosophy rests on an understanding of the fact that our real welfare lies in poverty, that our destiny is not enjoyment, voluptuousness, riches. The Creator in subjecting all living things to the necessity of eating in order to live, designed for us not an epicurean way of life but one of asceticism leading to a life of the spirit, in which our vocation is to cultivate the heart as well as the intellect. Moreover, the law of temperance or poverty has from ancient time always been proclaimed by prophet, poet and philosopher, by Christ, Horace, Virgil, Seneca, who were agreed at least in their contempt for luxury. *Blessed are the poor in spirit*, and Christ taught us to ask of God that we be granted materially no more than our daily bread. Proudhon is seen at his noblest when he draws in prose of great force and simplicity the sharp contrast between the needs of man, together with his fellow creatures in nature and his condition in what he chooses to regard as civilization.

The horse eats his oats, the ox his hay, the pig his mast, the chicken her fine corn. They do not vary this food, and do not find themselves in any way inconvenienced thereby. I have seen the labourer of the field make his meal each day of the same black bread, the same potatoes, the same porridge, without appearing to catch any harm from it: excessive labour alone made him thin. But the civilized worker, he who has received the

---

[1] Ibid., p. 394.

first ray of the illuminating Word, needs to vary his diet. He consumes wheat, rice, maize, vegetables, meat, fish, eggs, fruit, dairy produce; he avails himself sometimes of wine, beer, cider, honeydew, tea, coffee; he salts his food, seasons it, gives it every kind of preparation. Instead of covering himself simply with a sheep or a bear skin dried in the sun, he wears clothes woven of wool, hemp or cotton; he uses linen and flannel, dresses in one fashion in summer and another in winter ... Such is progress: which does not prevent humanity from remaining poor, since it has as always only what suffices, and is unable to lose a day without famine making itself felt in an instant.[1]

The basic distinction is that between pauperism and poverty: pauperism is the reverse side of luxury, that which remains to the family man after paying the levies imposed on his day's labour to maintain the army, the revenue, property, luxury, the budget of the bankers, the entrepreneurs, the merchants, the officials. It is a wretched average of 3 francs 50 centimes a day. Poverty, in sharp contrast, is the simple austerity of a man who labours for the sake of life, who does not seek riches, and who is free. 'Poverty is decent; its clothes are not full of holes like the cynic's cloak; its habitation is clean ...'[2] It is not good that man should be at ease, exempt from the goad of daily renewed need. Poverty is the noblest truth that Christ preached on earth to men.

And because we ignore this truth, because we inculcate the worship of wealth and productivity as fitting goals for a man's life, because we despise both the wisdom of the ancients and the touching simplicity of Christ, because, in a word, we exalt the appetites at the expense of the spirit, we create a world in our own image, a world in which the poor share the values of the rich, the workers the values of parasites, a world finally in which no escape lies for such twisted consciences other than into crime and war.

War, he concludes, is a thing that is ultimately a psychological phenomenon, a canker rotting the soul of man. It is endemic in the facts of our current situation. It arises inevitably from them; and ministers, field marshals, diplomats and statesmen simply make pronouncements to accord with the facts of the situation as they have evolved at any given moment.[3] To suppose that they control these

---

[1] *La Guerre et la Paix*, p. 337.

[2] Ibid., p. 338.

[3] He cites as examples the reasons given for the Crimean war: to protect Turkey, to destroy the treaties of 1815, to serve the revolution, religious zeal to

events is an illusion which they themselves are naturally anxious to create in order to justify their positions of importance and power in their own eyes as well as in the eyes of those whom they are supposed to lead.

> War, for reasons already indicated, is always inherent in the facts, a fact that princes do not control according to whim, and for the production of which they can choose only the pretext and the hour.[1]

He illustrates this thesis from the immediate war situation from which France had just emerged, ostensibly as a result of Imperial decree. The real author of the campaigns in the Crimea and the subsequent one in Lombardy was not the Emperor Napoleon III, but the situation itself created by public opinion. Although the nation was never formally consulted, it has applauded events, and that because they saw or thought they saw in these two campaigns a war against the counter-revolution, the heirs to the Holy Alliance and the European aristocracy. It is the people who ultimately make war; and it is the people, the broad masses who made the great Revolution, who alone have it in their power to establish the reign of peace. Peace can be brought about not by meetings, subscriptions and conferences, but only by a radical revolution in ideas and customs. War has always represented a manifestation of the universal conscience of mankind; in order that it should be abolished it is necessary that the will to peace should come to represent that universal conscience. Nothing less will do. Nothing less will be strong enough to subdue the armies of the globe.

In *La Guerre et La Paix*, Proudhon applied the political theory he had developed in *De la Justice* to the problem of war and its cause. His diagnosis remains the same. The analysis is not original to Proudhon. It is, as he himself insists, already clear in the pages of Machiavelli. Machiavelli's *Prince* scandalized princes and pontiffs, who, to their honour (says Proudhon) defended themselves against the charge of *raison d'état* as from a monster. They were sincere in this, demonstrating thereby that they had always intuitively followed the logic of

---

protect the Church's interests; and the reasons given for the Italian war: the independence of Italy, to serve the revolution, to diminish Austria. He then demonstrates from the historical evidence that none of these reasons could in fact have been the real reasons (which he does not profess to know) for imperial policy in these two wars.

[1] Ibid., p. 391.

raison d'état without knowing it. Even today scholars treat *il Principe* either as a calumny on statecraft or as a caricature or sometimes as irony. The masses in contrast have never been scandalized by it; it was merely what for them went under the name of Justice. Machiavelli correctly saw that political instability has as its primary cause the inequality of fortunes, which necessitates a permanent conflict of interests. This, Machiavelli in common with everyone else from Plato and Aristotle onwards accepts as inevitable—like the climate itself, in the nature of things. Because of this inequality, the State cannot perform its true function, namely, the dispensation of Justice, the essence of which is Equality. Therefore the State, finding itself obliged to defend that which is not just and is based on ignorance and pre-judice, acts in a way that is self-contradictory. In the perpetual war between wealth on the one hand and numbers on the other, the political régime always ends by succumbing. Dynasties change, con-stitutions are amended, democracy replaces monarchy; but political instability is constant, for the simple reason that in the eyes of all parties inequality of conditions remains a necessary fact, never to be questioned. Pagan culture explained the phenomenon in terms of fate or destiny; Christianity has offered a metaphysic of Divine Providence and a psychology of 'original sin' to account for the same phenomenon. The last word in the politics of the ancient world was subjection to *raison d'état*; Christianity in adding to this *raison du salut*, has changed nothing. Certainly it has not sanctified it.

Although men of intelligence, believing that war is no longer of this century, sought a peaceful solution to the quarrel that erupted in 1853 in the war of the Crimea, the Church did not raise its voice on the side of peace. War is a part of the plan of Providence, and the Church must always take this into account in her reckonings. The army is also a church, the church terrible, whose will obeys no religion, no morality, whose *raison d'état* is simply authority, *Orders, la consigne.*

> The soldier knows neither family nor friends, nor citizens, nor Justice, nor country: his country is his flag; his conscience, the order of his commanding officer; his intelligence, at the end of his bayonet. That is why the Eternal God is a warrior. *Dominus vir bellator*, as well as a God of peace, *Deus pacis.*[1]

War is the permanent lot of humanity because Justice cannot be expected to obtain between prince and prince, when it is not even to be

[1] *De la Justice Dans La Révolution et Dans L'Église*, op. cit., Vol. II, p. 228.

found between prince and subject. Moreover, the army like the church looks after its own and in so doing jeopardizes public morality. The military oath is the only allegiance it recognizes. Crime is considered to be serious only if it compromises the High Command, the hierarchy, by threatening to undermine discipline. 'Does he fight well?' asked a general of a soldier, court martialled for rape. 'Yes'. 'Be lenient.' And it is the same with the Church. She defends not the people's interest, but her own. That is why she is to be found on both sides in conflicts of war. She defends her own interests thereby, the same cause, the same truth.

> By virtue of the pact with Charlemagne, renewed from century to century by pragmatic sanctions and concordats, the Church remains the spiritual sovereign of nations, whom she directs, on one side by her pontiffs, her bishops, her legates, on the other by kings and emperors, her sons, according to the law of a perpetual state of siege.[1]

Such then, he concludes savagely, is the system of belief which goes under the name of Christianity: 'Suspension of Justice and morality in perpetuity, for the glory of God, the triumph of the Church and the safety of empires.'[1]

Why, Proudhon asks, do men worship power when it is thus contrary to Justice and therefore to their own real interests? They did so originally because, although the collective force has always been of transcendent importance, the hub of the political universe, it is not accessible to sense perception and therefore seemed an emanation of divinity. It was worshipped with religious veneration. In a word, men submitted, as they did to the gods. With the passage of time men found it more difficult to believe that their rulers were themselves gods, and so the belief was modified to the effect that the ruler exercised the collective power by right divine, while his local representative enjoyed a parallel *droit de seigneur*. These beliefs in their turn losing their efficacy with age have given way to the doctrine of the sovereignty of the people, that government is legitimate by right democratic. And today men submit themselves as readily as ever to the authority and domination of a single individual. What further proof could we require of the vanity of all these theological and political theories when the facts which they purport to explain or justify remain constant, independently of the rise or collapse of the theories?

People do not understand the nature of the force that they obey; but

[1] Ibid., p. 229.

ill defined as it is and for the most part inaccessible to conscious thought, men intuitively obey it because they feel lost and disoriented immediately they feel their connection with the collective force threatened. Like Rousseau, like Hegel, Proudhon senses the enormous importance played by the collectivity in the life of the individual, who is dependent on it, and who feels himself falling into the void when cut off from it. The body of the nation, uniting within it the forces of individuals and of groups is a unity: 'it is a real being, of a superior order, the movement of which draws along every existence, every fortune'.[1] And it is this power that they willingly obey. Rulers resort to terror, keep up a constant barrage of propaganda to ensure that they rather than their rivals should occupy this throne, but the throne itself needs no terror, no seductive arts to maintain it. For without its protective, invisible presence, the people are no more than a frightened flock of sheep. That is why they will readily acknowledge allegiance to any charlatan, anyone who declares himself father of the nation, any figure whose effigy is stamped on a coin, so long as he genuinely expresses the collective force. And immediately he seeks to govern against that force, he is overthrown. The ruler only imagines that he rules; he is in fact a mere puppet, the creature of the social force, the least free of men.

In the natural order the collective force is the result of all the particular forces which exist for purposes of production, defence and the exercise of Justice. But in existing society this power has been alienated to such an extent that men actually believe that the social power which they themselves generate is generated by the goverment, the prince, the ruling caste, who, like God, is the sovereign dispenser of welfare, defence and Justice. Consequently the prince is preoccupied not with the advancement of the collective welfare but with maintaining his own position, and constraining by army, police, and taxation his subjects to obey him. When Napoleon I said 'my army, my navy, my ministers, my prefects, my government', he spoke no more than the truth. For these forces, far from belonging to the nation, work against it.

Thus we live under the permanent paradox that Justice, whose essence is equality and the very negation of power, is conceived as something which emanates from power. In principle all men, all societies must obey Justice or perish, and therefore men are ungovernable. Governments naturally cannot understand this, since their *raison*

[1] *De la Justice Dans La Révolution et Dans L'Église*, Vol. II, p. 267.

d'être is supposed to be their capacity to govern; but the proof of the illusion is seen in the fact that all governments end badly and are replaced by other governments.

> In fact, the so-called governments, liberal and absolute, with their arsenal of laws, of decrees, of edicts, of statutes, of plebiscites, of regulations, of ordinances, have never governed anyone or anything whatsoever. Living a life quite instinctive, acting at the will of invincible necessities, under the pressure of prejudices and of circumstances that they do not understand, most frequently allowing themselves to drift with the current of the society which from time to time breaks them, they cannot of their own initiative do anything apart from disorder.[1]

The major premise of all Proudhon's reasoning is that men are by nature meant to dwell at peace one with another in conditions just to all. He therefore anticipates the objection that a vision of perpetual peace is contradicted by the evidence that war is natural to man, has its principle 'in the unfathomable depths of the human heart', is sanctioned by all religions, and is as indestructible as the duel. War, he replies, is not natural, nor is it, as the rationalists of the Left suppose, the result of the ambition of princes or of popular passion. It is a direct function of economic disequilibrium. A nation in which production is in the hands of monopolists and the public power exploited for their own purposes by the monopolists is by that very fact a nation at war with the rest of the world. The principle of monopoly of wealth in the interests of inequality knows no national frontiers, and will not exhaust itself until all peoples have been enslaved by it.

In fact, Proudhon proffers a sociology of war, in which the phenomenon is studied as an objective moral force with its own objective causes. Such an analysis leaves no room for a theory of causality in terms of the event-changing capacities of extraordinary charismatic leaders. In reply to the question as to the significance of the influence of the initiative, the counsels, the genius, the virtues, the crimes of statesmen, he is content to quote the dictum of Fenélon: 'man bestirs himself and God leads him'. Man represents the blind will to absolute power, inexperienced, untamed, avid to conquer all the kingdoms of the earth. God is manifest through the social law (Rousseau's 'real will') which unconsciously tames and directs, socializes and enlightens the blind impulse to power. Beginning in history with naked, uninhibited force and combat, man through recognition of the law of the collectivity is

[1] Ibid., Vol. II, p. 271.

led to Justice. No government, no statesman can do anything either to advance or impede this process. It is entirely a matter of the conscience of humanity, through whose gradual illumination we move inexorably to a life natural to man.

> What will be the life [of humanity] when it will no longer have a prince to lead it to war, nor priests to assist it in its piety, nor great personages to sustain its admiration, nor scoundrels nor poor to excite its sensibility, nor prostitutes to satiate its luxury, nor buffoons to make it laugh . . .[1]

It will, he says, dwell in the garden of Eden and comply with the philosopher's recommendation in Voltaire's *Candide* by cultivating the garden. The work of the field in ancient times assigned to the slave will become the prerogative of the free man, the tumult of his senses quietened by the serenity of his spirit.

But it will be objected that to be possible of realization such ideas would have to be disseminated among the people, and this cannot be done. The people, brutalized by servitude, ignorant and prejudiced, are plunged into apathy. And secondly, your attempts to penetrate this apathy will be slandered by the press, the pulpit and the universities, will invite severe punishment in the courts, will in brief be gagged by bourgeois power. Therefore, the revolution, it would seem, if it is to have any chance, must begin with the government, as democrats have always argued. 'Plausible, but false!' answers Proudhon. If you first make the revolution without having first established the idea, your revolution can of necessity change nothing. Everything depends on the free conscience of humanity. The existing order is doomed not only by the famished bellies of the workers which it exploits, but even more by the tortured consciences of the secure and privileged unable to close their minds to the increasingly evident falsehoods of authority, inequality, predestination, eternal salvation, *raison d'état*. The whole task of good men consists in teaching the people to say 'No'. The king's fool asked the vital question: 'What would you do, sire, if, when you say yes, everyone said no?' Let the people say this 'No'. Nothing else is necessary, nothing else will do.

Finally, in this brilliant argument between his imaginary opponent and himself, he faces the root question: how can the right survive the violence of so many vested interests in injustice? In logic he concedes that it might be extinguished for ever. But humanly this is impossible, because the human conscience always protests. Men thieve, but they

[1] *De la Justice Dans la Révolution et Dans L'Église*, Vol. II, p. 291.

will never prescribe theft. They lie, but they will never decree false-hood. Falsehood wears many faces. In politics, *raison d'état*; in econo-mics, *laissez-faire*; in religion, faith above morality; in aesthetics, art for art's sake. Against all the forces of reaction, its metaphysic, its machiavellism, its army, religion and courts, Proudhon appeals solely to the voice of the free human conscience, and he is confident that that is a sufficient shield.

To sum up, the revolution in human thought which Proudhon was attempting to pioneer was of far greater consequence even than the celebrated Copernican revolution. The latter may by substituting the heliocentric hypothesis for the Ptolemaic have resulted in an enormous shrinkage of man's sense of his own importance in the universe. Proudhon's revolution was aimed to restore man's sense of his own dignity by rescuing it from its abasement at the hands of Power. Men do not revolve around Caesars and Napoleons, and draw their strength and sustenance from so-called great men. Quite the contrary! Each man revolves on his own axis, and in so far as the Caesars and Napoleons have any power, it is drawn from the collective power of countless individual wills. Proudhon himself, if he did not make the analogy explicit, drew a comparison with the work of Kepler. Kepler laboured prodigiously for seventeen years to arrive at the formula for his three famous laws. It is necessary to advance by similar metaphysical as distinct from algebraic operations in order to learn something in the realm of social movements where everything is yet to be done.

Proudhon saw clearly that the worship of 'genius' in intellect or action was not only metaphysically false, but that it destroyed a man's self-respect at the roots and fatally undermined his capacity to find himself and develop his own talents. The consequences were so crippling to the individual's self-assurance that, burdened by an irrational sense of his inferiority, he remained in the state of servitude that 'genius' was only too anxious to encourage him to regard as his own natural or rightful dependency status. Proudhon's splendidly modest but defiant assertion of our dignity by refusing to bow the knee to any sort of genius added cubits to the stature of each one of us. The equality in which he believed with his entire soul and with complete integrity was of the kind, he said, which 'ought one day to extend to the intel-lectual faculties'. While readily admitting that he was no Kant or Leibnitz, not because of any deficiency of nature but of fortune, he has learnt 'to consider without fear all those great geniuses which the vulgar so justifiably admire'. Without boasting, he is confident that he, like any other man of sound constitution, could by work and discipline acquire a comparable intellectual power to those geniuses who are in fact much nearer to us than is apparent to us. Our present intellectual deficiencies are *anomalies*, and, he adds, 'a day will come when the vast majority of human beings, without being identical, will be equal in capacity, as they will be equal in wages'.

Proudhon diagnoses the true source of inequality, fear. The best thing in all Proudhon is the simplicity with which he summons man to free his soul of fear of those who, whatever their pretensions, are no more than his fellows. With great insight he observes that the tyrant's greatest weapon is to make men fear virtue. But in the end the free spirit always asserts itself, and, weary of obedience and self-abasement, revolts. The idols of his imagination, of his own creating, begin imperceptibly to lose their thrall.

> Talent and genius! Sublime words with which society loves to reward . . . the most precocious of its children; but fatal words, which have produced more slaves than the name of liberty has made citizens. Talent and genius! at these magic words, as at an invocation of Divinity, the human flock prostrates itself; in the subjugated consciences will expires; the mind is arrested, drawn along by the hypnosis of fear. [Nero trembled before his mother] and history testifies that the cruellest of the Caesars was at first only a pusillanimous child. Let there be no doubt of it, all these vile courtesans of a usurped greatness, all these thinkers without energy, these writers without character, these servile imitators are all children of fear. 'We are all born *originals*,' cries the untamed poet of *Les Nuits*; 'how does it come about that we die, almost all of us, copies?'[1]

Proudhon wrote as he lived: without fear. He called upon the disinherited, the oppressed, all those deprived of their spiritual nourishment to throw off their fetters and assert their mental freedom.

Proudhon had no need to tell us that he loved equality from the depths of his soul—it shines through everything that he wrote. But he did not love freedom equally. Consequently, although he admits that coercion of any kind compromises the purity of the ideal of Justice, he by no means rejects coercion as an instrument of equality. For instance, regarding allegations that certain races of mankind are biologically inferior or decadent—beliefs then openly avowed— Proudhon refuses to commit himself. 'I do not know', he says with far

---

[1] *Lettre à M. Considérant*, quoted by Sainte Beuve, *P.-J. Proudhon*, op. cit., p. 131.

from disarming modesty. But, he adds, it does not matter. For, if they are inferior, if the Africans, Red Indians and aborigines are inferior to the caucasian, and if they cannot be improved by crossing with the superior race, then like weak, deformed, or sick individuals in civilized society, they will be weeded out, they will be assimilated and finally become extinct. 'Equality or Death' is the moral he draws from this singularly unedifying piece of reasoning.

It was this side of Proudhon that called forth sharp criticism from friends like Herzen, who, if they remained themselves something of the *grands seigneurs*, found themselves shocked by Proudhon's calm acceptance of violence, when he thought it conducive to equality. Herzen wrote in *My Past and Thoughts*:

> The Latin world does not like freedom, it only likes to struggle for it; it sometimes finds the force for setting free, never for freedom. Is it not melancholy to see such men as Auguste Comte and Proudhon setting up as their last word, the one a sort of mandarin hierarchy, the other his domestic penal servitude and apotheosis of an inhuman *pereat mundus, fiat justitia!*[1]

It purports to be a rational religion—the religion of Justice, but for all its humanity, it is cold at heart, for its respect ceases at the point where it professes to find an absence of dignity. We must treat all men with justice, that is to say, as equals, because we recognize in them the same dignity of which we are conscious in ourselves. But Proudhon can find no dignity in the beasts—either he knew nothing of them or his ability to recognize dignity was limited by the demands of his belly—and so it is legitimate to set traps for them, treat them with violence and treachery, strip them bare, exploit them, sell them, eat them, all without remorse or murmuring of conscience. Not content with this, he proceeds to pour scorn on current attempts to remind us of our duty to the beasts arising out of the principle of universal charity. This 'pantheistic verbiage' he castigates as 'one of the most deplorable signs of our moral and intellectual decadence'.[2] Animals should be fattened and well cared for so as to maximize their contribution to the larder, he concludes, no doubt tucking in his napkin in anticipation. The reason is clear. Proudhon could not abide cant of any description; he did his best to keep 'a good table' within his modest means, as is the common practice. And he refused to be mealy mouthed

---

[1] *My Past and Thoughts*, op. cit., Vol. III, p. 232.
[2] *De la Justice*, op. cit., Vol. I, p. 418.

about it. It nevertheless makes painful reading, since all that he says on this subject is false—and is moreover completely irreconcilable with his own unconsciously eloquent tribute to the dignity of the beasts in the passage quoted above. (Cf. p. 95.)

Proudhon also rarely misses an opportunity to excoriate the law of love or Christian charity which he insists on identifying with the kind of charity that perpetuates and is designed to perpetuate pauperism. Again Christian humility he construes only as insincere subservience, something that is false, which he contrasts with modesty, a genuine virtue and a form of Justice, although not one which Proudhon himself could always be relied upon to evince. The law of love evokes in him strong feelings. He appears to feel as strong a hostility towards it as towards the law of egoism. Neither will advance humanity on the path of progress; the only moral law is the law of Justice. He reproaches his friend, La Châtre, himself an anti-religious spirit, because his letter betrays a spirit unduly 'affective', 'passional' which cannot be redeemed by the famous principle: Do unto others . . . 'Believe me, dear Monsieur La Châtre, it costs less to do love or charity than to do justice . . .'[1] Which is quite simply false.

But the world owes a great deal, a very great deal to Proudhon, and it would be churlish to take leave of him on a critical note. His influence in his own time, and even more so since his death, was great and overwhelmingly directed against the forces of repression, inequality and injustice. Moreover, the extent of his influence is still far from having been adequately recognized. The reason for this immense influence is that Proudhon esteemed one thing even more highly than Justice, although he would have insisted that they were inseparable, that is, the truth, which, according to his light—and it was undimmed to the end—he always spoke without regard for personal consequence. In nothing that he said does he more closely resemble Tolstoy than in the following sentences:

> The truth is one, but it appears to us in fragments and from very different angles. Our duty is to express it as we see it, no matter whether we contradict ourselves in reality or in appearance.[2]

His vision of the purpose and meaning of human life had both depth and dignity, and he held to it with a high degree of courage and

---

[1] Quoted by Jeanne Duprat, *Proudhon: Sociologue et Moraliste*, Paris 1929, p. 233.

[2] Quoted by George Woodcock, *Pierre-Joseph Proudhon*, London 1956, p. 254.

generally of consistency also. In a world where many debase themselves by preoccupation with the trivial and ephemeral concerns of
appetite, Proudhon never faltered in his firm adherence to the life of
the spirit. He accordingly had great dignity, which he unconsciously
makes his readers share with him. His abiding purpose was a purpose
conceived as rational and temporal, of the earth earthy, entirely
independent of transcendental or supernatural illumination or sanction,
a purpose of the humanly dedicated spirit. 'To be men,' he wrote, 'to
raise ourselves above earthly fatalities, to reproduce in ourselves the
image of God, as the Bible has it, and finally to realize on this earth
the reign of the spirit; that is our end.'[1]

[1] Ibid., p. 255.

6

Leo Tolstoy
'God sees the truth, but does not quickly reveal it'

Bertrand Russell, writing to Lowes Dickinson in 1904, expressing his admiration for Tolstoy's power of right ethical judgement, dismissed his theorizings as worthless. 'It is the greatest misfortune to the human race that he has so little power of reasoning,'[1] he added. Sir Isaiah Berlin, writing in 1964, quoting a Russian critic of the eighties to the effect that Tolstoy was generally considered to be an outstandingly good writer of fiction and a bad thinker, comments that 'this almost universal verdict'[2] has gone virtually unchallenged through the hundred years that have elapsed since the writing of *War and Peace*. More recently it seems to have been decided that the author of *War and Peace*, *The Kingdom of God Is Within You*, *Anna Karenina*, *Resurrection*, and innumerable other works of the very highest order, was capable of thinking after all; and that he is to be considered as a rather curious mixture of eighteenth-century European rationalism and anti-progressive, anti-liberal, Eastern quietism.

But what has not changed and what, moreover, shows no sign of changing is a total refusal on the part of all the critics to permit Tolstoy to state in his own direct, unmistakable way what it is he has to say about the human condition, and to consider in full seriousness the implications for our present situation. The reason for this is not difficult to understand. It is unwittingly made plain in a statement in an essay on Tolstoy by Leo Shestov. 'Many people', he wrote, 'in the effort to calm themselves and dissipate the uneasiness which seizes them on reading Tolstoy's works, have thought to explain his struggles

---

[1] *The Autobiography of Bertrand Russell, 1872–1914*, first American ed. 1967, Vol. I, p. 288.

[2] Isaiah Berlin, *Tolstoy and Enlightenment*, reprinted in *Tolstoy, A Collection of Ciritical Essays*, edited by Ralph E. Matlaw, New Jersey 1967, p. 28.

and his wild outbursts as the result of his fear of death.'[1] This is at one and the same time a fair statement of a very widespread reaction to Tolstoy and an example of it. (No one in his writings is less prone to 'wild outbursts' than Tolstoy, while his fearlessness in the presence of death was attested on more than one occasion.) Tolstoy's readers, finding themselves bereft of their wonted self-contentment, are apt to deal with their rising anxiety not by scrupulous analysis of their vulnerable selves, but by a hasty search for imagined failings in the author who has had the temerity to wound them in their self-esteem.[2]

More than any writer who ever lived Tolstoy was prepared to sacrifice everything that made life comfortable to his love of the truth. Everything he wrote bears the peculiar hallmark of this transcendent quality; and it is this quality which so transfixes his readers. Witness George Trevelyan, the liberal historian, writing in 1904:

> Tolstoi's letter in *Times* has set me thinking very uncomfortably—or *feeling* rather. It fills me with (i) a new sense of doubt and responsibility as to my own manner of life (ii) as to this of war. I feel as if we were all living in the City of Destruction but I am not certain as to whether I ought to flee—or whither.[3]

Trevelyan writes with unusual and refreshing self-candour of his apprehensions as to whether and whither he should flee the City of Destruction—ten years were to elapse before the City finally blew up in 1914. Trevelyan's City was of course a granite refuge compared with the City in which we dwell today, with the result that people now in the presence of Tolstoy's Truth are ever more inclined simply to shut their ears tight—so great is the fear aroused.

There are those like Herzen, who, if only in his weaker moments, seek to defend their peace of mind against menacing shafts of truth by persuading themselves that it is all too potent a solvent for human strength to cope with; and that those who ask us to drink of the cup

[1] Leo Shestov, *The Last Judgement: Tolstoy's Last Works*, reprinted in Matlaw, op. cit., p. 163.

[2] Since Tolstoy's death, an immense quantity of critical writing has been devoted to him; but it is very rare for a writer to allow Tolstoy's arguments in support of the doctrine of non-resistance to evil—the essence of Tolstoy—to be heard. The methods of Tolstoy's critics do not change. They were described by Tolstoy himself in 1893: 'long, clever, elegant and pretentious discourses and writings . . . about questions nearly related to the subject, though shrewdly avoiding contact with the subject itself'. (*The Kingdom of God Is Within You*, World's Classics 1946 ed., p. 51.)

[3] *The Autobiography of Bertrand Russell*, op. cit., Vol. I, p. 294.

undiluted not only mean us no good but are themselves an ominous warning of what will befall those who are rash enough to come beneath its spell. Acknowledging that truth is often very difficult to face and tell plainly, Herzen asks:

> And is it necessary? It, too, is in its way an obsession or a disease. 'The truth, the bare truth and nothing but the truth!' All that is very fine; but is the seeing of it compatible with our life? Will it not corrode it, as too strong an acid eats away the sides of a vessel, and is not the passion for it a terrible infirmity that bitterly punishes one who cherishes it in his heart?[1]

To which, I can only reply, 'Yes, it *is* necessary. It *is* compatible with our life; it will *not* corrode it. On the contrary, it is our only sure refuge—one that will never betray us, and the source of all enduring strength.'

The only person to trace in some detail the sources of Tolstoy's political ideas, as they inform *War and Peace*, has been the great Russian scholar, B. M. Eichenbaum. He shows conclusively the closeness of Proudhon's influence and to a lesser, but still significant extent, that of Pogodin, the Russian Hegelian philosopher. Particularly since Eichenbaum's work has unfortunately not been translated into English, it is necessary to summarize Eichenbaum's account in order to come to grips with Tolstoy's philosophy as expressed in *War and Peace*.

After spending a fortnight with Herzen in London, Tolstoy visited Proudhon in Brussels in March 1861. Tolstoy left no record of this meeting, although in conversation he expressed admiration for Proudhon's strength of character as a man with the courage of his opinion. Proudhon in a letter to Gustave Chaudey (7 April 1861) related that Tolstoy told him that he was widely read in Russia, but that Russians found it difficult to understand the importance Proudhon attached to Catholicism, because in Russia the church was nothing. 'Only now after I have been to England and France have I understood how right you were.'

Unfortunately, however, Eichenbaum does not make plain that Tolstoy's basic criticism of Proudhon related to the latter's identification of Catholicism with Christianity. Replying in May 1893 to Felix Schroeder, who had written an account of Tolstoy's religious outlook, Tolstoy took exception to the suggestion that he had been influenced

---

[1] *My Past and Thoughts*, op. cit., Vol. IV, p. 162.

by two peasants, Sutaev and Bondarev, ready though he always was to acknowledge cultural indebtedness to the peasants. His views, he insists, are not original, having been repeated thousands of times by a variety of sectaries from the Paulicians to the Quakers and others. But what an odd notion that one should borrow one's ideas from disciples, when the teachings of the Master himself are freely available. He then comments:

> This error can be committed only by those who take for the teaching of the Master the teaching of a bad disciple, of a traitorous disciple. And this is the case with almost all Catholics. All those who have been brought up in the Catholic principles, whether scholars, religious or literary figures, thinkers, philosophers, like Proudhon, Renan, and others, can never rid themselves of the illusion that the Catholic religion is synonymous with Christianity, and that every other conception of Christianity is an arbitrary invention, which has no direct relation with the true religion.[1]

When Proudhon met Tolstoy, Proudhon had only just completed the introduction to his *La Guerre et la Paix*, about which he was immensely enthusiastic. Publication was delayed owing to the understandable apprehensions of the publishers. But in 1864 a Russian translation appeared in two volumes. Eichenbaum points out that Tolstoy was influenced by Proudhon in his decision to write not simply a historical novel but a war novel with digressions on the theory of war and philosophy of history. He also draws attention to the importance Tolstoy attached to the title. The novel is not simply an alternation between battles and domestic scenes or of a society at war portrayed both on the battle front and on the home front. It is a theory of war and peace, conceived as a basic dichotomy or conflict within the human soul. 'War and Peace is a correlative expression' is one of Proudhon's chapter headings. He defines peace as 'a suspension of arms, caused either by the exhaustion of the powers, or by the equality of their forces, and regulated by a treaty', adding that 'the knowledge of peace consists entirely in the study of war'. A passage quoted by Eichenbaum from the penultimate chapter of Proudhon's book, emphasizes the interdependence of war and peace:

> War and peace which the mass of mankind perceive as two orders of things, mutually exclusive, constitute in turn the conditions of life of the peoples. Mutually they give rise to each other, are defined by relation to each other, re-enforce and maintain one another as opposite, equal and

---

[1] L. N. Tolstoi, *Polnoe Sobranie Sochinenii*, Moscow 1953, Vol. 66, p. 334.

inseparable antinomian terms ... Peace presupposes war; war presupposes peace ... And so, war and peace are correlative occurrences, equally valid and necessary, essentially the two principal functions of mankind. They alternate in history, as in the life of the individual—waking and sleeping as with a workman—losing his strength and renewing it, as in political economy—production and consumption.[1]

Since, he urges, war exists in its own right like poetry, justice, religion or freedom, we ought to study it seriously, not as a military man would study it for tactical or strategic interest in battles or sieges, but as a manifestation of universal consciousness.

There is no people which would not have its Iliad. The epic is the people's ideal, outside of which there exists for the people neither inspiration, nor popular plays, nor dreams, nor oratory, nor art; but the principal base of the epic is war ... War, which, it is said, the muses of peace flee, is on the contrary a necessary condition of their existences, their eternal subject ... Of all the subjects, capable of inspiring the poet, the historian, the orator, the novelist war is the most inexhaustible, the most various, the most inviting; the crowd prefers it to all others, and can never have its fill of it; without it poetry would become sickly and insipid. Try to destroy this sacred connection, which makes war a necessary material for the creation of the ideal, and you will see how man is debased, how by such hateful dullness individual and social life will be stricken. If war did not exist, then poetry would invent it.[2]

The relevance of all this to Tolstoy's interests needs no underlining. He was himself a veteran of the Crimean campaign as well as having experience of frontier war in the Caucasus. His intention of writing a historical novel centring around the Decembrist rising was already indicative of his powerful historical interest. But in addition Tolstoy had considerable moral affinities with Proudhon. Eichenbaum lists some of Proudhon's characteristic subjects on which he wrote books: women, war, an attack on literary property, art, the Gospels—all themes on which Tolstoy himself was to write at length. And although Tolstoy later in life was decisively to reject Proudhon's paradoxes concerning war and violence, he was never to reject, on the contrary he sharpened, the radical political analysis. The extract from his notebook for 13 August 1865 endorsing Proudhon's attitude to property remained Tolstoy's verdict to the end. '*La propriété c'est le vol* will remain more truthful than the truth of the English constitution as

[1] Quoted by B. M. Eichenbaum in *Lev Tolstoi*, Nachdruck der Ausgabe Leningrad 1928/31, Munich 1968, Vol. I, p. 386.   [2] Ibid., pp. 386–7.

long as the human race exists. This is an *absolute* truth, but arising out
of this there are also relative truths—applications.'[1]

The one thing that Eichenbaum singles out as differentiating
Proudhon from Tolstoy is his attitude to Napoleon. He speaks of
Proudhon's constantly enthusiastic tone of reference to Napoleon and
attributes this to his German Hegelian orientation. It is true that here
too Proudhon is not entirely free from ambivalence, but a close
reading of *La Guerre et la Paix* will leave the reader in no doubt as to
Proudhon's basic hostility to Napoleon. And Eichenbaum subsequently retracted his earlier view. In his later work Eichenbaum lists the
following characteristics of Napoleon as seen by Proudhon as well as
Tolstoy: smallness of soul, arrogance, vanity, deep egoism, complete
absence of humanity, contempt for people, charlatanism, braggadocio,
contradictoriness, contempt for principle. He further suggests a useful
comparison between Proudhon's notes on Thiers' Napoleon with
Prince Andrew Bolkonski's soliloquy in Tolstoy's *War and Peace*
(pp. 108–9). Indeed, as has been shown in the previous chapter,
although Proudhon's picture of Napoleon is less scathing than
Tolstoy's, his conception of his 'event-making' role or rather his
impotence to control the forces of history is strikingly akin to Tolstoy's. This gives even greater force to Eichenbaum's astonishment at
the complete failure to notice or rather silence on the part of the
critics and correspondents of Tolstoy regarding the latter's affinities
with Proudhon, particularly since only four years separated the
publication of the two books in Russia—*La Guerre et la Paix* (1864),
Tolstoy's *War and Peace* (1868). The exception that he cites is an
article by H. Michailovskii which appeared in *Fatherland Notes* (1875,
No. 7) entitled *The left hand and the right hand of Count Tolstoy*.
Defending Tolstoy from the charge of self-contradiction in the sense
that implies a failure of integrity, he denies that Tolstoy's contradictions are of this kind.

> I would compare them with those which it is possible to find with some
> frequency in Proudhon. I note that in his cast of mind but partly in his
> outlook as well Tolstoy in general recalls Proudhon. That same passionate
> attitude to a cause, that same striving towards the broad generalization,
> that same boldness of analysis and finally, that same belief in the people
> and in freedom.[2]

---

[1] L. N. Tolstoi, *Polnoe Sobranie Sochinenii*, Vol. 48 (1952), p. 85.
[2] Quoted by Eichenbaum, op. cit., Vol. II, p. 293. (In this German edition of
the Russian text, the two volumes are published as a single work.)

Eichenbaum is interested in the sources of Tolstoy's ideas, not at all in Tolstoy's analysis of the cause of war as a vitally important subject in its own right. Consequently he mentions only briefly as further evidence of Proudhon's influence that Tolstoy shared his contradictory attitude to war. Both writers express great indignation at the immorality of war. But Proudhon also echoes de Maistre's 'War is a divine fact'; while Tolstoy describes it triumphantly as a terrible and mysterious affair, 'which is carried out not in accordance with men's will, but in accordance with the will of that which guides peoples and communities'. Proudhon dilates at length on the right of force, on which alleged right his whole theory of war rests—might is revered because of its crucial role in determining the forms and shape of human development, much as Darwin's law of evolution rested on the survival of the fittest. *The Origin of Species* first appeared in 1858, just three years before Proudhon's book. Eichenbaum finds an echo of this doctrine in Tolstoy's reference to the significance of the murder of the Duc d'Enghien in Napoleon's rise to imperial power.

> *Chance* sent d'Enghien into his hands and accidentally forced him to kill, convincing the multitude by that very means, more powerful than all others, that he had the right as he had the power.[1]

Two further points are made by Eichenbaum as illustrative of Proudhon's decisive influence on Tolstoy. In the introduction to his book Proudhon cites the myth of Hercules to illustrate the popular worship of strength or superhuman power, but concludes '... heroism is a wonderful thing, but its time has gone ... I respect power. ... But I do not want Hercules peoples or Hercules governments, nor military courts ...' And in the epilogue to *War and Peace* Tolstoy refers to the ancients' view that power was of divine origin and that this viewpoint having been subsequently repudiated, we cannot now unlearn the lesson. The following sentence Eichenbaum suggests is an almost direct quotation from Proudhon: 'This power cannot be that direct physical power of a strong man prevailing over a weak one, a predominance based on the application or the threat of the application of physical force—like the power of Hercules.'[2]

The second point refers to the fact that as in Proudhon's book there is a special reference directed against the emancipation of women, so in Tolstoy women do not understand war—Princess Lise, Marya

---

1 Quoted by Eichenbaum, ibid., pp. 304–5.
2 Second epilogue to *War and Peace*, op. cit., p. 1315.

Bolkonski, Countess Rostova. Proudhon wrote: 'War establishes a huge inequality, irremediable by any means, between men and women.' While, however, it is true that Tolstoy's women do not understand war, their role always centring around the events of domestic and family life, it may not be inferred from this that Tolstoy shared Proudhon's view of the inferiority of women—quite the contrary!

But the link which overshadows all others in binding Tolstoy to Proudhon—a link which Eichenbaum does not so much as discuss—is the analysis of the *nature* of power and its relation to the cause of war. It is here where Proudhon's influence is most vital, and it is here where Tolstoy's development of Proudhon's analysis constitutes his own crucial and unique contribution.

Eichenbaum further draws attention to the influence of de Maistre, particularly for his letters from St. Petersburg, *Correspondance Diplomatique*, letters which were written at the time of events the ultimate outcome of which could not then be known to the author. He cites Tolstoy's indebtedness to de Maistre for certain scenes, such as Prince Vasili's conversation with *l'homme de beaucoup de mérite* regarding the appointment of Kutuzov as Commander-in-Chief, and more significantly, of de Maistre's observations on the crucial importance of morale in battle being echoed by Prince Andrew in explaining the reasons for the Russians' defeat at Austerlitz.[1]

Eichenbaum's most valuable contribution is perhaps his skilful portrayal of the influences on Tolstoy's developing viewpoint. Tolstoy's focal point of interest and stance had shifted notably as he reached the latter part of his work written some five years after the undertaking was launched. Eichenbaum notes the extent to which interest in the sixties focused on history and in particular on the problem of reconciling individual freedom with historical necessity. Chernyshevsky caused a considerable stir with his article *On the causes of the fall of Rome*. Stasulevich summarizing Buckle's thesis wrote:

> People have explained all movements in history by two hypotheses: either they have referred to *predestination* which they represent as theologically based or to man's *freedom of the will*, arising from a metaphysical view;

---

[1] But de Maistre's influence, as we have seen, concerned above all Tolstoy's reflections about the nature and role of power. Tolstoy himself makes a cryptic reference to this in his diary entry for 1 November 1865. 'Finally finished Bilibin and am content. Am reading Maistre. Thought of the free giving back of power *svobodnoi otdache vlasti*).' L. N. Tolstoi, *Polnoe Sobranie Sochinenii*, Vol. 48, . 66.

neither one is true: history is the modification of man by nature and the modification of nature by man.[1]

Whereas in the forties under the influence of Hegel and Schelling interest had centred on theory of knowledge and phenomenology of mind in history, by the sixties Buckle more exactly reflected the more practical interest in philosophy of history as a source of *weltanschauung* and personal behaviour patterns. Eichenbaum sees this intellectual trend reflected in the modification of Tolstoy's original anti-historicism to an interest in the laws of history. However he rejects the suggestion of those such as N. V. Lopatin that Tolstoy was directly influenced by Buckle who was widely read by the Russian intelligentsia in the sixties. Tolstoy himself twice refers to Buckle in *War and Peace* but only to demonstrate his lack of helpfulness. Buckle, Eichenbaum concludes, was an influence that came too late; much of Buckle, it is claimed, was anticipated by Pogodin. Eichenbaum argues conclusively that Tolstoy was much influenced by his own friends, Professor N. P. Pogodin and S. S. Urusov, author of *Review of the campaign* of *1812 and 1813*. Urusov was a long-standing friend of Tolstoy's whom he mentioned in his *Letter to the Swedes* as the officer who proposed that the bloody struggle for the Fifth Bastion at Sevastopol in which they participated should be settled instead by a game of chess.

Eichenbaum amply substantiates the view of the importance of Pogodin's influence, but the lengthy extracts from his *Aphorisms of History* relate mainly to the least interesting part of Tolstoy's philosophy of history. For example, the term 'differential of history' is taken from the foreword to Pogodin's book. Both writers illustrate their view of history with comparisons drawn from physics, mathematics or mechanics. Eichenbaum goes so far as to say: '. . . an understanding of Tolstoyan philosophy of history is impossible without a knowledge of Pogodin's book'. Certainly two of the aphorisms quoted have an authentic Tolstoyan flavour. For example,

> Every man acts for himself, according to his own plan, but accomplishes a more general activity, fulfils another higher plan and from the taut, thin, decaying biographical threads weaves the hard fabric of history.[2]

This is, of course, the main *leitmotiv* of the philosophy of history informing Tolstoy's *War and Peace*.

[1] Quoted by Eichenbaum, op. cit., Vol. II, p. 320.
[2] Quoted by Eichenbaum, ibid., pp. 335–6.

Tolstoy was very fond of metaphor and reasoning by analogy—methods of reasoning, he points out in his portrait of Speranski, alien to the bureaucrat. The following aphorism from Pogodin is characteristically Tolstoyan both stylistically and in relation to Tolstoy's central concern with the cause of great historical movements, and in particular of Napoleon's invasion of Russia.

> Take a look at the river in Spring for a minute before the thaw: how peaceful and still are its frozen waters. But suddenly the ice cracks, the water rises, the shifting blocks in turbulent sequence are carried one after the other to the distant estuary. There you have the universal movement of peoples in the fourth and fifth centuries.—But who gave them that first propulsion? Why were they, hitherto at peace in their lands, suddenly, links in an electric circuit, imbued with a single force, and rushed in whatever direction they gazed, as if not in possession of themselves?[1]

S. S. Urusov's friendship with Tolstoy was later strained although not altogether severed by Tolstoy's break with the Orthodox church. Urusov, himself an author of a book on the 1812 campaign, was intensely interested in military strategy and the laws of war. His affinity with Tolstoy may be discerned from the following extract from his writings on the Crimean campaign.

> Armies in essence are most unfree societies; established under civil laws, united by military discipline, they form up, move, diminish and disappear altogether with such correctness that from time immemorial there has been conceived strategy—the science of war. In armies there is observed a communal spirit, a common power, flowing from the vanguard or the rear, and no discipline whatever, no generals whatever could struggle against such an influence. It follows that over armies such kinds of control are possible as we must necessarily be familiar with from many phenomena of social life. If we are to learn the laws of war, we must get a clear understanding of popular movements, for example, an understanding of popular will. But as soon as this subject is made clear, that is, of the social will, then the whole of history will unfold itself before us, just as though it had all taken place before our eyes.[2]

Urusov expresses the metaphysical belief that human societies function according to laws which are discoverable by plumbing the secrets that govern the wills of immense numbers of people. And if such movements are governed by law, they must be predetermined. In a letter to Tolstoy in March 1868, expressing his admiration for the

---

[1] Ibid., pp. 336–7.   [2] Ibid., p. 354.

fourth volume of *War and Peace* which had then just appeared, Urusov also expressed his concurrence with the metaphysics: '... I see that this is not *Turkish fatalism*, but simply, that which we call predestination.'

And the interest in military strategy which he shared with Tolstoy, fellow veteran of the Fourth Bastion at Sevastopol, was not motivated by a primary interest in war but in sociology. The behaviour of armies claims priority to be investigated, because in armies and military organization we see in its purest form the principal of social organization. In the army freedom is at a minimum; laws of movement and direction can therefore be most easily discovered. In society at large there is more freedom, but the same principle obtains and necessity ultimately governs. But methodologically speaking, it is clear that the student of sociological or historical law, the student of the relation between freedom and necessity will be better placed if he does not try to run before he can walk. In short, we must begin with the army. Urusov expresses it thus:

> Laws, established by men, that is, those which are called subjective, are also subject to investigation: but it would be irrational to begin the business from the end, to take the tenth step before we have taken the first. And so, first of all it is necessary to study objective historical laws and moreover in such societies as have the least freedom, that is, as has already been said, in armies.[1]

To this end, Urusov wrote his own book to examine the leading strategists down to Clausewitz and thus discover the laws of war. To unravel the complexity of cause and effect in history is not given to us. We must be more modest and confine ourselves to the possible task of understanding the general laws which govern the mass. In his Introduction to his own book, Urusov states succinctly the central thesis of Tolstoy's *War and Peace*.

> We cannot know the cause according to which is established one and not another law of the event, nor the cause of every event in its particularity; but we can know the law itself; we can know those unchanging rules by which one phenomenon is transformed into another, and one event follows from other events.[2]

The great value of Eichenbaum's researches is self-evident. He concludes his survey of the intellectual influences on Tolstoy during

---

[1] Quoted by Eichenbaum, pp. 354–5.
[2] Ibid., p. 355.

the years when *War and Peace* was being composed, with the judgement that the military theory informing the book, including the interpretation of Kutuzov, motivated by the desire to correct the bias of the
historians (and in particular of Bogdanovich), was the work of a circle
of friends, the most important of whom being Urusov. Tolstoy was
unmoved by the latter's mathematically based positive laws, but did
accept the justice of his polemic against the historians and also much
of his method of approach to sociological problems.

Eichenbaum is the one exception—an outstanding exception—to the
habit of Western scholars whereby Tolstoy is never considered as a
significant thinker in his own right—the rule that assigns Tolstoy an
unrivalled place as an artist and denies him any significant role as
philosopher and thinker. We are indebted to Eichenbaum for making
a sizeable hole in this tradition; but Eichenbaum again stops short at
actual analysis of what it is that Tolstoy is saying. With patient schol-
arship he illuminates the sources of influence on Tolstoy; he recreates
with great skill the intellectual milieu in Russia in the sixties; but
Tolstoy's own analysis of the issue of war and peace so momentous
to mankind is not discussed directly; and the general impression with
which Eichenbaum is careful to leave the reader is that Tolstoy should
not be overlooked by students of the history of ideas; and when they
go to the subject, they will in fact find that whatever interest attaches
to Tolstoy's ideas derives largely from the ideas of Tolstoy's predecessors or contemporaries. If Tolstoy was after all a thinker, he was not,
it would appear, an original thinker.

An obvious and unusual feature of Tolstoy's *War and Peace* is the
attempt to portray the realities of human society and development at
two levels, the private, personal level and the public, collective level.
It was unusual since the two are commonly regarded as quite distinct
and as requiring different modes of treatment, the former being the
characteristic subject matter of novels and romances, and the latter of
history or political studies. The plan of *War and Peace* is almost
exactly described by Herzen in speaking of a French novel, *Arminius*,
which influenced him in his youth. From the early days of Christendom, he says, we have been familiar with the meeting and conflict of
the two worlds of ancient effete culture and the chaotic forces of the
forest savage like the beasts. We have known, that is, the public side,
the official side of this clash of events as a whole, but we have no knowledge of the lives of those anonymous hosts of individuals whose un-
chronicled lives directly depended on them.

The author of *Arminius*—I have forgotten his name—tried to reproduce these two worlds—one coming from the forest into history, the other going from history to the tomb—as they met at the domestic hearth. Universal history, when reduced to personal gossip, comes nearer to us, more within our grasp, more living.[1]

Tolstoy had, as he himself tells us in the prologue to an early story, *The Raid*, always been interested in the life of 'the forest', brutal, simmering, violent, namely, war. His interest was not strategic but moral.

War always interested me: not war in the sense of manœuvres devised by great generals—my imagination refused to follow such immense movements, I did not understand them—but the reality of war, the actual killing. I was more interested to know in what way and under the influence of what feeling one soldier kills another than to know how the armies were arranged at Austerlitz and Borodino.[2]

He was interested not so much in the abstract movement of large masses of men as in the psychology and morality of the life of the individual caught up in the momentous events of mass movements. What happens in the soul of an individual peasant or landowner caught in the toils of history, and what is the connection between the two, between the life of the individual and the life of the collectivity? In what sense may the individual, engaged with large numbers of others in civil or military activities, be said to be free, and how far is his life determined by forces over which he has no control? This is the kind of question which absorbed Tolstoy and which he sought to answer in his epic portrait of the clash between East and West which rent Europe in the early part of the nineteenth century. In a letter to Pogodin in March 1868 he wrote:

My thoughts about the limits of freedom and independence and my views on history are not a mere paradox that has occupied me in passing. These thoughts are the fruits of all the intellectual efforts of my life, and they are

---

1 *My Past and Thoughts*, op. cit., Vol. IV, p. 23.

2 The above-quoted passage from the Maude translation in *Tales of Army Life* (World's Classics) is not included in most editions of *The Raid*. In the Russian Jubilee Edition of Tolstoy's *Collected Works* it is also omitted, but is given in the text variations, Vol. 3, 1932, p. 228. Of equal interest as an expression of Tolstoy's youthful attitude to war—he was not yet twenty-four when he wrote *The Raid* (1852)—is the following passage: 'War! What an incomprehensible phenomenon! When one's reason asks: "Is it just, is it necessary?" an inner voice always replies "No." Only the persistence of this unnatural occurrence makes it seem natural, and a feeling of self-preservation makes it seem just.' (Maude translation, op. cit., text variation in Russian edition, op. cit., p. 234.)

an inseparable part of that philosophy which I have achieved, God alone knows with what striving and suffering, and it has given me complete calm and happiness.[1]

He immediately added that he had, however, no illusions that critics and readers would be willing to appreciate his book on that level of understanding, nor was he in error about this. When, however, he wrote that by his philosophy he had achieved 'complete calm and happiness', he expresses that which he longed for rather than the reality. At the height of his powers, a decade after the completion of *War and Peace*, Tolstoy experienced a profound religious crisis, the nature of which he described imperishably in his *Confession*. The philosophy which guided Tolstoy through the last thirty years of his life and which did bring him complete calm and (so far as depended upon himself) happiness, was the fruit of that crisis at the age of fifty. But when he wrote *War and Peace* his crisis had not yet erupted, for the seeds of the conflict within him lay beneath the surface, and he still struggled to contain the conflict. It was much later when even his enormous energies could no longer contain the contradiction that he resolved the conflict by the radical but only rational way open to him.

Consequently the essential clue to *War and Peace* is not to be found without at the outset bringing into the open the contradiction at the heart of the book. It has close kinship with the contradiction at the core of Proudhon's *War and Peace*, but in Tolstoy's case it is explored and probed far more ruthlessly and in infinitely greater depth. Tolstoy describes war with unprecedented realism from direct experience and with his incomparable imaginative power; and he tells us that terrible though it is, it is the result of a mysterious and inevitable force that guides the destiny of men. War is a force that rules the destiny of men and nations, and there is nothing that rational men can do about it other than bow their heads humbly in submission to the awful decrees of Fate. Kutuzov, for example, the only one of the world's 'great men' portrayed in the novel to be conceded as 'great' by Tolstoy, is so considered because of his humility in the presence of the mysterious Force or Fate or Divinity that governs history. On the other hand, Tolstoy makes no attempt to conceal the horror, revulsion and disgust which war evokes in him. War, he says bluntly, is a crime, a dreadful crime. Further, he diagnoses with his unique honesty and extraordinary

---

[1] Quoted by Ernest J. Simmons in *Leo Tolstoy*, New York 1960, Vol. I, p. 311. The Russian text of this letter is in the *Polnoe Sobranie Sochinenii*, op. cit., Vol. 61, p. 195.

skill the causes of war; his diagnosis is detailed and richly circumstantial; the cause is seen in a specific moral defect in man. Tolstoy, moreover, does not confine himself to analysing the cause of war; he also affirms loud and clear the moral principle that man is possessed of reason and freedom of the will whereby he may not only recognize evil but also overcome it. Therefore, war is evil, not inevitable but remediable, and it is man's manifest duty to eradicate it. This is an impossible contradiction and Tolstoy had not succeeded in resolving it in the years during which he composed *War and Peace*. In order to do so, he had to overcome very powerful inner resistances, which even he was able to do only at the cost of intense struggle and great suffering. But the irresolution of this conflict in *War and Peace* is responsible for a certain ambiguity and lack of incisive clarity in argument which in turn makes it easier for the reader with his own powerful inner resistance to truth which Tolstoy uncovers, to avoid seeing that truth.

Reference has already been made to Urusov's approving remark concerning Tolstoy's emphasis on the laws of history—not a fatalism *à la Turke*, so much as predestination. Tolstoy feels himself forced back on some such explanation because of the central paradox in the behaviour of men as characterized in the phenomena he has elected to describe, namely, the invasion of Russia by Napoleon's hordes. This paradox, inexplicable to reason, is that millions of men should agree to obey a few weak individuals to undertake a project in defiance of all reason, which would necessitate the commission of countless unutterable crimes and bring inevitably in its wake immeasurable suffering to themselves as well as to others. These events therefore must be accounted irrational, but, in Hegelian terms, whatever is has a logic of rationality. If it appears otherwise, it must be simply that the reasons are not intelligible to us, which leaves us with an explanation in terms of Fate or predestination. The individual, in living for himself under the illusion of free will, is in fact the tool of history which uses him for the fulfilment of its predestined laws. 'But', Tolstoy insists, 'there are two sides to the life of every man: (a) his individual life—which is the more free the more abstract its interests (b) his elemental swarm-life in which he inevitably obeys laws laid down for him.'[1]

This division between the individual and the swarm, between the free and the unfree, is fundamental to Tolstoy's thought, and he enlarges upon it in the short but highly significant note which in response to criticism he published in 1868 on *War and Peace*. There he attempts

[1] *War and Peace*, London 1943, p. 665.

to illustrate briefly his crucial distinction between the two categories of actions, the free and the unfree.[1] I can write or not write, read or not read, raise or lower my hand in the air. I am incontrovertibly free in this category of actions, namely, self-regarding actions which concern me alone. Conversely in the category of non-self-regarding actions which concern others besides myself I am no longer free. The examples he gives are the inability to choose to lower his hand to strike a child or not to raise it to stop a dog attacking a child or to act out of step with all the rest of the regiment when on parade. These examples are singularly unfortunate and serve only to confuse the vital distinction which Tolstoy is making, but of which he himself is evidently not yet fully aware. It is confusing because the vital distinction between the life of the individual bound by conscience and the life of the individual obeying the swarm is a moral distinction—for example, a man who cannot strike a child because his conscience will not permit it, and a man in uniform who does strike or even kill a child in obedience to an order from a superior within the organization or 'swarm'. Whereas the distinction between self-regarding and non-self-regarding acts blurs this vital moral distinction by lumping together in the category of unfreedom acts where the 'unfreedom' is arising from acts in obedience to conscience and acts in obedience to the demands of swarm life—as in the above example where inability to act out of step with the regiment is bracketed with inability to strike a child.

The confusion arises because of the inadequacy at this stage of Tolstoy's moral development of his definition in categorizing the realm of the free. He defines it not as the realm of conscience but as the realm of the ego or of the highest abstractions of individual existence. We are more free the more abstract our interests. Tolstoy is contrasting with the love of power the quality of disinterestedness, of pursuit of an abstract idea. The contrast is not of like with like, for love of power is an emotion, whereas disinterestedness and commitment to abstract ideas is primarily an intellectual quality. The correct contrast with love of power, of the realm of unfreedom, is with love, the essence of the realm of freedom. But in *War and Peace*, while it is abundantly evident that Tolstoy intuitively grasps this distinction, he has not yet brought it to the level of consciousness and thus is unable to make it a clear and explicit basis of his theorizing. In sharp contrast to the ambiguity and confusion in defining the realm of the free, the realm of the unfree, of the swarm life, is incisively probed with devastating realism. Confusion

[1] *Some Words about War and Peace*, appended to *War and Peace*, op. cit., p. 1351.

arises, he says, when we wrongly transfer the notion of freedom which we rightly associate with self-regarding actions (actions of conscience) to those acts which we perform in conjunction with others and which depend not simply on our own mind and conscience but upon the contingency of other wills coinciding with our own. And the great paradox which lies at the heart of *War and Peace* is that the supreme example of man's unfreedom, that is to say, of his being bound by the chains linking his activities to those of others, is when a man enjoys what we term *power* over the lives of other men. Men seek power in order to impose their will on others, to do that which they want to do and which they want others to do, which, being in a less powerful position they fear they would not be able to do. But, insists Tolstoy, a man is free in proportion to his non-possession of power. And the most powerful are the most unfree.

> The strongest, most indissoluble, most burdensome, and constant bond with other men is what is called power over others, which in its real meaning is only the greatest dependence on them.[1]

The significance of this principle for the understanding of history is momentous. For conventional historians regard power not at all in the sense of Tolstoy's paradox but in the way that the vast mass of mankind understand it. History is made by men of power, so historians write of the activities of statesmen, generals, kings and diplomatists, men who are visibly possessed of power. Tolstoy does not quarrel with this at the level of actuality—he does not dispute its *descriptive* truth. But he relegates it to the despised status of the predetermined, swarm-life of mankind, the life of enslaved men, living lives not free and thus not worthy of men.

> The higher a man stands on the social ladder, the more people he is connected with and the more power he has over others, the more evident is the predestination and inevitability of his every action.
>
> 'The king's heart is in the hands of the Lord.'
>
> A king is history's slave.
> History, that is, the unconscious, general, swarm-life of mankind, uses every moment of the life of kings as a tool for its own purposes.[2]

The truth expressed so sharply here by Tolstoy was graphically caught by the French cartoonist who under the caption 'Two Tsars in Russia'

[1] Ibid., p. 1352.
[2] *War and Peace*, op. cit., p. 666.

depicted a pygmy Nicholas II complete with crown, sceptre and orb and sumptuous royal robes, side by side with a giant Tolstoy, clad in a tattered peasant's smock, carrying a giant scythe across his broad shoulders.

For thousands of years men thought that the sun revolved around the earth; and when Copernicus told them that the truth was the precise opposite, they made a great resistance since they felt that the status of the earth itself had been dethroned, and with it their own status. But that resistance, great as it was, prolonged for more than a hundred years was as nothing to that which is aroused by Tolstoy's Copernican revolution. For Tolstoy exposes as a false god mankind's most consistent and oldest religion, the worship of power. Moreover, he documents his case with a vast wealth of circumstantial detail. At the end only those whose eyes have been put out by the love of power which he is excoriating can fail to see the truth of the picture he draws with such life-like verisimilitude. Men have believed, still do believe that they must submit to the powerful, that their lives revolve round the sun-king, *le roi soleil*. Pure illusion, says Tolstoy. It is not simply false, it is the precise opposite of the truth, which is that it is the king who is the slave, history's slave, the slave of the swarm-life of mankind, that which is least worthy of man.

> In historic events the so-called great men are labels giving names to events, and like labels they have but the smallest connexion with the event itself.[1]

For centuries, men have cried: 'The king is dead. Long live the king.' It is time, says Tolstoy, for men to grow up, to cease to be duped, and to realize that the king has always been dead, that his life is no more than an illusion born of the people's fear and liability to be gulled. *War and Peace* sounds the death knell not just of kings, but of power itself. It is not only a very great book; it is a profoundly subversive book, one that is much and deeply feared.

The conflict at the heart of *War and Peace* is the moral conflict between good and evil, the conflict which is the central concern of all genuine art. The forces of evil are diagnosed unerringly and with unrivalled penetration; they derive from the love of power within the human soul. But the forces of good are less surely diagnosed or rather with some ambiguity, because when Tolstoy wrote this book, although he saw quite clearly that war was evil, the clarity of his moral vision was still confused by his belief that war and therefore evil in the

[1] Ibid., p. 667.

world was inevitable, was decreed by Fate, that force which governs men and worlds, and against which men are powerless to struggle. When Pierre Bezukhov, exhausted from his experiences on the field of Borodino, drops off to sleep in the inn yard at Mozhaysk, he dreams a dream, in which he hears his benefactor's words pronounced as by someone outside himself: 'To endure war is the most difficult subordination of man's freedom to the law of God ... If there were no suffering man would not know his limitations, would not know himself.'[1]

It is significant that the voice was that of 'someone *outside* himself'— Pierre is the most clear, most successful, most sympathetic of all Tolstoy's projections of himself in fiction—but nevertheless this false judgement dogs Tolstoy persistently throughout the book; he cannot throw it off, although his basic analysis of society is quite incompatible with it. He cannot throw it off, because he has not yet clearly discovered the antidote to the love of power and its embodiment in war.

The love of power at its most ruthless is naturally to be seen in the public arena of politics and war; and accordingly Tolstoy's most astringent portraits of individuals in whom the power drive finds its purest fulfilment are those of Speranski, Rostopchin, Murat, Davout and above all, Napoleon. But these public figures, playing what is generally considered to be their key roles in historic events, were themselves once private figures, and in private as distinct from public life Tolstoy shows us their counterparts. Foremost among these is Pierre's evil genius, Prince Vasili, whose single-minded egoism and wooing of the powerful in his own interests wear the mask of genial benevolence, half paternal—half patronizing. Not a conscious Machiavellian, he would not dream of doing anyone a deliberate injury to further his own plans. 'He was merely a man of the world who had got on and to whom getting on had become a habit.' He did not consciously seek to exploit or use others to his own ends. 'But when he came across a man of position his instinct immediately told him that this man could be useful, and without any premeditation, Prince Vasili took the first opportunity to gain his confidence, flatter him, become intimate with him, and finally make his request.'[2] Such a man is not actuated by malice, but he does evil, because he is intuitively guided only by the dictates of his own appetites which do not permit him the luxury of any genuine independent integrity. Such a man is in

[1] *War and Peace*, p. 933.
[2] Ibid., p. 215,

no position to afford the risk of unpopular views; his own views accordingly mirror the prevailing opinions as faithfully as a weather-cock. When Kutuzov is out of favour, Prince Vasili has little or no good to say of him; as soon as Kutuzov returns to favour, Prince Vasili is among the first to discover the great hidden merits of Kutuzov.

A younger version of Prince Vasili, portrayed in rather more depth, is Boris Drubetskoy. Whereas Vasili is an accomplished *arriviste*, Drubetskoy is an apprentice to the trade who wins his spurs between Olmütz and the crossing of the Niemen. His original position on the staff he owes to his mother's assiduous pressure on Vasili himself. His rapid climb up the ladder he owes to his own perspicacity and efforts at place-seeking. Prince Andrew Bolkonski, whose pride will not permit him to seek preferment on his own behalf, enjoys using his influence on behalf of others. Boris accordingly seeks him out at headquarters at Olmütz, in order to be introduced to Dolgorukov, adjutant-general to the Emperor.

> Boris was excited by the thought of being so close to the higher powers as he felt himself to be at that moment. He was conscious that here he was in contact with the springs that set in motion the enormous movements of the mass of which in his regiment he felt himself a tiny, obedient, and insignificant atom.[1]

The occasion also advances his education by showing him that even generals await abashed while Captain Prince Andrew engages in casual conversation with a mere Lieutenant. The discipline imposed by the military code was transcended by another unspoken, more important social mode of subordination.

With yet more experience he learns a further unwritten code, that success, that is to say promotion, depends not on effort or achieve-ment, courage or perseverance but on knowing those possessed of powers of patronage. He was surprised not only by the ease of his advancement but also at the naïveté of others who failed to grasp these small essentials. 'He made friends with and sought the acquaintance of only those above him in position and who could therefore be of use to him.' When Prince Hippolyte criticizes the Russians for fighting for *le roi de Prusse*, Boris's smile is circumspect so that it may be construed as ironic or appreciative according to the reception of the *mot*.

By the time the Emperors meet at Tilsit to agree an armistice, Drubetskoy has acquired the hallmarks of the professional courtier.

---

[1] Ibid., p. 269.

It is crucial to Boris's rising status to have it known that he was present at Tilsit, but his problem is how to engineer an invitation for himself. 'I should like to see the great man,' he says to a General, powerful enough to take him along. 'You are speaking of Buonaparte?' asked the general. . . . 'I am speaking, Prince, of the Emperor Napoleon,' replied Boris.[1] The general perceived at once that Drubetskoy was through ambition reliable and possessed of that perspicacity of judgement to assess accurately the moment when the winds of power were shifting. Boris was accordingly taken to Tilsit. He was thus able to notice and inwardly digest that Napoleon took care to step onto the raft in the Niemen first so as to be the Emperor who welcomed the other aboard.[2]

Boris's advancement thereafter was so rapid that he became rich, no longer needing patronage but on an equal footing with the highest of his generation. When news is brought of the French invasion of Russia, he is even adroit enough to be strategically placed to overhear the news being conveyed to the Emperor by Balashev, and so to impress others by the importance that accrues to those who are first to have access to knowledge of important events.

Far more complex than Drubetskoy is that other son of an aged widow and doting mother, Dolokhov. A man of immense courage, driving energy, proud, independent, tough as whip-cord, he commands respect. But a streak of cruelty combined with his essential egoism and arrogance put him in the ranks of those who are not on the side of the angels. The complexity is to be seen on the eve of the Borodino battle when the man who had seduced Bezukhov's wife and then provoked the cuckolded husband to a duel begs forgiveness of him whom he had wronged. Surprising, perhaps, and yet not out of character, either. But the essential defining trait of Dolokhov which, despite his undoubted virtues, by its ascendancy ranks him as a predominantly evil force in the world, is his single-minded drive to reduce all with whom he associates to submission to his own imperious will. Among the most sinister episodes in the book is the scene in which Dolokhov, smarting under the rejection of his suit by Sonya, sets out to gain his revenge by ruining Nicholas at cards. By force of his savagely hypnotic will he deprives his victim of any vestige of

---

[1] *War and Peace*, p. 440.

[2] On another occasion, however, Alexander's ambassador redressed the balance. When Napoleon allowed his handkerchief to fall for Balashev to pick up, Balashev had the presence of mind to drop his own handkerchief.

independent will or self-respect. It is this quality which is at the heart of Dolokhov that makes him so deadly. It is the explanation of his closest personal relationship, that with Anatole Kuragin: '. . . the very process of dominating another's will was in itself a pleasure, a habit, and a necessity to Dolohkov'.[1]

Berg, Vera's husband, is a minor character, and scarcely differentiated from Boris Drubetskoy in type. He would be contemptible were he not pathetic by the triviality of his stature, the pettiness of his concerns, and his total absence of humour. What animates himself he spells out without the slightest embarrassment or sense of shame, since it has never occurred to him that anyone is or could be moved by other considerations. When he marries, the decisive consideration governing not only when but if the marriage shall take place is the size of the dowry, which is carefully negotiated in advance. When Moscow is abandoned by its inhabitants and the Rostovs are in the full crisis of organizing their own evacuation, Berg appears out of the blue to touch his father-in-law for money to buy Vera a chiffonier with a secret drawer going cheap at an antique dealer's. A derisory figure, almost! But what prevents him from being negligible, what gives him some stature in the eyes of the world is success, modest success but stable and secure by virtue of Berg's sure knowledge of its secret and his single-minded pursuit of it. Berg, Tolstoy tells us, measured his life not by years but by promotions. Berg himself explains to his wife the importance this has for their social relations, necessitating that they seek acquaintance always with those above them in order to ensure maximum satisfaction:

> My comrades are still nobodies, while I am only waiting for a vacancy to command a regiment and have the happiness to be your husband. [For one in Berg's walk of life Vera was a splendid match] . . . And how have I obtained all this? Chiefly by knowing how to choose my acquaintances.[2]

None of these people are evil in the sense that they actively do evil, but by their values they contribute their full share of the world's evil. Prince Vasili's children, Anatole and Helène Kuragin, are in a somewhat different category in that they actively do evil, that is to say, by their own actions knowingly and unfeelingly wreck other people's lives. Anatole is a rake and libertine who has no scruples about luring an innocent, momentarily infatuated young girl to her doom for the sake of his own lusts. His sister uses people for the sake of her own

[1] Ibid., p. 624.   [2] Ibid., p. 508.

social advancement and desire for wealth and position. She is beautiful, heartless, a calculating and successful schemer who sells herself at great price. And because she is immensely rich and powerful, dances with the Emperor, has the ear of the great, she is greatly admired and sought after. There is one exception—gruff, honest Marya Dmitrievna, a conservative *grande dame* of inflexible standards, who amidst general silence at a Petersburg ball calls Princess Hélène a harlot to her face. The Kuragin brother and sister in their respective ways wield great power for evil, respectively they are responsible for the undoing of the two strongest characters in the work, Prince Andrew and Pierre. But the evil they do is not entirely of their own making. It requires the weaknesses of many others to wreak its havoc. Moreover, the retribution it brings upon itself is so terrible that it is impossible to hate even the Kuragins.

There is one other private person who ought perhaps to be included as an example of one who lives according to the code prescribed by the structure and ritual of power—I refer to the diplomat, Bilibin, a minor character drawn with exceptional skill. A friend of Andrew Bolkonski, endowed with an outstanding intellect, a polished, suave, highly informed diplomat on the verge of middle age, he has all the makings of the successful elder statesman of the second rank. He understands the charade of power with peculiar intimacy, subtlety; he even affects to despise it; but for all his irony and wit he is himself the embodiment of the man who has surrendered everything to the requirements of his profession, and whose very soul, despite the truthfulness of his powers of observation, becomes a diplomatic soul. It was Bilibin's suggestion that Napoleon be addressed as 'Usurper and Enemy of Mankind'; but the actual form of address decided on by the Russians—*Au chef du gouvernement français*—was Bilibin's also. And we catch our last glimpse of him advising Princess Hélène that if she marries the old wealthy Count, there is every reason why with a little patience she may catch the young handsome Prince as well in the role of young and wealthy widow. 'A masterly woman' is his opinion of Princess Hélène.

Most subtle and complex of all the characters in whom will is uppermost is the old Prince, Nikolai Bolkonski. The tyranny he wields over his entire entourage is real enough, and he is capable of unmerciful bullying, especially of his daughter who loves him and whom after his fashion he loves. At first sight, an almost impossibly contradictory character, a bully who is kind, an affectionate man hiding deep emotions who inspires universal fear, a man of great dignity and courage who is yet on one plane essentially a comic figure, he convinces by the sincerity of his soul which is compounded first and last of the pride of the Bolkonskis, pride of family, pride of caste, pride of country, pride of tradition and even of a Voltairean rationalist culture. For in culture too the contradiction holds—a combination of anti-clerical Enlightenment with de Maistrean worship of power and caste based on a belief in the necessity of submitting to the Divine will. But although he commands respect, his fierce pride is ultimately egocentric; he loves himself more than anyone else, including even his saintly daughter, Princess Mary; and his chief pleasure is derived from the unbridled, unchallenged dominion he wields over all in his household. If this assumes irresistibly comic proportions when he orders his servants to replace the snow they have laboriously swept from the drive as a mark of respect for the status of a visiting minister, it assumes a streak of cruelty in his scandalous treatment of his prospective daughter-in-law, Natasha, calling to pay her introductory respects. The old Prince, whose final passing amid the ruins of his country engulfed by foreign invasion seems to symbolize the passing of the old autocratic Russia, is a masterly creation. While we are not permitted to see the inner conflict at close quarters, as is the case of the central characters, we are shown very vividly the play of contrast in the external behaviour traits of a character containing violently contradictory elements.

It is always more difficult to portray that which is good than that which is bad. The latter assumes a thousand forms in human character, though always deriving ultimately, as Tolstoy in his characterization reveals, from the love of power or dominion over others, expressed either by satisfaction in its possession or frustration and resentment at not having it or as much as one would like of it. But goodness is very simple and always takes the same form, and is known to all of us, and is very difficult to define or describe directly. Tolstoy is unique among all the world's writers in two respects. Firstly, he commands our respect to a degree that no other writer does by virtue of his love of truth. Like all human beings he is liable to error, but as we read him we soon realize that for Tolstoy in all things truth—to get it right, exactly right—matters more than anything else; that for this one value he will not count the cost in personal suffering, isolation or risk of ridicule. It is this which gives him his unique moral authority. But there is another respect in which Tolstoy is unique among writers

—that is in the degree to which he moves our inmost and deepest feelings. The reason for this lies in Tolstoy's goodness and his love of goodness which shine steadily and unwaveringly through everything which he ever wrote. Tolstoy in his life, more especially in his youth, sometimes did things which were not good. But never at any time in his life did he falter in his love of goodness, which he sought to understand and obey with all the strength of his soul. For this reason when he writes of our sufferings and of the most poignant moments in life of joy or sorrow, his understanding and compassion are so great that we can only read through eyes that are wet with tears.

Princess Mary Bolkonski is far from being Tolstoy's greatest achievement in characterization—although she is portrayed with exceptional love and skill and in some depth—but she more than any other of his characters embodies his ideal of religious perfection. She is generally considered to have represented Tolstoy's idealization of the mother whom he never knew—he was only two at the time of her death; she is unmistakably good and the beautiful nature of her soul irradiates the plainness of her features. If she does not entirely convince, it is perhaps that her goodness appears too easy, too effortless. But she knows envy, she experiences fear, she is not entirely devoid of the Bolkonski pride; but she recognizes these things in the main for what they are and struggles against them. She is introduced to us as a young woman, thin, graceful, plain but with beautiful eyes. Her beliefs are at once made plain through a letter to her friend, Julie Karagina. While she herself, she says, has never been in love, this does not prevent her from understanding such feelings in others, but it seems to her that this kind of feeling is not worthy to be compared with Christian love of one's neighbour and one's enemy. She thinks well of Pierre, whom she knew as a child, because of his excellent heart, the quality she values most in people. She regrets the more the news of his great inheritance, since riches bring temptation, and it is easier for a camel to go through the eye of a needle than for a rich man to enter the kingdom of heaven. She thinks it better to read the Gospels than works of mysticism contrary to Christian simplicity. And she is opposed to war, having just witnessed heart-rending scenes in the village as the conscripts took farewell of their wives and children. Whereas Jesus preached love and forgiveness of injuries, men consider it highly meritorious to kill people in war.

When a suitor comes to request her hand, and she is torn by conflict between her religious aspirations and her irrepressible longing for earthly love, her prayer finds answer in her own heart: 'Desire nothing for thyself, seek nothing, be not anxious or envious . . . but live so that thou mayest be ready for anything.'[1] Her father is not only brutally insensitive to her femininity and the delicacy of her feelings, but goes out of his way to torment her where he knows she will be most hurt, namely in her love for her orphaned nephew and in her religious devotions. But Princess Mary forgives easily (too easily) the old Prince's cruelty and injustice to her. She does so because it is her religious duty. She is critical of her brother for wishing to bind his happiness to another woman, Natasha, after the death of his wife, Lise; she is critical of her father for objecting to the marriage on the grounds that the Rostovs are not a sufficiently distinguished family for a Bolkonski to marry into. The ground of her criticism, which her love will not permit her to voice, is as always religious. We are put into a world dominated by evil not to seek happiness but to learn to be good in the face of ceaseless temptation, and therefore it is necessary to suffer without repining. We are on probation, so to speak. We should love not because the object of our love is worthy of our love but because, love overflowing within us, we cannot help loving all God's creatures. To neglect this spiritual activity in the quest for ephemeral earthly happiness is irrational as well as damaging to our immortal souls. This is the essence of Tolstoy's own inmost religious teaching and where he departs most radically from the secular humanism of the Enlightenment or the Proudhonian worship of Justice which he rejects not simply because it lacks the warmth of divine love but because essentially it is false and leads to power conflict.

> And what is justice? The princess never thought of that proud word 'justice'. All the complex laws of man centred for her in one clear and simple law—the law of love and self-sacrifice taught us by Him who lovingly suffered for mankind though He himself was God. What had she to do with the justice or injustice of other people? She had to endure and love, and that she did.[2]

The teaching is irreproachable—a single sentence reveals the abyss that separates those who see the Absolute manifest in Justice and those who put love above every other consideration including even that of Justice where the two are not immediately reconcilable. But there is a high degree of idealization in the characterization at this point. Tolstoy's intuition in matters of characterization is almost infallible;

---

[1] *War and Peace*, p. 236.   [2] Ibid., p. 524.

but such maturity of character as Tolstoy here attributes to Mary Bolkonski would not be possible for a youthful daughter of a father so consistently guilty of petty tyranny as the old Prince. A Princess Mary in reality, barely on the threshold of adulthood, however remarkable her wisdom and truth of religious understanding, would necessarily resent her father's treatment deeply. If her filial obligation and religious devotion did not permit conscious recognition of that resentment, repressed unconscious conflict would inevitably ensue, and would be productive of more serious behavioural blemishes than merely involuntary envy of Natasha's youth and happiness and of Prince Andrew's love for her. Princess Mary's subsequent marriage to Nicholas and, notwithstanding her religious beliefs, her loyal support of her husband in his belief that a man should subordinate himself and obey the State, is not at all out of character. Views akin to Princess Mary's religiously based conservatism were held by Tolstoy's Aunt, Countess Alexandra Tolstoy, and the attack launched by Tolstoy on them after his religious conversion temporarily strained their relations. Tolstoy died before Freud had been assimilated, and while Tolstoy understood far more clearly than Freud the deviousness of the mind bent on evading self-convicting moral truth, he did not, I think, understand fully the unconscious consequences for those suffering from the domination of others, no matter how stoic or even Christian their motivation. In dealing with Prince Andrew and Pierre, his intuition serves him impeccably; and both men achieve by cathartic release personal liberation from the will of another, old Bolkonski and Prince Vasili respectively. But in metaphysical terms little significance would seem to be attached to this by Tolstoy.

The other character in *War and Peace* who after Princess Mary most clearly reveals the qualities most valued by Tolstoy is the peasant, Platon Karataev. His is a comparatively small part in the novel—although he is of crucial importance in resolving Pierre's spiritual crisis—and he is highly idealized as well as being denied development in depth. He is intensely spontaneous, natural and wholly unconscious of his own thought processes. He reacts directly with no *arrière pensée* or even ability to recall what he has already said. He lives fully and wholly in the present, facing life whole in all its aspects and vicissitudes with resignation, with joy, without repining. He responds to all men (and indeed all animals) alike regardless of rank, of nationality, with kindness and full acceptance of them for what they are, be they Frenchmen, officers, prisoners, peasants. Physically he is a round person who in his arduous circumstances of captivity sweats and smells. He is without any personal attachments of his own and so lives affectionately with all. His every word and action naturally express his inner life, of which he appears to have no direct consciousness. The proof that it is there is his life—a life of self-reliance and ability to attend to all his simple needs, a life of submission to the will of God, a life of endurance, the personification of simplicity and truth. When he prays, he prays to Christ, St. Nicholas and the 'horses' saints', Frola and Lavre. When he talks, he talks simply but from a plain metaphysic investing the commonest events with dignity. His wholly unreflective philosophy is of a piece: '—things happen not as we plan, but as God judges'—'if we grumble at sickness, God won't grant us death'—'where there's law, there's injustice'. He loves most to tell and listen to stories illustrative of the moral qualities of life, and his favourite tale is that of the innocent merchant who forgives the guilty man whose crime has cost him a decade's imprisonment, the tale Tolstoy subsequently retold as *God Sees The Truth But Waits*. Karataev, supremely tranquil for all his sufferings, awaits death with the same rapturous joy with which he told his stories but with an added solemnity; and Pierre, who amidst the cumulative horrors of the retreat from Moscow dare not give way to such profound emotions, cannot, as the moment of Platon's execution approaches, any longer bear to look his friend in the eye.

Princess Mary and Platon Karataev illustrate the religious qualities most esteemed by the author—the qualities of simplicity and acceptance of fate by a heart unable to do other than to love all creatures, hostile as well as friendly. Neither of these characters has or desires any power over others. Both suffer much in body and spirit from the power of others, which they do not approve but at which they do not repine. Mary and Karataev, each in their individual way, illustrate goodness in its essentially religious qualities. In their secular aspect, the qualities most esteemed by Tolstoy are admirably illustrated in two of his minor characters, Captain Tushin and Natasha's 'Uncle'. Tushin is modest and unassuming, knows his job thoroughly, is intensely practical, and people automatically rely on him. He is inarticulate, kindly and considerate towards all, and so absorbed in the task in hand that he is wholly unconscious in his heroism. When he is called to account by General Bagration for having lost two guns, he is not even aware that in fact it was his battery's heroism that was largely responsible for the victory of Schöngraben. He is only conscious of the fact that if he speaks the truth, namely that he was deprived of protective infantry supports, he may get some other officer into trouble. The irony lies in the fact that the officer responsible for removing Tushin's supports was General Bagration himself. Tushin is called to account by authority as a result of his quite unconscious heroism, and he is prevented from exonerating himself from the charges by his additional virtue of loyalty to colleagues.

Natasha's 'Uncle', a distant relative of the Rostovs but of humble social position, in many ways resembles Tushin—simple, unaffected, natural, honest, down-to-earth, entirely without pretension, and wise enough to avoid all association with authority on the grounds that he can't make head or tail of that sort of thing for which he is quite unfitted. Generally known and respected throughout the province for his disinterested and honourable nature, he is accustomed to being confided in, having his advice sought, requested to settle disputes and act as executor. But against all pressures to accept public office of any kind he is adamant, preferring to ride his bay gelding in spring and autumn, and for the rest to potter in his home and garden.

I have been at pains so far simply to isolate and illustrate Tolstoy's values as seen through his characters, to get a clear understanding of his conception of the nature of good and evil. For this provides us with the key to the whole book, concerned as it is with life as perceived on two planes, the private and the public. At the private or personal level the central subject matter of the book is to be found in the way the conflict between the contending forces of good and evil work themselves out in the lives of the three principal male characters, Nicholas Rostov, Andrew Bolkonski and Pierre Bezukhov. The other principal character is Natasha Rostova, but although she is perhaps the world's favourite fictional character, she is only of sub-sidiary interest to our theme. With the exception of Anna in *Anna Karenina* profound inner moral and spiritual conflict is an exclusively masculine phenomenon in Tolstoy's fiction. Conflict is hinted at in Natasha—contrast her attempts to test out her power over the servants in the Rostov household with her spontaneous compassion for the wounded soldiers stranded in the courtyard of their Moscow home. But essentially Natasha is a unity—all of a piece—beautiful in the intensity, spontaneous naïveté, directness and naturalness of her character. She is emotional, intuitive, overflowing with the vitality of youth, completely unselfconscious (a great Tolstoyan virtue), absolutely unable to believe that everyone in the world would not be bound to love her and therefore unable to betray her trust. And when she finds she is mistaken, like a wounded fawn she turns in her anguish to the person whom her intuition tells her is the one above all whom she can trust absolutely, namely, Pierre.

I will deal first with the conflict in Nicholas, where as in all honest conservatives, pillars of society, the conflict is no more than glimpsed and the source of anxiety immediately repressed. In Andrew the conflict is profound. Although the truth is as emotionally unacceptable to Prince Andrew as it is to Nicholas, reason, intellectual integrity and personal pride are so highly developed in him that the repression of the painful, the evasion and self-deception of Rostov are simply out of the question in Bolkonski, a figure of altogether greater dimension and stature. The conflict is so terrible that Bolkonski unconsciously resolves it in the only way compatible with his nature, by choosing death. Bolkonski's mortal wound on the battlefield is not fortuitous— it is a response to the profound need of a nature which has ultimately turned its back on life. And thirdly, I shall sketch the conflict in Pierre who, when he perceives the truth in the great central crisis of his life, does not turn his back upon it but strives with all the strength of his soul to embrace it.

Nicholas Rostov is a young man of uncomplicated energies, who lives unreflectingly by virtues which he does not question—the virtues of his caste—honesty, loyalty, family tradition, patriotism, love of the land, hunting, love of his regiment, pride in his country and its heritage. Indeed his values are very much those of old Bolkonski with whom Nicholas never comes into contact. His weakness lies in his conventionality and fear of appearing to be in the least non-conformist within the social milieu where he feels secure. So great is his dependence on this milieu for his basic identity that although he prizes truthfulness very highly—so much so that when his Colonel accuses him of having spoken an untruth he wants to challenge him to a duel— his moral weakness stems precisely from his inability to be wholly truthful with himself. When in camp near Olmütz he tells Boris and Berg how he was wounded at Schöngraben, he in fact tells them not what actually happened but what sounded well and was in harmony with his own desires and fitted the model of such stories as they are generally told illustrative of courage and modesty and *sang froid*.

Rostov was a truthful young man and would on no account have told a deliberate lie. He began his story meaning to tell everything just as it happened, but imperceptibly, involuntarily, and inevitably he lapsed into falsehood. It is very difficult to tell the truth, and young people are rarely capable of it.[1]

Just as Baron Pesth in Tolstoy's second *Sketch from Sevastopol* after his first skirmish with the enemy in which he killed a Frenchman related not his confusion, panic and horror at what he had done but simply boasted that *he* had killed one too, and was duly congratulated by his commanding officer.

Since Nicholas is not rigorously accurate in his reportage of events, he is not of the metal to listen to his own inner doubts when he finds that society's values do not countenance his own misgivings. When he discovers that a fellow officer is a thief, he also discovers that the colonel and all the officers of the regimental mess take the view that it is he, Nicholas, who is betraying the honour of the regiment in making public behaviour which can only bring dishonour on the entire regiment. The good name of the regiment, Nicholas dutifully learns, is far more important than the truth that a member has besmirched that good name. Again, when between Drissa and Vitebsk Rostov's hussars charge the French dragoons, Nicholas overtakes and strikes a fleeing, frightened dragoon, he loses all his animation, is confused and disturbed by the act of deliberately cutting down a man like himself. But so far from being reprimanded for his behaviour, he is awarded the cross of St. George for bravery—conclusive proof for Nicholas and everyone else of the righteousness of his actions.

Only once is Nicholas's inner conviction that all is right with the world in which he is asked to be brave, straightforward and devoted in the service of the Tsar and his country, seriously threatened. And the moment of frightening truthfulness is immediately buried deep in his unconscious. That moment occurs at Tilsit, where the two Emperors meet to bury the hatchet and establish a *modus vivendi* between them. Nicholas himself is freshly arrived not only from the experiences common to every soldier in the front line, but from the dreadful experience of the field hospital with its dirt and disease, its terrible stench of dead and putrefying flesh, its mutilated and amputated legs and arms. He now witnesses the feasting of the senior staff-officers, the respect and honour shown by his beloved Tsar to the upstart Bonaparte, whom he had been taught to regard as the foe incarnate. The enemy had now turned out, it appeared, to be gallant allies after all. 'Then why those severed arms and legs and those dead men?'

[1] *War and Peace*, p. 258.

Terrible doubts, hitherto inconceivable thoughts of a profoundly subversive nature began to arise in Nicholas's simple, uncomplicated soul, and he is momentarily frightened. But it is only momentary, the hidden inner conflict is immediately stifled. He shouts and bangs the table to reassure himself.

> If we are ordered to die, we must die. If we're punished, it means that we have deserved it, it's not for us to judge. If the Emperor pleases to recognize Bonaparte as Emperor and to conclude an alliance with him, it means that that is the right thing to do. If once we begin judging and arguing about everything, nothing sacred will be left! That way we shall be saying there is no God—nothing![1]

And so Nicholas restores his equanimity, and retains the security of his inner self intact for life. '. . . it's not for us to judge'.

Tolstoy projects himself as a central character in all his major works of fiction, but nowhere does he do it so successfully as in *War and Peace* where he actually brings off the double, so to speak. Both Pierre and Andrew are individualized and wholly inseparable from the world in which they move and develop in a way that is not true of Levin in *Anna Karenina* or of Nekhlyudov in *Resurrection*, for example. Of the two Andrew is presented as the senior and stronger character, but he suffers from a fatal weakness which undoes him in life and brings him to premature death. Whereas Pierre, originally the seemingly weaker, more unsure and confused character is most completely the poetic embodiment of Tolstoy himself, and in his maturity becomes a person of commanding strength—commanding because he has learnt the futility of all commanding. Andrew has many and high virtues, his remorseless truthfulness leads to bitterness and wounded pride, whereas Pierre is saved by the humility that lies behind the bewildered kindliness of his quest for truth. For both characters are for ever imprinted upon the imagination of the world by virtue of the nobility and sincerity of their seeking after the truth of the meaning of life.

Andrew is the son of old Bolkonski, a retired general, one of the most remarkable men of his time, and a man who has wielded absolute powers—sometimes tyrannically—over large numbers of men. The son is proud like the father and anxious to achieve worldly distinction, fame or glory, worthy of his heritage. He is a man of high honour and integrity but one in whom will—a scornful, aristocratic will—is uppermost. Unhappily married through his inability to give love and

[1] Ibid., p. 450.

his contempt for the frivolity and triviality of his wife's social pleasures, he regrets having encumbered himself in this way prematurely since it is liable to act as a brake on the one thing of supreme importance, the advancement of a career in the world worthy of a prince of the Bolkonski blood. He is introduced to us as a young man, ambitious, of high intellect, occupying an envied social position, scornful of those of smaller mould in Petersburg society—a man full of admiration for Bonaparte as the embodiment of power and glorious achievement, the quality of which may not be measured in the scales of ordinary personal morality. With Machiavelli, Prince Andrew believes that statesmanship forges its own moral laws which transcend those of private individuals. His constant dream is of the opportunity that may come his way when he too may seize destiny by the throat on the model of his hero at Toulon. He learns from Bilibin that the Russians have been cut off as a result of the French crossing the Thabor bridge over the Danube in Vienna.

> As soon as he learned that the Russian army was in such a hopeless situ-
> ation it occurred to him that it was he who was destined to lead it out of this
> position; that here was the Toulon that would lift him from the ranks of
> obscure officers and offer him the first step to fame![1]

Himself too proud to stoop to seek favours on his own behalf, he is not above doing so on behalf of others like Drubetskoy since this affords him the double pleasure of dispensing patronage and of keeping in touch with the highest circles whence success is conferred. On the eve of Austerlitz, his imagination, fired by his dreams of power and fame, takes full possession of him, and fantasies of wish-fulfilment arise in his soul.

> All are struck by the justness of his views but no one undertakes to carry
> them out, so he takes a regiment, a division . . . and gains the victory
> alone. . . . The dispositions for the next battle are planned by him alone.
> Nominally he is only an adjutant on Kutuzov's staff, but he does every-
> thing alone. The next battle is won by him alone. Kutuzov is removed
> and he is appointed . . . but if I want this—want glory, want to be known
> to men, want to be loved by them, it is not my fault that I want it and
> want nothing but that and live only for that. Yes, for that alone! . . .[2]

Not his 'fault' perhaps, but not inevitable either; and he has already been exposed to experience which has sharply jolted his faith in the

[1] *War and Peace*, p. 172.
[2] Ibid., p. 282.

rationality of such values. After Kutuzov had successfully engaged Mortier's division, he despatches Prince Andrew with the news of the victory to the Austrian court at Brünn. Andrew full of the exhilaration and pride of victory expects to be given a significant welcome for news of an encouraging nature coming at a time when the allies were suffering defeats at the hands of the French. He is therefore bitterly disappointed when he finds the Austrian war minister quite indifferent to his tidings and his subsequent reception by the Emperor purely perfunctory. The soldier fresh from facing death in direct encounter with the enemy is shocked to discover that their lives are simply pawns in the hands of politicians, themselves absorbed in the intricacies of diplomacy, into the subtleties of which Bilibin seeks to initiate the naïve Andrew. The Austrians, he explains, smarting under the humiliation of General Mack's defeat, were already preparing the ground behind the scenes to do a deal with Napoleon, already ensconced in Vienna, and therefore had little cause to be interested in Kutuzov's skirmish with Mortier. Andrew, deeply mortified (but not able to adjust to reality by the self-deception resorted to by Nicholas when similarly shocked at Tilsit), hastens to exchange the scene of high diplomacy and its sordid intrigues for the more familiar and cleaner one of the army. There however an even more severe shock awaits him in the episode of the heroic stand of Captain Tushin's battery at Schöngraben. It is only due to the chance of Andrew's own presence and integrity that the hero of that action did not find himself in severe trouble on account of an order by General Bagration himself. This revealing episode is compounded of the humility and loyalty of a brave man chastised for his pains, the cowardice and falsehood of staff officers, and the inability of the commander-in-chief in the confusion of battle to grasp the consequences of his own orders. Bagration's own contribution consisted not of his command of operations he was no more able to control than anyone else, but in the tact with which he fulfilled the role expected of him, thus serving to support and strengthen the morale of his staff.

Andrew's education is advanced still more rapidly when he is wounded at Austerlitz, and from the radically changed perspective of one hovering between life and death he obtains a glimpse at first hand of his hero, Napoleon.

Looking into Napoleon's eyes Prince Andrew thought of the insignificance of greatness, the unimportance of life which no one could understand, and the still greater unimportance of death, the meaning of which no one alive could understand or explain.[1]

He has reached this stage of his development when he suffers the misfortune of losing his unloved wife in childbirth. Indeed it is more than a misfortune since he now suffers the anguish of guilt for the love he owed his wife and can now never give. She reproaches him from the tomb, and he draws in more and more upon himself, austere, near misanthrope, saturnine. To such straits has his proud, ambitious, aloof, highly intellectual, loveless soul brought him. He is saved from himself by the kindliness and unwavering honesty of his friend, Pierre, who calling on him in his rustic retreat first overcomes his jaundiced self-hate by engaging him in honest argument and secondly, on the raft crossing the ferry at evening, by raising the question of immortality in the light of the universality of evil in the world we know, penetrates to Prince Andrew's humanity and essential nobility of soul. His 'cure' is finally accomplished and he is restored fully to life by Natasha's love. That such happiness was possible, he had not dreamed. But again he is destined to be cheated, and again by the encumbrance of his family heritage, by the pride of the Bolkonskis, father and son. The old prince, more testy and despotic with age, is loath to see his domestic certitudes invaded by a newcomer, and one not an equal of the Bolkonski blood at that. The son, who for all his pride shares something of the general fear of his father, yields to the extent of delaying his marriage for a year. In the meantime Anatole Kuragin attempts his abortive elopement with Natasha, and Prince Andrew's pride is outraged beyond all possibility of forgiveness of his fiancée's momentary infatuation born of frustration.

Prince Andrew departs for the front once more, this time intent largely on finding self-forgetfulness and vaguely in the hope that he may come up with Kuragin and exact his revenge. On a brief visit to Bald Hills, observing his father's unseemly behaviour with his son's governess mainly in order to humiliate Princess Mary, he at last finds the courage to stand up to the old tyrant and assert his independence. Although the actual clash is conveyed with all Tolstoy's customary skill, there is no indication that Tolstoy really appreciates the full significance of this act of liberation from paternal domination. Tolstoy's own father died when he was only eight years old, and Tolstoy is not of the psycho-analytic age. Not of course that Tolstoy did not fully

---

[1] *War and Peace*, p. 313.

grasp the moral significance of one human being dominating the will of another. Witness, for example, the effect of Pierre ordering Prince Vasili out of his house and conversely the effect of Nicholas's inability to throw off the hypnotic domination of Dolokhov.

In June Prince Andrew reaches Barclay de Tolly's army where he witnesses the various factions struggling for dominance within the high command. The sense of futility he had experienced when through his contacts with Speranski he became chairman of a committee to revise the legal code, is now reinforced by his observance of the interested motives and lack of contact with military reality characteristic of the members of the Tsar's war council. He reflects that the concept underlying all the discussions—that there exists a science of war of which Armfelt, Toll, Paulucci, Wolzogen, Pfuel and the others were exponents—is entirely bogus.

> What theory and science is possible about a matter the conditions and circumstances of which are unknown and cannot be defined, especially when the strength of the acting forces cannot be ascertained?[1]

The presence of a single coward or a single brave man at a crucial moment when all the combatants are necessarily in a highly emotional state, can make all the difference to victory or defeat. And this factor of morale is not one that can be predicted or allowed for in advance. So he concludes that the very notion of a military genius is a spurious one; and he recalls the picture of Napoleon's 'limited, self-satisfied face' on the field at Austerlitz. Not that there are not good and bad military commanders; but in order to be a good one it is necessary to be possessed of virtues which are not virtues. He requires not the qualities of tenderness or love or philosophic enquiry, of humanity or love of justice or a disposition to pity but the absence of all these. He must be limited and convinced of his own importance, stupid or absent-minded. The reason why they are called geniuses is simply that they are possessed of great power. Animated by such reasoning, Prince Andrew shocks his confrères and loses his standing in court circles for ever by asking the Tsar to assign him not to the imperial staff but to active service with his regiment. And there it is on the field of Borodino that he receives his fatal wound. As the shell spins on the ground, his pride, that fatal aristocratic pride which destroyed his happiness in life, will not permit him to fling himself to the protection of the ground in the presence of his men.

[1] Ibid., p. 708.

On the eve of the battle he meets his friend Pierre, and it is interesting to compare this, their last conversation in life, with the one with which the book opened, when both men were Bonapartists defending the essence of the doctrine of *raison d'état*, that statesmen must be governed only by the laws of power and are exempt from the principles of private morality. Shortly afterwards, the two discuss the war to which Andrew is about to depart. Pierre says he would fight in a war for freedom, but is not willing to assist the English and the Austrians against 'the greatest man in the world'. To which 'childish words' Andrew merely replied that if wars were to await upon men's private convictions, there would be no wars, and that will never be. It is sufficient reason for him to go to the wars that he is unhappy at home.

Now almost at the end of his short life, he has come to adopt the substance of Pierre's original position, but incisively sharpened. War he has learnt to see truthfully and he condemns it, except such a battle as the present one in defence of the fatherland and of Russian freedom. As for the doctrine of *raison d'état*, he has learnt that great issues are not decided by statesmen and generals anyway, but by ordinary people.

Overhearing Wolzogen and Clausewitz agreeing on the need to extend the war and to weaken the enemy irrespective of casualties, Prince Andrew reflects with disgust on what the war has done to his dying father and sister at Bald Hills. His bitterness is directed both against military strategists, who presume to fight war as though it were a game of chess and against the French who in invading Russia have brought carnage, rapine and destruction down upon millions of innocent heads. It is necessary, therefore, he concludes, to strip war of its false sentimentality and rules of chivalry which mask the real barbarity of war. Paradoxically he feels that if the Russians were to take no prisoners and execute the French as criminals, it would not only be in tune with outraged Russian patriotic feelings, but would also serve to remind men that war is not a game but something grotesque and horrible, not to be undertaken as a pastime for professional staff-officers but only as a last desperate measure in defence of freedom. It is time to put an end, if not to war—that is not possible—at any rate to the conception of war as a conventional and glorious distraction for the idle, frivolous but greatly honoured military caste.

> The aim of war is murder, the methods of war are spying, treachery, and their encouragement, the ruin of a country's inhabitants, robbing them or stealing to provision the army, and fraud and falsehood termed military

craft. The habits of the military class are the absence of freedom, that is, discipline, idleness, ignorance, cruelty, debauchery and drunkenness. And in spite of all this it is the highest class, respected by everyone. All the kings, except the Chinese, wear military uniforms, and he who kills most people receives the highest rewards.

They meet, as we shall meet tomorrow, to murder one another; they kill and maim tens of thousands, and then have thanksgiving services for having killed so many people . . . and they announce a victory, supposing that the more people they have killed the greater their achievement. How does God above look at them and hear them?[1]

He has learned much in those seven short years between Austerlitz and Borodino, and the burden of such truth he does not find easy to reconcile with the need to go on living. He echoes the old adage—expressed by Herzen, too, it will be recalled—that 'it does not do for man to taste of the tree of knowledge of good and evil'. But his honesty and strength of intellect do not permit him to take the way out so commonly taken, the way of self-deception. So how is he to go on living? The answer is given to him only after he has been relieved of the necessity of going on living. Himself mortally wounded he at last catches up with his hated enemy—Anatole Kuragin, sobbing convulsively on the operating table as he is shown his amputated leg. Andrew's hatred had been even more futile than his ambition, and he is flooded by compassion and love for this piteous creature, his brother in agony, whom he had pursued as an enemy. And in his last days the love for the Natasha who is returned to him is a love that is purified of all earthly desires. On the point of death, he muses just like Tolstoy's Ivan Ilych, created some thirteen years later, 'Is it possible that the truth of life has been revealed to me, only to show me that I have spent my life in falsity?'

Pierre Bezukhov is a man of less assurance and greater humility, more inclined to speculation and philosophizing than Prince Andrew. Less a man of action, he is nevertheless capable of furious energy, and this energy he seeks to harness to his quest for the truth about human life. But deeply as he loves truth, there are very powerful inner resistances to be overcome. It costs him an effort, for example, to confess his illegitimacy. He is clumsy, rather bewildered, joins in the life of the young man about town for want of any more serious purpose. He yet conveys an intuitive sense of great latent strength, he is kindly and above all he is searching for something. Politically he supports

[1] *War and Peace*, pp. 858–9.

Bonaparte because he identifies him as a symbol of the Revolution in France, and Pierre regards himself as a liberal. When he finds himself the heir to the Bezukhov millions, he finds himself quite out of his depth and passively submits to Prince Vasili's eagerly offered tutelage, although he notices and mentally records that the attitude of people perceptibly changed towards him the day after he was known to be the new heir—in general a more deferential and flattering if not obsequious note was struck by those addressing him.

Pierre's marriage to Prince Vasili's daughter, Helène, is a masterpiece of comedy, which at the same time sends a cold shudder down our spines. Although he is attracted only by Helène's beautiful body, he weakly allows himself to be engineered into a *fiançailles accompli.* Looking upon the rise and fall of her exquisite bosom, he felt it incumbent upon him to say what the occasion required of him, but could not recall the necessary phrase. Later it came to him—'*Je vous aime.*' He has the feeling that what is happening, although of the highest importance to him, is inevitable and that he is being borne along by the tide of events. In other words, unless we have a clear idea of our own identity and moral purpose, we are very likely to find ourselves the involuntary tools of the Vasilis of this world, the upshot of which we are likely to attribute to Fate or Destiny. He does not, however, remain long in servitude, as he awakens to his guilt in having married Vasili's daughter out of lust and under the father's blandishments. The scene where he frees himself for ever from the father-in-law's domination reveals with complete accuracy and in few words the immense psychological significance of the discovery by one man that his soul really is his own and the realization by another that not all men are pliant tools for him to possess and use.

> He was so used to submitting to Prince Vasili's tone of careless self-assurance that he felt he would be unable to withstand it now, but he also felt that on what he said now his future depended— ... 'Prince, I did not ask you here. Go, please go.' And he jumped up and opened the door for him. 'Go!' he repeated, amazed at himself and glad to see the look of confusion and fear that showed itself on Prince Vasili's face.[1]

Pierre is very gentle, peering cautiously out through his spectacles, curious, kindly, sympathetic, but behind the awkward exterior lurks the bear-like strength of honest outrage when his essential simplicity of soul is mistaken for weakness or gullibility. Like Tolstoy

[1] *War and Peace*, p. 393.

himself, he is infinitely gentle and compassionate. Like Tolstoy he has a towering strength which power and egoism confront at their peril.

Pierre's venture into Freemasonry is perhaps the least successful of all Tolstoy's writing. It has a quality of forced artificiality very rarely present in Tolstoy; and it is exceedingly difficult to imagine a man of Pierre's character engaging in elaborate fantasy rituals. The intention of the author is, however, plain enough. Pierre, seeking to find the purpose of life, is attracted by the seriousness of moral purpose apparently informing masonic teachings. It does not take him long to be disillusioned by the cold reception given to his own moral enthusiasm which takes the naïve form of a proposal to establish a 'universal government' to carry out the essential principles of Christianity by non-revolutionary, non-violent means. The other false path pursued by Pierre trying to set his house in order is his attempt to use his power as a landowner to do good to his serfs. He is shown to be again naïve in his lack of understanding both of people and of the truth that good cannot be done to others by means of external power. Tolstoy rarely resorts to overt irony. When he does, it is administered with effect and maximum economy. 'How easy it is, how little effort it needs, to do so much good,' thought Pierre, 'and how little attention we pay to it.' And yet for all his naïveté and error, it is his simplicity of soul and a moral earnestness not to be deflected from its purpose that penetrates the barrier of Prince Andrew's aloof reserve and moral scepticism in the dialogue at the ferry already referred to.

And how pointed is the contrast in the reactions of the two men to Natasha's youthful folly. Although Andrew's love is genuine, it is not sufficient to overcome his wounded pride, and his inability to forgive costs him much suffering. Pierre also loves Natasha, although he may not admit this to himself since, although estranged from his wife, he is still married to her, and therefore is not free. He too is shocked by Natasha's behaviour, but where Andrew has pride, Pierre has humility. In all Tolstoy I know of nothing more moving than Pierre's involuntary forgiveness of Natasha for consenting to elope with 'that bad man' Kuragin. Natasha stands before him in tears, filled with shame and self-abasement, protesting that all is over for her and that her life is worthless. And Pierre, although he still understands nothing of how she could have behaved as she did, feels only love and compassion for her which momentarily under the stress of emotion overflow his normal restraints and raise her up again to his own level.

'All over?' he repeated. 'If I were not myself, but the handsomest, cleverest and best man in the world, and were free, I would this moment ask on my knees for your hand and your love!'[1]

Pierre is intensely unhappy because of the severity of his inner conflict, from which he seeks endlessly repeated distraction in the shape of wine, gossip, as a *bon viveur* at the clubs, buying pictures, above all reading. On the one hand he knows that life is a serious business, that it is intolerable to live it other than purposefully, and that he has been endowed with a conscience to that end. On the other hand every possible occupation in life—and it was necessary to have an occupation in order to live—seemed corrupt and so far from improving the lot of men only made it worse.

> He had the unfortunate capacity many men, especially Russians, have of seeing and believing in the possibility of goodness and truth, but of seeing the evil and falsehood of life too clearly to be able to take a serious part in it.[2]

He, like everyone else, knows the good and yet is expected to acquiesce in a life that is not only bad, but absurd, self-contradictory, offensive to reason. On the very day that the Catholic clergy in France give thanks to God for a victory over the Spaniards, the Catholic clergy of Spain thank God for the victory over the French. His wife whom he has the best of reasons for knowing as heartless, stupid, empty of soul and vain, because of her wealth and eminent social position is universally respected and praised for her intelligence and grace. In the name of Christ who preached love and forgiveness army deserters are knouted to death. How is it possible to live under the burden of contradiction so obvious, inescapable and painful? It is not so possible, Pierre concludes; and so each man, like himself, according to taste seeks to escape from life and still the pain by the opiate of diversion. They find it in a variety of ways: 'some in ambition, some in cards, some in framing laws, some in women, some in toys, some in horses, some in politics, some in sport, some in wine, and some in governmental affairs'.

When war comes and Moscow itself is threatened, although he believes in the justice of a war in defence of the country, he is inhibited from joining the armed forces partly because of distaste for the fashionable gust of patriotism, partly by Freemason teachings against the depravity of war, but mainly by a feeling that destiny has marked him

---

[1] *War and Peace*, p. 659.   [2] Ibid., p. 590.

out for a special role: the role of assassin of Napoleon, the anti-Christ, as he now believes him to be. The absurdities and crimes which men become capable of in times of national crisis as a result of self-dramatization, hysteria and wholly artificial belief in the efficacy of external power to alter the main direction of events are illustrated on a number of occasions in Tolstoy's treatment of the advance of the French and the occupation of Moscow. When the Tsar calls a council of nobles to raise levies, and Pierre attempts to make a reasoned statement, he is astonished by the fury and irrationality of chauvinistic attacks upon him by men who normally are simply genial club companions. When Rostopchin sees his own status threatened by the flood of events which he imagines it is his function as Governor of Moscow to control, he loses his head, and perpetrates a crime the guilt of which for ever haunted him. He did in fact incite a mob of frustrated city defenders to divert their anger onto the defenceless head of Vereshchagin, a pacifist leafleteer dubbed 'traitor' whom they brutally murdered.

Pierre, under the influence of his consuming notion that Napoleon is the author of all this engulfing misery, sets out in a dazed stupor to murder him. He finds himself, however, deflected from his theatrical assassin's path by the sight first of a distraught mother whose child has been left in a burning building, and secondly of a beautiful Armenian girl threatened with assault by soldiers. His customary humanity and simple directness of response immediately reassert themselves and he recovers from his temporary insanity.

Having thus narrowly escaped the loss of his normal humane self under the impact of the mass hysteria generated by war, he then himself almost perishes at the hands of others in the grip of this same terrible and mysterious force. This force, the culmination of the will to power, indicted consistently throughout the entire work, is experienced in all its horror by Pierre when he is led to execution as an alleged incendiary. The veil which was torn from the eyes of Prince Andrew resolving his conflict at last, recalling him to life, as he lay on the operating table, mortally wounded, next to the mutilated Kuragin, is torn from Pierre's eyes as he gazes with horror upon the execution of his companions. And the essence of the evil that destroys men is symbolized in the drum—the drum of the parade ground, of military discipline, of the triumphal march, of the charge, of an execution, of the dehumanization of men in the service of a vast machine designed for murder.

'There it is! . . . *It* again! . . .' said Pierre to himself, and an involuntary shudder ran down his spine. In the corporal's changed face, in the sound of his voice, in the stirring and deafening noise of the drums, he recognized that mysterious, callous force which compelled people against their will to kill their fellow-men—that force the effect of which he had witnessed during the executions. To fear or to try to escape that force, to address entreaties or exhortations to those who served as its tools, was useless. Pierre knew this now. One had to wait and endure.[1]

Pierre is reprieved, but with the mainspring of his life, his faith in humanity, of all that made sense of life, of his own soul wrenched out and broken by the terrible crime he had been compelled to witness. But it is just at the moment of despair and of his greatest need that he finds, amidst the extremities of hardship as a prisoner in the French retreat from Moscow, the answer to his life's quest. It comes in the shape of the life, the example and conversation of Platon Karataev, a man who owns nothing, who is wracked by illness from sufferings previously inflicted upon him, and who is yet beyond the reach of privation or wickedness to touch him. The reason is that he is the embodiment of a man who has conquered in himself the last surviving remnants of that will to power which has wrought such terrible evils, and is thus able genuinely and with simple sincerity to serve and strengthen all those with whom he meets upon life's way.

In creating an immense host of characters and setting them in motion one with another, Tolstoy creates a world which mirrors his vision of human reality. In order to do this, he has of course to select from the infinite fragments of his experience those which are to him significant. Tolstoy's criteria for inclusion and exclusion derive from standards imposed by his art, his purpose being to give his readers a vision of reality, human and physical, moral and political as seen and experienced by himself. My own criteria of selection in thus drastically summarizing the interplay of character in *War and Peace* have been determined by the intent to reveal the basic principles at the heart of Tolstoy's moral universe. In so doing, it is my contention that those principles are made quite plain, that they are very simple, and that they are true; that is to say, that they inform not only Tolstoy's moral universe, but our moral universe, too—the one in which we all necessarily dwell. But the principles thus elucidated are clearer to us *now* than they were to Tolstoy *then*. They are the principles which became wholly conscious and consistently articulate in Tolstoy only

[1] *War and Peace*, p. 1118.

after his great religious crisis at the age of fifty. When he wrote *War and Peace* during his late thirties, his fundamental moral understanding of life, although strongly developed, as we have seen, was still only latent, encumbered by much else which prevented it from rising to full consciousness.

In personal relations Tolstoy perceived quite clearly that an individual's unpleasant qualities productive of evil consequences to himself and others were always associated with the will to power, domination or self-aggrandisement; and that these qualities were evil because they could only be exercised and fulfilled at the expense of some weaker person or persons. He also saw that good qualities were the negation of these, namely, patience, humility, suffering rather than resisting power, equality, concern for others, compassion, love, self-sacrifice. But in addition to perceiving this, he perceived equally sharply that the principle of power and domination, of hierarchical command is necessarily present wherever organization of human activity on a large scale is involved, and nowhere more so than in matters of military business, that is to say, of war. Since the latter aspect of experience is well-nigh universal and pervades our life at all levels, it seemed by its very ubiquity to carry with it some degree of validation or legitimacy, notwithstanding the fact that it contradicted the clear knowledge that in personal relations the principle of power and domination was uniformly evil in its consequences. And so Tolstoy, albeit reluctantly and with great latent inner turmoil, has to have recourse to some such principle as is expressed by Pierre and Andrew at the opening of the novel—the principle of *raison d'état*. Napoleon in murdering the Duc d'Enghien was doing something which, if it had expressed no more than a facet of their purely personal relations, would have been morally indefensible. But as an act of state, undertaken not as a result of personal animosity but in order to stabilize the precarious Bonapartist dynasty in the interests of French political stability, might it not be morally validated? Tolstoy of course nowhere suggests that it might. On the contrary, it is obviously profoundly repugnant to his every moral value and runs counter to the whole tenor of the book. But in so far as war and violence, albeit allegedly defensive violence, are not rejected as morally indefensible, some such rationalization is inescapable. And Tolstoy, although it is clear that he hates war, does not in *War and Peace* reject war. Quite the contrary: the Russians are fighting a just war in defending their sacred soil against a foreign and cruel invader. It is this which constitutes the essence of the epic quality pervading the book; at this level it is the prose equivalent of Tchaikovsky's *1812*. It is Tolstoy's account of the great patriotic war—an interpretation *de rigueur* with all Soviet commentators—and it is true that there is no more Russian Russian than Tolstoy. Nevertheless Tolstoy was never a chauvinist; he was always much too truthful to make this possible. The military conflict is described objectively and fairly without nationalist partisanship or biased rancour. Indeed, since Tolstoy devotes far more space to describing the Russian side of the conflict than the French, his astringencies concerning the vices and moral weaknesses of the generals relate in detail to the Russian rather than the French—with the obvious exception of the two principal protagonists, Napoleon and Kutuzov—the one, the 'aggressor', the other, the 'defender'.

This ambivalence towards the question of war itself is the key to the lack of clarity and confusion in the philosophic reasoning underpinning the whole work and made explicit in the very important but puzzling second epilogue. The following extracts will make this clear: first, Tolstoy's condemnation of war as such. It suffuses the whole atmosphere of the book, and most clearly of all in the central character of Pierre who observes war closely at first hand but does not himself participate in it. Prince Andrew, who plays a significant part in the military events both at Austerlitz and Borodino and who is far from rejecting war as such, nevertheless on the eve of his last battle says: 'War is not courtesy but the most horrible thing in life; and we ought to understand that, and not play at war.'[1] The author himself, speaking directly of the war of 1812, an event 'opposed to human reason and to human nature', says:

> Millions of men perpetrated against one another such innumerable crimes, frauds, treacheries, thefts, forgeries, issues of false money, burglaries, incendiarisms, and murders, as in whole centuries are not recorded in the annals of all the law courts of the world, but which those who committed them did not at the time regard as being crimes.[2]

But Tolstoy, incomparable as he is as a narrator and descriptive writer, is first and foremost an artist; and it is as an artist that he evokes in his readers the fullest measure of horrified revulsion against and condemnation of war—a role in which even in the torrent of writing provoked by the world wars of the twentieth century Tolstoy has never been surpassed. I refer to the death of Petya, Natasha's sixteen-

[1] *War and Peace*, p. 858.   [2] Ibid., p. 663.

year-old brother, killed in a partisan affray. Although only a minor
character, in the few pages of his presence, he enables us to capture
unforgettably the vibrant enthusiasm of first youth, the sheer exuberant
delight in being alive in such a marvellous universe, the boyish anxiety
to impress on adults that he too is fully grown up, his generosity and
spontaneous compassion, above all his warm naïveté and unbridled
nervous energy and curiosity. Then brandishing his newly sharpened
sword, galloping amidst the excitement of the mêlée, in a fraction of a
second he is transformed into something unrecognizable—'. . . his
arms and legs jerked rapidly though his head was quite motionless. A
bullet had pierced his skull.' Shortly afterwards, his body was carried
to a hole freshly dug. That is all—in the perspectives of 1812 and the
horrors of the retreat from Moscow, a trifling episode, hardly worthy
of mention. The account of this death is terse, laconic, wholly free
from comment. Tolstoy reserves the full force of his unique literary
genius to describe the impact of the news of the death of her beloved
boy on his mother, the Countess Rostova. In those pages of human
agony, of horrified incredulity and total inability to accept, of the
transformation of a woman in the prime of life into an old woman,
lifeless and broken, we observe and feel at first hand the monstrous
criminality of war, as no other writer has made us experience it.

But Tolstoy, like everyone else, has to live in a world saturated with
this all-pervasive violence, taken for granted as the necessary basis of
the entire inherited culture, and therefore he too at the time he wrote
this work sought to come to terms with it. As the day of carnage at
Borodino drew to a close, Tolstoy describes the scene in the following
terms:

> But though towards the end of the battle the men felt all the horror of
> what they were doing, though they would have been glad to leave off,
> some incomprehensible, mysterious power continued to control them, and
> they still brought up the charges, loaded, aimed, and applied the match
> . . . The cannon-balls flew just as swiftly and cruelly from both sides,
> crushing human bodies, and that terrible work which was not done by the
> will of a man, but at the will of Him who governs men and worlds,
> continued.[1]

And in the second epilogue, he again writes:

> Why war and revolution occur we do not know. We only know that to
> produce the one or the other action people combine in a certain formation

---

[1] Ibid., p. 904.

in which they all take part, and we say that this is so because it is un-thinkable otherwise, or in other words that it is a law.[1]

War, it appears in spite of everything, is not only necessary—a world without war being 'unthinkable'—but it is the work of God—it is no doubt significant that Tolstoy resorts to the euphemism 'Him who governs men and worlds'. 'War is divine,' wrote Proudhon, 'Humanity wants no more war.' The contradiction (politely but inaccurately termed 'paradox') at the core of Proudhon's *La Guerre et la Paix* is precisely the same as that devouring the heart of Tolstoy's *War and Peace*.

War is the will not of man but of God; but war is contrary to all reason, Tolstoy insists again and again. Then perhaps human life can-not be an affair of reason. And even this conclusion, Tolstoy, the supreme rationalist, does not hesitate to draw. In discussing the hostility of the 'progressives' to the 'reactionary' policies of Alexander I at the end of his reign, Tolstoy asks rhetorically what would have happened to the activity of his opponents if Alexander had not been reactionary. It would not have existed; there would have been no life, nothing. 'If we admit that human life can be ruled by reason, the possibility of life is destroyed.'[2] Compare this with Pierre's dream at Mozhaysk (cf. p. 126 above). 'If there were no suffering man would not know his limitations, would not know himself.' Keats, a writer at the opposite pole of the philosophical spectrum from Tolstoy, expressed the same thought:

> Do you not see how necessary a world of Pains and Troubles is to school an Intelligence and make it a Soul?

From St. Augustine to Kant this argument has found ever-renewed currency. The obvious danger which attaches to it is that it should undermine or weaken man's most vital protection, namely, his aspira-tion towards self-perfection. No one held this aspiration in greater reverence than Tolstoy. His favourite maxim—almost the last words that he wrote—was '*Fais ce que tu pourras, advienne que . . .*' and such arguments as the above come oddly from Tolstoy's lips.

[1] *War and Peace*, p. 1328. We kill one another in war, he says in *Some Words About War and Peace* (*Russian Archive*, 1868), although we have always known it to be immoral, because by so doing we fulfil the same 'elemental zoological law' that the bees obey when they kill each other in the autumn. Tolstoy develops *in extenso* this simile of the bees in a queenless hive to convey his picture of the evacuation and destruction of Moscow.

[2] Ibid., p. 1248.

This contradiction in Tolstoy's attitude to the status, the morality of war is naturally reflected in the other crucial question: the cause of war. Tolstoy, seeing clearly the wickedness of war and seeing equally clearly the principal source of individual wickedness, has no difficulty in relating the two. The love of power corrupts the individual, and collectively this results in the supreme human wickedness, war. But the other Tolstoy, sensitive to the universality of the phenomenon of war and the fact that his entire surrounding culture is based on violence, and thus needing to adjust to this reality, argues that the cause of war is inscrutable. On this premise, war is caused not by the love of power in man which is evil, but by God's inscrutable purpose, expressing itself through men in a particular combination of human activities. A minority who take responsibility, elaborate justifications and define purposes, issue orders which seem to them relevant, who in fact wield what is called power but who do not themselves do any of what is being organized, combines with a majority who actually perform the necessary actions, although themselves relieved of all responsibility for performing them. On this hypothesis war is actually the work of common soldiers who determine the outcome by their killing activities, by their courage or their cowardice, their confident morale or their defeatism, while the responsibility for the wars belongs only ostensibly to the statesmen and the generals, but in reality to God alone, using these peculiar combinations of men for his mysterious purposes. The advantage from Tolstoy's point of view of this argument is that it enables him to excoriate Napoleon, the aggressor, for arrogance and *hubris*, while idealizing Kutuzov as the defender of the fatherland for his humility in realizing that destiny is decided not by his petty, insignificant, uncontrolling commands but by the activities and heroism of thousands of soldiers reflecting ultimately God's will. Why not simply present Kutuzov in a good light for fighting a just war and Napoleon in a bad light for fighting a war of aggression? Tolstoy's truthfulness will not permit this, since he knows all too well how all armies resemble one another, particularly in the arrogance and ambition of their staffs. In short, he is not blind to these vices on the Russian side, and knows that war as a universal phenomenon is not the result of nations being divided into good and evil, but by the presence of the love of power and ambition to dominate to be found in men of all nations.

This contradiction also provides the explanation of another major source of confusion that bedevils the reader throughout the book.

The attack on Napoleon and other power figures is twofold but mutually contradictory. They are attacked on the one hand for their callousness in accepting responsibility for and ordering the slaughter of men and causing incalculable suffering. In short, they are attacked for their power which is evil. But they are also attacked for their *hubris* and arrogance in naïvely supposing that they, puny individuals that they are, can order and thus cause these momentous historical events, made up of the contributions of millions of men. Thus their *hubris* rests on the illusion of power, which in reality they do not possess.

And out of this confusion there develops yet a further contradiction. Since men do not possess the power they falsely attribute to themselves, since all men alike who are involved in any historical event contribute to the outcome, and since the power resides ultimately in the divine will, it follows that human history is predestined and governed by law. In order to elucidate these laws, it would be necessary to examine and integrate the contributions of each individual involved in any way in the events. Thus a science of history is in principle possible, but in practice not possible because of the impossibility of anyone ever being able to amass all the necessary evidence. Nor is this all. Although human activity is governed by the divine will and therefore predetermined, that is to say, not free, every one of us knows indubitably that we are possessed of free will, and that this alone constitutes the meaning and responsibility of our life. Tolstoy is thus committed to the further impossible task of attempting to reconcile a doctrine of determinism with a belief in freedom of the will.

But this being said, it would be quite wrong to conclude that Tolstoy's contradictions were sterile. What we are in reality witnessing is the struggle of a very great thinker wrestling with a predicament that is universal, more rigorously and sincerely than any of his predecessors. And out of the irreconcilable antinomies is laid the foundation on which a decade later in great inner turmoil he finally resolved the contradictions. Herzen, Proudhon, Stendhal and many others felt the inhumanity of war. But no one before Tolstoy had evinced such a deep and lasting revulsion to its horror and presented it as simply a monstrous crime. By the force of his imagination every subject to which he addressed himself comes incredibly to life, and nowhere more so than when he is describing the actual conditions under which war is waged—conditions of great danger with which, objectively and psychologically speaking, he was intimately familiar especially through his regimental experiences at Sevastopol during the Crimean campaign.

Secondly, his knowledge of the true cause of war, if not made explicit in *War and Peace*, is apparent from the clarity of his moral understanding, which never for a moment failed him in handling his hundreds of human characters. War is caused by the will to power in man.

Thirdly, he succeeds by remorseless and painstaking analysis in pricking the bubble of power as no one before him had ever come near to doing. Man, he said, is in subjection to the forces of power. Ostensibly—at this stage of his development—he also said that there is nothing to be done about this. It is inevitable. But emotionally he could not accept this. It disgusted him whenever he observed it in individual character, and its consequences in action horrified him. So he set about analysing the nature of this thing called power, demonstrated that while it was a reality—a grim reality—in terms of human behaviour, it corresponded to no moral or metaphysical reality, and was therefore simply a myth, a cheat, a fraud. The consequences of this discovery were inevitably revolutionary, for they plainly pointed to the fact that war, resting on the will to power in men, was not inevitable after all. It rested upon a fraud, and if Tolstoy was right, then eventually others would be obliged to arrive at a similar conclusion; and man would then come to free himself from the thrall of power, leading to violence and war. But again, Tolstoy when writing *War and Peace* was not yet psychologically and morally ready for this bold conclusion to rise to consciousness and conviction. And so the implications of his analysis of the nature of power for what he calls 'the science of jurisprudence' or political theory, are explicitly ruled out of his field of consideration.

> The science of jurisprudence regards the State and power . . . as something existing absolutely . . . it follows that jurisprudence can tell minutely how, in its opinion, power should be constituted and what power—existing immutably, outside time—is . . .[1]

In *War and Peace* Tolstoy's central subject of concern is the answer which history must give to the question of the nature of power, and for history power and its mutations *in time* is not an absolute but simply one phenomenon among others to be studied objectively.

I will conclude this study of *War and Peace* with a summary of Tolstoy's view of power as revealed by history. For despite the

[1] *War and Peace*, p. 1315.

confusions, referred to above, the analysis of power in history is substantially the same as that which after his intellectual crisis he finally applied to 'jurisprudence' with radically revolutionary consequences. In *War and Peace* Tolstoy's case study of power in history is essentially the campaign of 1812, Tolstoy's version of which, severely condensed, is as follows:

Napoleon advanced on Moscow not because he foresaw and guarded against the perils of over-extending his lines of communication or because the Russians successfully lured him on to his doom, but because Napoleon, who himself thought every advance was a triumph, was led on step by step not by his own plans but by the intrigues, quarrels and ambitions of his officers and men. And on the Russian side, Bagration's delay resulted not from strategic considerations, but from his hatred of Barclay de Tolly.

The great battle of Borodino was not the result of respective decisions of the French and Russian high commands. The only possible outcome of such a battle was that the Russians would continue to retreat with disastrous consequences for the French. The French attacked and killed their enemies because there was no holding them back at that juncture, weary with their endless march and feverish to reach the promised goal of rest, provisions and winter quarters in Moscow. The events proceeded along their predestined course not as a result of Napoleon's orders or plans, but as a result of the contributions of all the scores of thousands of participants. '. . . human dignity—which tells me that each of us is, if not more, at least not less a man than the great Napoleon—'[1] Since Borodino constituted Napoleon's first major military check, it was suggested that this must be attributed to the fact that he was suffering from a cold at the time, and was thus not up to his best form. Tolstoy therefore examines in detail his battle orders in order to demonstrate (*a*) that they were neither better nor worse than usual and (*b*) that they were in any case irrelevant since in the event it was impossible to execute any of them. Napoleon's actual role in the battle is described in much the same terms as is the role of the most respected of the Russian generals, Bagration:

> . . . but with his great tact and experience of war, calmly and with dignity, he fulfilled his role of appearing to command.[2]

---

[1] *War and Peace*, p. 867.

[2] I have preferred to translate this literally, since the Maude translation (op. cit., p. 869), in putting the adverbs at the end of the sentence, weakens, if it does not entirely lose, the force of the 'fictitious commander'.

The Russians on their side also obeyed an inevitable logic, retreating to Fily, and then abandoning Moscow not as a result of decisions by Kutuzov but because there was no alternative. The decision was made in a series of steps, at Drissa, Smolensk, Shevardino, Borodino, and 'every day, every hour, and every minute of the retreat from Borodino to Fily'. And just as Kutuzov was a fictitious commander on the Russian side, even more illusory was the idea that Rostopchin by his orders caused the evacuation of Moscow by the civilians, an event brought about by a myriad individual decisions.

> The lady who, afraid of being stopped by Count Rostopchin's orders, had already in June moved with her negroes and her women-jesters from Moscow to her Saratov estate with a vague consciousness that she was not Bonaparte's servant, was really, simply, and truly carrying out the great work which saved Russia.[1]

And the city, being made of wood, once abandoned by its inhabitants and given over to looting soldiery, burnt down as a matter of course, due neither to Rostopchin, Russian patriotism nor French savagery.

While the French occupied Moscow, Napoleon's command was again purely illusory. He issued orders to stop pillage, to re-establish trade, to reconcile the clergy and reopen the churches, to reopen the theatres, to establish the assignat as accepted currency. His orders in every case remained a dead letter. Moreover, to remain in Moscow until October and then on the onset of winter, emerge with the debauched remnants of his army, not to give battle or to pursue Kutuzov but to withdraw through devastated country to Mozhaysk, was an act of mass suicide. Almost any course of action would have been more sensible. Provisions were adequate for six months in Moscow; he could have marched on Novgorod, he could have pursued Kutuzov —in theory. Nothing could have been more predictably disastrous than what he did do. Why? Napoleon was not stupid. He did what he did because as always he was at the mercy of events. The soldiers were ill disciplined after the long horrors of the invasion, they could not be prevented from pillaging nor would they be induced to leave their hard-won refuge until they panicked on news of the battle at Tarutino and on hearing that the supply convoys had been seized on the road to Smolensk. When Napoleon finally ordered the great retreat via Smolensk along the same route by which they had come, but one now

[1] Ibid., p. 921.

strewn with their own relics, skeletons of men and horses and shattered, abandoned equipment, he again bowed to the inevitable.

If others, French historians in Egypt unchecked by witnesses, German historians in Austria and Prussia having to explain the humiliating surrender of whole army corps intact, if such writers consider Napoleon a genius, there is no need for Russian writers to engage in such self-deception. They have no shame to hide; they have on the contrary paid a high price for being in a position to evaluate the facts truthfully. And Tolstoy's conclusion is that:

> During the whole of that period Napoleon, who seems to us to have been the leader of all those movements . . . acted like a child who, holding a couple of strings inside a carriage, thinks he is driving it.[1]

But his supreme contempt is reserved for the last act of the tragedy or rather for the self-deception of the historians who are unable even to describe Napoleon's personal abandonment and flight from his exhausted troops for what it was: an act of cowardly betrayal. Since for the historians, Napoleon is great, a concept transcending all considerations of good and evil, in the name of tactical wisdom or military genius he is acquitted of all responsibility for the atrocities he committed. 'For us', comments Tolstoy, 'there is no greatness there where simplicity, goodness, and truth are absent.'[2]

The same points about the illusory nature of Napoleon's control of events are made equally forcefully about the Russian commanders. The Russian generals at Fily advocated a further retreat to Nizhni Novgorod; the Russian army in fact turned round Moscow and made a flanking movement via Kaluga to Tarutino. This, Tolstoy argues, it would have done even if it had had no commanding officer, since it intuitively moved in a direction where there were more provisions, munitions and remounts. But the vanity of the leaders (except Kutuzov) was such that they genuinely believed that their decisions and plans guided the events. With the death in action of Bagration and the withdrawal of Barclay after Tarutino, replacements were necessary.

> Very serious consideration was given to the question whether it would be better to put A in B's place and B in D's, or on the contrary to put D in A's place, and so on—as if anything more than A's or B's satisfaction depended on this.[3]

---

[1] *War and Peace*, p. 1111.
[2] Ibid., p. 1180.   [3] Ibid., p. 1094.

And the basic reason for the impotence of the high command is that the play of contingent forces is so great in battle as to make the actual conditions impossible to foresee in advance. These forces, fluid like mercury, are especially uncontrollable in warfare since man is never more uncontrollable than he is during a battle when his very life is at stake. It was Kutuzov's great merit—not his strategic genius, a spurious concept—that he alone understood what was happening and did what little he could not to obstruct these inevitabilities. He alone understood why the victory the French claimed at Borodino was in reality a defeat for them, he grasped the significance of the French inactivity on occupying Moscow, he did all in his power to restrain the Russians from undertaking more battles with unnecessary loss of life, leaving the French to hasten their own end. For which wisdom and humility he was scorned both by the Emperor Alexander and subsequently by the historians. 'The hatred and contempt of the crowd punishes such men for discerning the higher laws.'[1]

War and Peace is at once a critique of 'history' as it has generally been understood and an attempt to write a three-dimensional account of a momentous event in the history of Russia and Europe. Historians falsify reality by violating continuity through arbitrarily selecting and treating particular events in isolation, but above all by attributing the power of causation to individual 'heroes' or leading men of action. Tolstoy's epic seeks to maintain continuity by the device of the first epilogue, where we become involved in the growth of a new genera-tion, as the events of 1812 recede into memory and the conflict cul-minating in the Decembrist rising of 1825 is foreshadowed. And while the leaders of the nations are presented as vain individuals in the grip of a delusion that they control historical events, the events in question are shown to be the work of huge numbers of individuals, each playing his part according to his individual character with his hopes, fears and ambitions. The 'novel' is meant to exemplify the correct method of presenting history: what the analytic Tolstoy calls the art of observing and integrating 'the infinitesimally small unit'.

The question which *War and Peace* is ultimately concerned to answer is what is the nature of the power which moves history, which causes the movement of peoples, which, in a word, causes war and peace. The answer, implicit in the structure and characterization of the work, is made explicit in the second epilogue, together with the reasons for rejecting the conventional answers to this question.

[1] Ibid., p. 1197.

Although contemporaries imagine that they have outgrown primitive attempts to understand historical causation in terms of the will of the gods and subsequently in terms of god-like Emperors or other heroes, in practice contemporaries fall back on modes of explanation as superstitious as those of any of their forefathers. They describe the activities of a handful of individuals, selected by virtue of their alleged 'power'—statesmen, kings, diplomats, generals, and perhaps also philosophers, reformers, publicists, orators, professors—and assume that these individuals are causing by their activities the realization of or movement towards a given end, which varies according to the nationality and political leanings of the historian in question—viz., the glory of France, the expansion of the British Empire, the advancement of progress or of European civilization or the promotion of liberty and equality or of democracy. Whether the nature of this power of control and change is seen as the will of charismatic heroes or as the ideas of outstanding and seminal thinkers, it is equally illusory, since the allegedly causal forces are obviously unequal to the consequences allegedly resulting therefrom. It is as absurd to say that Rousseau by conceiving the doctrine of the sovereignty of the general will caused men to revolt and kill one another in many different parts of France, as it is to say that Napoleon by issuing an order caused 600,000 men to move from West to East across the face of Europe. The absurdity lies in supposing that the activities of large numbers of men can be caused by the activities of one or a few among them, however exceptional he or the few might be. Therefore in order to write a true history of events it would be necessary to describe the force commensurate with the vast movements of nations, and that force can only be the activities of 'all, absolutely all' the participants. Such a history alone would have no need to fall back on the bogus concept of 'power', on which existing historians all rely.

Again we run up against contradiction at the heart of Tolstoy's analysis—power is so great and terrible a reality that the whole book is concerned to get at the roots of its nature. On the other hand Tolstoy so loathes it and is so anxious to exorcize it that he sometimes speaks of it as though it were a bogus entity. And however much it ought not to exist, it is only too plainly a grim and all pervasive reality. The problem therefore remains: what is the nature of power? What is the nature of the relationship between government and governed, between the commander and the commanded?

If 600,000 men obeyed Napoleon and invaded Russia, whence came this mysterious power? A child might believe that he was a god-like figure possessed of divine power or that he was endowed with unique hypnotic or charismatic or moral or Herculean physical power, but a rational adult cannot be so duped. Perhaps a clue is to be found in the view of political theorists that the sovereign ruler has the necessary power to command events because the will of the whole people is vested in him. He is the representative of the people and speaks and acts in their name and on their behalf. '*L'État, c'est moi.*' The king is the representative of the collective consciousness, the general will, the common 'I'.

But in that event, much is left to be explained. How are we to account for the frequency of transfers of this power both domestically and internationally, through internal palace revolutions and through foreign conquest? Are we to assume a coincidental shift in the will of the people to correspond with the transfer of sovereign power to the new rulers? And if this shift of opinion, conferring legitimacy, is subject to the fulfilment of certain conditions, who is to determine the conditions if not the *de facto* ruler? Besides, the facts of history do not bear out this theory. Whatever the alleged conditions, the fulfilment of which authorizes the ruler to claim to speak in the name of the whole people, it cannot be said that Charles I or Louis XVI were obviously guilty of non-fulfilment of conditions fulfilled by all the other Charles's and Louis's who did not lose their heads and were not removed from their thrones. How did it come about that for centuries the collective will of the people was not withdrawn from the reigning sovereigns in France, and then suddenly during the half-century between the National Convention and Napoleon III it was transferred no less than ten times? If it be admitted that these transfers are not the result of genuine popular will but are the result of accident, of the way in which the cunning and skill or errors and weaknesses of rulers and party leaders operate, then we have abandoned the theory and have to fall back on the view that the power of the ruler rests simply on usurpation, that is to say, that power is power.

It is true that whenever an event occurs, a man or men appear by whose will the event seems to have been caused. But the illusion of cause and effect derives from the fact that we remember only the commands that were given that did turn out to correspond with what actually happened, and forget about all the other commands that were given that were not blessed with corresponding, seemingly conse-quential events. 'Every command executed is always one of an immense number unexecuted.'[1] Long after the cessation of the Crusades, popes, kings and knights continued to urge the necessity to free the Holy Land, but the peoples were no longer willing to go. On no single venture did Napoleon expend so much organizational effort and energy as on the invasion of England, but the people invaded not England but ultimately Russia.

Tolstoy therefore concludes that a command can never be the actual cause of an event, but of course does not deny that commands are related to events. What then—and this is the crucial question—is the exact nature of the relation between a command and the subsequent event, if it is not a causal one?

Whatever activity men undertake in common, they organize themselves on a hierarchical basis of which the army offers the most perfect example. The purpose of an army is to kill the enemy, but the principle of organization is precisely the same whenever men combine together for any common purpose, be it agricultural, industrial, commercial, or administrative. At the base of the pyramid is the private soldier who is immediately responsible to the NCO who in his turn must obey the junior officer, and so on right up to the commander-in-chief. While the activity of each depends upon the nature of the joint enterprise, the relationship between the hierarchical ranks is always the same, independently of the common activity. That relationship is such that the most direct share in the common activity is undertaken by the majority at the base and the less direct share is taken by the minority higher up the pyramid. In the case of the army, the private soldiers do the killing, the NCOs do so less frequently since they are already to a small extent engaged in commanding, the officers rarely kill, the generals never, being exclusively commanders, and the C.-in-C. is frequently not even present at the place of engagement.

From this basic organizational analysis Tolstoy concludes that the actual work of the world which collectively constitutes human history is always undertaken by the common people, the vast majority; while the function of their rulers is not to engage directly in the work but to 'devise considerations, justifications, surmises concerning what has happened'. Tolstoy had illustrated this process in action in Moscow after the news of the defeat of Austerlitz had been received.

> The men who set the tone in conversation . . . [five names are mentioned] . . . did not show themselves at the Club but met at private houses in

---

[1] *War and Peace*, p. 1323.

intimate circles, and the Moscovites who took their opinions from others
. . . remained for a while without any definite opinion on the subject of the
war and without leaders. . . .[1]

But then the top people reappeared and everyone began speaking
clearly and definitely, finding reasons for the disaster that excused the
Russian army.

The actual examples that he cites in the course of his sociological
analysis relate to the French Revolution and the subsequent military
events. After the noyades and killings, the explanation appeared that it
was necessary for the realization of liberty and equality. When the
killing stopped, the explanation was given that it was necessary to
centralize power in order to resist the Coalition Powers. The French
drove Eastwards across Europe: and the explanation was that it was
necessitated by the glory of France or the baseness of England,
according to taste.

In conclusion, Tolstoy infers that essentially there is a twofold
division of 'labour' in the organized activities of men which make up
history. Physically, the activities are carried out by large numbers who
do what is required by Providence but without personal responsibility
for what they do. To absolve them from responsibility is the purpose
of the *ex-post facto* explanations and justifications provided by the
rulers, who do not themselves ever directly do any of the things that
collectively make up history. Thus does Tolstoy finally arrive at his
definition of the nature of power.

> Power is the relation of a given person to other individuals, in which the
> more this person expresses opinions, predictions and justifications of the
> collective action that is performed, the less is his participation in that
> action.[2]

The total analysis of the meaning and significance of the organization of human life in the continuum of history, although less than
satisfactory, is nevertheless vitally important and breaks new ground
in our understanding of the cause of war. It is for this reason that it has
been so studiously ignored—not at all, as is alleged, because Tolstoy,
though admittedly a great artist, indeed a 'genius', is not worth taking
seriously as a student of vital human problems such as war, power and
historical causation.

Tolstoy's argument is of course highly subversive, since its main
thrust is to devastate the claims of the powerful to be powerful. Never

[1] Ibid., p. 327.   [2] Ibid., p. 1327.

before have the powerful of the earth been so effectively deflated and brought low. This is done by demonstrating that their alleged power, for which they are both revered and feared, is illusory. The trouble is, however, that Tolstoy in *War and Peace* overplays his hand. If Napoleon's cold in the head is of no more significance than that of the last straggler in the ranks or if his contribution to the events is actually less than that of the least of his footsoldiers, our indignation at the horrific consequences of what takes place ought in logic to be reserved for the common soldiers, who actually do the killing. But this is not the conclusion that Tolstoy wishes us to draw. While the point of his analysis is to demonstrate that no one can be absolved from responsibility for his share in the events, it is also to insist on the much greater responsibility of the Napoleons of the world, who arouse—and he makes us feel, justly—his deepest censure. Tolstoy really cannot have it both ways. If Napoleon did not in reality exercise power at all, he does not constitute a legitimate target for moral indignation. If he is justly censurable, it is because he exercised great power for evil. Tolstoy, try as he will, can never in *War and Peace* escape from his impossible dilemma of seeking to indict power without actually condemning absolutely its most characteristic product, namely war. He cannot do this, because, although war revolts him, he is still in the grip of the theory of the just war. Napoleon's power is evil, but not Kutuzov's. And yet not primarily because of the justice of his cause—at bottom the Russian leaders are as squalidly motivated as the French—but because Kutuzov understands that he is a pawn in the hands of Destiny, while Napoleon does not.

The contradiction concerning the nature of power also shows itself in the analysis of the role of those who are commanded, who, that is, submit to power. On the one hand, Tolstoy asserts that commanders cannot command because nowhere are men more uncontrollable and unpredictable than in battle when the issue at stake for each man is a matter of life and death. On the other hand, he offers as an example of where a man is least free or most bound by his relation to others the case of the soldier in his regiment. Such is the power of military discipline, he says, that it is literally impossible for the individual soldier to refrain from attacking when all around him are doing so or to refrain from fleeing when all his comrades in the line are in flight.

Finally, there is contradiction in the analysis of historical causation. On the one hand, consistent with the belief in determinism is the assertion that laws govern human history and that it is necessary in order to elucidate them to study 'the differential of history', the individual, and then to integrate these separate units. But since these separate units exist in immense numbers, and are each possessed of freedom of the will, it is an absolutely impossible task to observe them 'all, absolutely all', let alone to integrate them. So that in practice there are and can be no laws of history. And Tolstoy, notwithstanding his indictment of the historians for providing explanations of historical events in terms of chance or Divine Will, is himself driven to fall back on a precisely similar explanation of history. But for him the chances are not the chances that befall diplomatists and monarchs but the chances of courage and cowardice in the hosts who constitute the rank and file; and Divine Providence realizes its purposes not through the will of men in command, falsely called 'great', but in the daily preoccupations of ordinary, allegedly powerless, men and women going about their business.

7

The Nature of Power

I have argued that Tolstoy in *War and Peace* made a remarkable advance in the analysis of the nature of human power; that this insight rested basically on his intuitive knowledge of the nature of good and evil in human psychology as revealed in the moral behaviour of all his characters; but that the general effect of his total analysis is still one of confusion, and that this confusion arises out of the inability to acknowledge unequivocally that war is evil, and as such should not exist.

Tolstoy knew more clearly than any man the full evil of war. As we have seen, the evidence for this already in *War and Peace* is overwhelming. Why then could he not accept this knowledge and build upon it? He could not then do so for the same reason that millions of human beings, also aware of the great evil of war, still cannot bring themselves to accept the knowledge and act upon it. With the growing cruelty and savagery of war, many people have revolted so far as their emotions are concerned; and some, essentially unreflective and conservative minded, have asserted that they will not take part in war, but for the rest are 'good citizens' playing their part loyally in all the essential functions of society as it is traditionally organized. Such people are perfectly sincere, and their contribution to the struggle against war is not negligible, because it rests on sane human emotions. But in so far as they are unaware of the real cause of war, they may not unfairly be termed 'sentimental pacifists'. Such a position is at once seen to be naïve by all sophisticated political conservatives, who are accordingly very tolerant of such a position, readily paying it all due respect. Books on this theme will generally be well received with appropriate encomiums and even approbatory leading articles in the national press. For the defenders of the existing order derive their political understanding, consciously or otherwise, from the Machiavellian–Maistrean tradition of analysis, and understand full well that 'sentimental pacifism' does not seriously threaten them. To the mature Tolstoyan analysis of war and its cause, the established Press will extend no such tolerance, only baleful silence; for they understand very well that this analysis is true and ultimately must destroy the entire way of life to which they are devoted. Proudhon was impatient with, indeed scornful of pacifism, since he understood by that only 'sentimental pacifism'. Tolstoy became a pacifist, but never a sentimental one. Like Proudhon, he had a very clear understanding of the logic of the nature and the reality of the exercise of power. He hated war but he knew full well that war was not simply an unfortunate excrescence, a wart on an otherwise healthy face that might be removed by a purely local anaesthetic, but that it was the basis of the entire existing culture. Every State derived its very existence from war, and survived only by its armed preparedness to defend the sphere of power that it had carved out for itself. Moreover, in every State the people who ruled and organized the defence of their power against their external rivals beyond the frontiers were invariably the richest group in their community and also organized the defence of their riches against any threat to property within the State.

Morally speaking, the entire structure with its attendant culture rested on an allegedly universal right to self-defence, which traditionally underpinned the theology of the 'just war'. True, this would not in logic explain the universality of the phenomenon of war; since war would then require an aggressor. But so far as convincing the mass membership of each particular sovereign State of the moral validity of their own stance was concerned, no difficulty ever arose due to the ease and skill with which all governments are practised in the art of demonstrating that aggression is the exclusive prerogative of their enemies, and self-defence the only possible basis on which they themselves invariably take their stand.

For a man as truthful as Tolstoy, possessed of his implacable integrity, to reject war outright, root and branch, would automatically entail a conflict to the death with his entire surrounding culture. It would involve a head-on collision with his entire inheritance—his social position, his wealth, his moral and literary standing in society, his relations with his family, his religion, his public relationship *vis-à-vis* Church and State, in a word his Russianness, and Tolstoy was very Russian. Above all, he had to begin the Herculean task of overcoming his own will to power, and rebuilding his inner life and therefore eventually his external life upon entirely new foundations, not simply different from the will to power, but its very antithesis. The wonder is not that he experienced violent inner resistance to the knowledge that war is an indefensible evil, but that he was ever able to marshal the necessary nervous and spiritual resources to resolve that conflict aright.

The story of that conflict or rather convulsion which rent him on the threshold of fifty Tolstoy has himself told in his *Confession*, one of the world's most significant religious documents. It is not my concern to analyse it here. The effect of that crisis was to remove the contradiction that had dogged him throughout the writing of *War and Peace*. The moral values which had always clearly guided his understanding of human character were now accepted absolutely as applicable to the whole of life. Double standards, plural moral universes, contradictory values were not admissible. What was good for Princess Mary, Platon Karataev and Pierre Bezukhov must be good for all men. Tolstoy's moral standards were not simply his personal preferences; he held them because he was not free to do otherwise, because they were objectively true. And if all men recognized this truth in accordance with their moral obligations, the institutions of the State and war which was the fruit of the will to power or evil in man could not exist. In short, Tolstoy cut the Gordian knot which bound him by totally rejecting violence and power, and thus set himself on a course which brought him into a head-on collision with Church and State, not to mention his own social, economic and family situation.

Tolstoy himself claimed that he was doing no more than rediscovering the original teaching of Jesus, which minority groups throughout the centuries, invariably proscribed and persecuted, frequently exterminated as heretics, had again and again sought to resurrect. If Tolstoy had been doing no more than he claimed, namely, to reapply ancient but conveniently forgotten principles to the contemporary context, this in itself would have had very great significance. For every generation has to rediscover the truth afresh for the first time and express it in its own idiom so that it becomes once again a living thing. And Tolstoy quickened everything in the white light of his imagination by methods similar to those of Michelangelo in stone. He hacked away at the dross and delusion, the pretence and dishonesty caked with custom until there stood revealed for the first time that which had always been there, but which without his aid we had been blind to see. But in fact Tolstoy's performance exceeded his own claims for it. Even 'heretic' Christians had not directly challenged the moral legitimacy of the State as such. They had said: 'if you wish to follow Christ, then you cannot participate in any office of State, you must not yourself be responsible for acts of violence in pursuit of "law and order" or of State security'. But they had not claimed to determine the rights and wrongs of the matter for non-Christians. No doubt it was proper for *them* to perform acts of State and accept responsibility for coercion; but what was not possible was to do so and at the same time be a Christian. Tolstoy radicalized this teaching. He held that we were here dealing with universals that determined the true welfare of all men; that if we did not recognize the universal truth of the principles that Christians had claimed as their own, then we would inevitably reap the harvest of a culture based not, as it should be, on the law of love, but on the law of violence.

Tolstoy's stand brought him face to face with the State, which he consistently denounced over and over again in a torrent of articles, letters, plays, tales, novels. Because of his immense moral stature and world-wide fame, the government in Russia did not dare to lay hands on Tolstoy. They confined themselves to imprisoning and banishing Tolstoy's courageous recusant followers, and to suppressing Tolstoy's polemical writings. But although the political repercussions of his stand were of the highest importance, the fundamental issue—as Tolstoy himself claimed, and as the Russian Orthodox Church, by excommunicating him, confirmed—was religious. The basis of man's welfare in this world was the Christian teaching of the law of love and non-violence, the law of suffering evil, of not returning it. The cause of man's evergrowing estrangement from the true law of his being lay primarily in the perversion of this teaching by the so-called Christian churches, preaching pseudo-Christianity. They, instead of serving the true cause of their founder, served the cause of the State which persecuted and crucified him, and which has never ceased to persecute or suppress his true followers. The greatest responsibility for all the man-made ills which afflict us, Tolstoy insisted, lay with the Church for poisoning the wells of pure water which alone could meet our needs. This metamorphosis occurred officially when Christianity passed from being a persecuted heretical sect into the official State religion of the Empire under Constantine—referred to by Tolstoy as 'that canonized scoundrel'. If Tolstoy is right about this, it should prove highly instructive to review the process by which this vitally important historical change came about. I propose therefore to quote here two relevant passages from the historian of the epoch whose account has never been surpassed, Edward Gibbon, a man who himself had no sympathy with Christianity.

The Christians were not less averse to the business than to the pleasures of this world. The defence of our persons and property they knew not how to reconcile with the patient doctrine which enjoined an unlimited forgiveness of past injuries, and commanded them to invite the repetition of fresh insults. Their simplicity was offended by the use of oaths, by the pomp of magistracy, and by the active contention of public life; nor could their humane ignorance be convinced that it was lawful on any occasion to shed the blood of our fellow-creatures, either by the sword of justice or by that of war; even though their criminal or hostile attempts should threaten the peace and safety of the whole community. It was acknowledged that, under a less perfect law, the powers of the Jewish constitution had been exercised, with the approbation of Heaven, by inspired prophets and by anointed kings. The Christians felt and confessed that such institutions might be necessary for the present system of the world, and they cheerfully submitted to the authority of their Pagan governors. But while they inculcated the maxims of passive obedience, they refused to take any active part in the civil administration or the military defence of the empire. Some indulgence might perhaps be allowed to those persons who, before their conversion, were already engaged in such violent and sanguinary occupations; but it was impossible that the Christians, without renouncing a more sacred duty, could assume the character of soldiers, of magistrates, or of princes.[1]

The essential original position of the Christians is here clearly indicated, although Gibbon might better have explained the logic of refusal of oaths. To suggest that oaths were repudiated because they offended the 'simplicity' of the Christians neglects the crucial importance of this issue. Oath taking is fundamental to military and therefore to political power. The oath of allegiance creates the legal basis for the maintenance of the disciplined unity of large numbers of men, on which all State power ultimately rests. When Jesus said, 'But I say unto you, Swear not at all; . . . But let your communication be, Yea, yea; Nay, nay . . .' he was indirectly striking at the roots of Caesar's military power.

Gibbon himself goes on to castigate this Christian attitude towards the defence of the realm as 'indolent or even criminal disregard of the public welfare'. What would happen, he asks rhetorically, as did the Christians' Pagan contemporaries, if in the presence of depredations by the barbarians, everyone were to adopt such a 'pusillanimous' attitude? To this reproach the Christians could make only 'obscure

[1] Edward Gibbon, *The Decline and Fall of the Roman Empire*, edited in seven volumes by J. B. Bury, London 1909, Vol. II, pp. 40–1.

and ambiguous' answer, since their own serenity in the presence of danger and refusal to defend themselves rested, according to Gibbon, on the delusion that the end of the world was imminent in comparison with which calamity the prospect of the collapse of the Roman Empire assumed a diminished significance. In the same breath that we are told that the Christians were 'pusillanimous', we are told that their courage can only be explained by their proneness to delusions.

After this account of the moral convictions of the first Christians, Gibbon proceeds to diagnose the cause of the steady erosion and falling away from the original professions, and to give the grounds for his belief that this was inevitable. But if Gibbon's premises concerning the limits of human nature are those of the perennial conservative defender of things as they are, this does not detract from the value of his clear and concise analysis of how Christianity came to be betrayed from within its own ranks.

But the human character, however it may be exalted or depressed by a temporary enthusiasm, will return, by degrees, to its proper and natural level, and will resume those passions that seem the most adapted to its present condition. The primitive Christians were dead to the business and pleasures of the world; but their love of action, which could never be entirely extinguished, soon revived, and found a new occupation in the government of the church. A separate society, which attacked the established religion of the empire, was obliged to adopt some form of internal policy, and to appoint a sufficient number of ministers, intrusted not only with the spiritual functions, but even with the temporal direction, of the Christian commonwealth. The safety of that society, its honour, its aggrandisement, were productive, even in the most pious minds, of a spirit of patriotism, such as the first of the Romans had felt for the republic, and sometimes of a similar indifference in the use of whatever means might probably conduce to so desirable an end. The ambition of raising themselves or their friends to the honours and offices of the church was disguised by the laudable intention of devoting to the public benefit the power and consideration which, for that purpose only, it became their duty to solicit. In the exercise of their functions, they were frequently called upon to detect the errors of heresy or the arts of faction, to oppose the designs of perfidious brethren, to stigmatize their characters with deserved infamy, and to expel them from the bosom of a society whose peace and happiness they had attempted to disturb. The ecclesiastical governors of the Christians were taught to unite the wisdom of the serpent with the innocence of the dove; but as the former was refined, so the latter was insensibly corrupted, by the habits of government. In the church as well as in the world, the persons who were placed in any public station rendered themselves considerable by their eloquence and firmness, by their knowledge of mankind, and by their dexterity in business; and while they concealed from others, and, perhaps, from themselves, the secret motives of their conduct, they too frequently relapsed into all the turbulent passions of active life, which were tinctured with an additional degree of bitterness and obstinacy from the infusion of spiritual zeal.[1]

This brilliantly written and remarkable passage shrewdly illumines the difficulty of the problem of striking at evil, and at the same time is unusually candid in identifying evil with the necessities of government. Gibbon would appear to be asserting four general propositions:

1. Human beings, whatever their religious zeal or ethical professions, are so animated by a 'love of action' that they find the urge to govern irrepressible.
2. Their psychology coincides with the necessities of their situation, so that even those who attack the evils of temporal government, are driven by the need to protect themselves to resort to the very governmental processes they condemn.
3. The moral conflict thus engendered is made tolerable by self-deception concerning the true nature of one's real motives, so that ambition for office is disguised under the mask of devotion to the public interest.
4. The habit of government by its very nature insensibly corrupts those who exercise it, however lofty their original aspirations.

There are, however, two important errors in this highly illuminating analysis. What Gibbon calls 'love of action' is inaccurately defined: what he is really referring to is 'will to power'. The action designated is not simply action, it is a peculiar form of action, namely, the exercise of control over others. The second point to note is that Gibbon wrongly attributes this 'love of action' to the Christians in general; whereas in reality this will to power was being asserted only by some, and that a minority of the Christians. Otherwise there would have been no Christians to rule over. With this modification, Gibbon's analysis—not his Pagan values concerning the alleged necessities of organized defence—can be accepted. It is certainly of the greatest significance that the one group in history to have recognized that power is evil and attempted to struggle against it themselves succumbed

[1] Edward Gibbon, pp. 41–2.

to it. But this proves only that the full depth of the problem posed by the nature of power has not been adequately analysed.

Let us, at this point, return to Tolstoy's definition of the nature of power in *War and Peace* (cf. p. 165 above) '... power is the relation of a given person to other individuals, in which the more this person expresses opinions, predictions and justifications of the collective action that is performed, the less is his participation in that action'. This is, of course, to reverse the commonly accepted way of regarding the matter. In the popular judgement, as in the minds of those at the top of the hierarchical pyramid, the leaders, if they do not actually of themselves cause the events certainly play a more significant and important role than those who merely carry out the activity itself which is being organized. But cause and effect in human affairs cannot be equated with command and obedience—it is an infinitely more complex affair because we are here dealing with the wills of a host of separate individuals, all of whom contribute their share, none of whom can be reduced to a nullity as a mechanical instrument of another man's will. And when analysing the different contributions, Tolstoy affirms common sense in sharp contrast to received opinion when he insists that those who do whatever it is that is desired to be done must be playing a more important role than those whose function is confined to expressing opinions and justifications. Such a view, anti-intellectualistic and radically subversive of power, would obviously be generally resisted by the articulate on that account.

In my view, Tolstoy's analysis is essentially correct, but it fails to convince, because it seems to underestimate the importance of the role of the leaders, given human beings with their present very confused understanding of the processes and nature of power. Tolstoy rightly sees that leaders are not by any means always obeyed, and that even when they are, they cannot be said to have caused an event. In short, rulers do not have the power that they imagine they have and that their subjects imagine them to have. From this it might be concluded that the whole concept of power is a figment of the imagination, a metaphysical entity corresponding to nothing real. Yet our experience tells us that it is something all too real, and productive of the most terrible consequences.

It might be tempting to explain the phenomenon in terms simply of fear. But apart from the problem of explaining how it would be possible for a few men to be able to recruit and control sufficient armed forces to intimidate tens of millions, experience again indicates that power is only in part compounded of fear—and that normally a relatively minor part—and that most people obey if not enthusiastic-ally, at any rate willingly. They do not require to be coerced. Psycho-logically speaking, they find their emotional security in conforming to the collective consciousness of the group with which they identify, and from which they receive in return an important part of their identity as individuals, in so far as they are individualized.

The reason for this is that most people have little or no understand-ing of the true nature of power, and genuinely do believe the content of the ideologies, projections of traditions and religions, whereby their organizations hold together and maintain their inner unity. Even the leaders themselves who live by the logic of power, daily practise it and only survive politically in so far as they understand that logic aright—even they to some extent manage to deceive themselves that the reason for all their activity is not love of power, but the necessity for upholding the alleged truth of the ideology of their particular organization. This ideological activity of the leaders, that which Tolstoy refers to as their expressing opinions, predictions and justi-fications, and which he sees as purely mythical, nevertheless plays the vital, indispensable role in the mystery of power. For it is these myths which retain the allegiance of the followers, of the rank and file of the organization, who would no longer willingly obey, if they ceased to believe that their activity was not essentially concerned to promote those particular values they adhere to, but only to make possible the power and authority of their established leaders.

In an exceptionally valuable study, an American scholar, Barrows Dunham, has surveyed the history of many of the great heresies, the espousal of which by their exponents led to their persecution and often martyrdom at the hands of the orthodox. Orthodoxy means of course 'the right opinion' in the sense of the opinion that has sufficient power to back it to make it the received opinion, and heterodoxy or heresy being 'the other opinion', that is to say, the one lacking at the time the necessary power to establish it as 'right'. As the generations pass, the ostensible issues about which men dispute change, orthodoxies become heresies, and heresies become orthodoxies with timeless repetition. Dunham in his study passes in review among others the following heresies, the upholding of which by their successive followers cost many lives: Docetic, Gnostic, Montanist, Arian, Nestorian, Pelagian, Manichean, Donatist, Vaudois, Albigensian and Cathars, the heresies of Abelard, Arnold of Brescia, Hus, St. Joan, Copernicus, Giordano

Bruno, Galileo, Tyndale, Luther, Servetus, to mention only a few—
the issues covering a vast range of theology, philosophy, astronomy,
sociology, some of them issues which seem incomprehensible or even
meaningless to subsequent generations, but all having in common the
capacity to stimulate the highest excitation among those contemporaneous with the beliefs. In reviewing the struggles generated over
the earlier heresies within the Christian Church, Dunham draws
attention to the highly significant fact that in determining, as they are
called upon to do again and again, where the 'truth' lay in successive
controversies, the Fathers of the Church were careful never to choose
a partial or sectarian view. Exhibiting a rare talent for organization,
they always chose the doctrine which had the merit of combining the
twin features of ensuring maximum unity among the rank and file with
the widest possible membership of the organization, in this case, the
Church.

For example, if the dispute was whether Jesus was man or God, the
son of the Father or sharer in the Godhead, the 'correct' decision
proved to be that he was both. In the controversy as to whether or not
a sacrament was valid if administered by a heretic, the 'correct' decision
proved to be that it was, but that the heretic remained a heretic. And,
of course, the converse of this significant generalization also holds,
namely, that the test of heresy is never a question of the objective truth
or falsity of the thesis being propounded, but the capacity of the
proposition, if accepted, to disunite and fragmentate the membership
of the organization, leading to a weakening and loss of power. For
example, St. Joan's 'heresy' in terms of doctrine was infinitely less
serious than that of St. Francis a century earlier, but Joan was declared
heretic where St. Francis was not, because of the changed political
circumstances.

Is this the same as to suggest that people, and especially the hierarchical leadership of an organization, are wholly cynical or hypocritical in determining matters of truth or falsity in terms not of logic
and evidence, but in terms of political convenience and the logic of
the struggle for power? That is not, of course, how the leaders themselves or, generally speaking, the majority of the rank and file see it.
They would protest the sincerity of their convictions or ideological
beliefs, but would also acknowledge what they claim to be an inescapable dilemma, arising out of their desire that 'truth' should prevail,
and not lose the day to their opponents' 'falsehoods'. As we saw in the
above quoted passage from Gibbon, the contradiction of *organized*

Christianity lay in the fact that the hierarchy in conducting the business of the Church were obliged to do certain things which their creed specifically forbad them to do, if the Church was to survive as an organization in a world where other organizations also sought pre-eminence. This dilemma is, of course, not peculiar to Christianity, but common to all organizations professing aims of human equality, justice, brotherhood and freedom. Many, almost certainly the vast majority of men, try to have it both ways in order not to suffer intolerable guilt from conscience but at the same time without disqualifying themselves entirely from hope of worldly success.

Henry Adams, writing in the context of the Church and St. Francis, gives a clear statement of the latitudinarian view of the matter.

> The Church, embracing all mankind, had no choice but to march with caution, seeking God by every possible means of intellect and study. Francis, acting only for himself, could throw caution aside and trust implicitly in God, . . . The two poles of social and political philosophy seem necessarily to be organization or anarchy; man's intellect or the forces of nature.[1]

But this is a facile view; it is not possible to sit on the fence in the attempt to get the best of both worlds—for one very good reason. The martyr in affirming his belief even unto death may of course be wrong about the objective issue in dispute, but about one thing—and that the crucial thing—he must always be right as against the organization leaders who excommunicate, banish, persecute or murder him. And that is, that he, unlike them sets the claims of truth above the claims of power. He boldly affirms complete and sufficient faith in truth alone, and defies power to do its worst, for truth by its very nature can never be reached by even the mightiest assemblage of human power. Dunham expresses this perfectly in a passage that deserves not to be forgotten.

> Excellence when punished is still excellence. A true assertion is still true when it is consumed by flames, and a false assertion is still false when it escapes them. It is no doubt possible to determine, by faggot or rope, how many men will attain excellence and profess truth, but it is certainly not possible, by any such means or indeed by any means at all, to change the

---

[1] Henry Adams, *Mont-Saint-Michel and Chartres*, London 1936 (first published 1905), p. 339.

essential nature of the values themselves. These exist as limits upon administration . . .[1]

Administrators may sometimes forget this, but they do so at their peril. However, when they are dealing with forces of counter-power, they are fighting on their own ground, and their opponents are at a hopeless disadvantage. The advantage always lies with those entrenched in power: possession is nine-tenths of the law. Their opponents are by the very fact of their seeking power always liable to be suborned by the magnet of the patronage and rewards of power. But against the invincible integrity of the individual, the greatest powers are ultimately impotent. That is why those in power have time out of mind gone to great lengths to destroy their opponent's integrity; the destruction of his body is a mark of their defeat, and the desperation born of impotence. Up to the final awful moment Farrel on Calvin's behalf did not cease to try every artifice to extort from Servetus an acknowledgement of error; when Joan recanted, the Inquisitors were satisfied to offer her her life; when she recovered her deathless courage, they condemned themselves for ever by taking it from her.

We at last come to the heart of the problem which Tolstoy so boldly and brilliantly dissected; the problem of the nature of power, and its inseparable connection with the cause of war. The largest concentration of power is to be found in the modern sovereign nation state, where millions of people customarily obey a relative handful of individuals in all essential respects exactly like themselves. (In so far as they differ at all, it is in the possession of an outsize will to power which differentiates them to their moral disadvantage *vis-à-vis* those over whom they rule.) This extraordinary phenomenon is achieved in part by the recruitment by propaganda (much of it deceitful) and privileged remuneration of armed forces, police and gaolers, in short, by direct intimidation or the threat of intimidation, made possible by enforced taxation of the fruits of men's labour. But this account of the matter is clearly inadequate; it fails to meet Tolstoy's legitimate test in the equation of cause and effect, an effect cannot be attributed to a cause of wholly disproportionate magnitude. Hundreds or even thousands of men, even armed men, cannot of themselves determine the behaviour of millions of men year after year, decade after decade. This is why

[1] Barrows Dunham, *The Heretics*, London 1965, p. 187. Compare with this Herzen: 'Is a man less right merely because no one agrees with him? Does the mind stand in need of any other warrant than that of the mind? And how can universal insanity refute personal conviction?' *(From the Other Shore*, op. cit., p. 131.)

doctrine, that is to say, concepts, ideas, argument, is of such critical importance. No organization grounded solely on fear can hope to long endure. Stability requires at least some measure of genuine consent. Therefore, an organization, and particularly one so powerful as a nation state, must explain and justify itself in terms which command the consent or at least the passive acquiescence of the bulk of the members. This explains the ferocity with which 'mere' ideologues, prophets, philosophers and intellectuals have been and are persecuted —and conversely, others richly rewarded for devising persuasive defences of the existing order. The hierarchy of any organization, the leaders and rulers of a nation state, capitalist or communist, fear nothing so much as loss of faith in the prescribed ideals on the part of the membership. When the rank and file lose even their declared intention, however vague, of supporting the organization and what it stands for, or is supposed to stand for, the organization itself is in mortal peril. At all costs, a doctrine must be maintained sufficiently plausible to secure the maximum unity of belief and support possible. As the late President Kennedy, speaking of the NATO organization, put it:

> The reality of purposes therefore, is that that which serves to unite us is right, and what tends to divide us is wrong. . . .[1]

From all of which I conclude that power consists of the obedience of the many to the few, an obedience which is secured in part by the intimidation made possible by the control of armed men, but (as this means is never of itself sufficient) even more by beliefs, purposes, justifications designed to persuade people that it is their duty to obey. Throughout all human history these theories have always existed, and have always played a vital part in securing unity and obedience of the many under the control of the few. These theories have always been subject to change; but the fact of submission and obedience has not changed. What the theories of legitimization, which themselves come and go, exist to explain, namely, the reality of power does not come and go, that remains a constant. It is the contention of this book that all the varieties of theory of legitimization are false, and that is why no single theory has ever been found to endure. They are false because they seek to do something which is impossible, like squaring the circle, namely, to explain how the exercise of power of man over

[1] Quoted by David Horowitz, *From Yalta to Vietnam*, Penguin 1967, p. 387, from the *New York Times*, 23 January 1963.

man can become morally legitimate. It cannot. And because men refuse to recognize this, we lurch onwards in an ever-widening circle of disaster, which has now brought us all to the very edge of the precipice of nuclear destruction.

In earlier times—more than two millennia ago—the ruled were told that although they looked like men, in reality they were not so, but 'pseudo-men' or slaves, who required in their own interests to be owned and controlled. And men believed it, but not indefinitely. Human gullibility is without limit, but it does not last. Eventually, despite Aristotle's ingenious arguments in defence of slavery, men awoke to the fact that they had been deceived. So then it was decided to tackle the problem from the other end. The controlled men were real men after all, but the men who ruled them were super-men, gods. And men believed this too, but not for ever. So this too was modified so as to read: the rulers are not actually themselves gods, but they are God's appointed representatives and they rule by right divine. This falsehood too was eventually seen through, and in our time, since Rousseau and the French Revolution a different myth got under way, achieving by the twentieth century universal currency in the West. This myth goes by the name of 'democracy', and maintains that the rulers are not after all God's representatives, but the people's representatives. It holds that when people obey a government that represents them, they are only obeying themselves and therefore are free. In Britain this principle is thought to find expression in such institutions as free elections, based on universal suffrage, a parliamentary opposition to ensure redress of grievance and the protection of minority right, *habeas corpus*, trial by jury, the rule of law and equality before the law. In the USA the same principle finds embodiment in similar institutions, with a slightly different emphasis. In addition to the above institutions, there is greater emphasis on a written code of individual rights, with a supreme court to uphold them, on the principle of the separation of powers, as well as the federal principle, in order to 'establish justice, insure domestic tranquillity, provide for the common defence, promote the general welfare, and secure the blessings of liberty'. While no single institution is held to be the *sine qua non* of liberty, the basic pattern is thought to constitute the essence of democracy. Countries enjoying such institutions or at any rate holding such values are held to be democratic or free in contrast to those countries which do not uphold those institutions or principles, which are said to be autocratic, authoritarian, totalitarian, in a word, not democratic, not free. Any growth in the power of such countries by armaments, territorial expansion, or even political prestige and conversely any diminution in the power of 'democratic' countries is held to be a threat to freedom and therefore to the peace of the world. In defence of such freedom we must all, if needs be, be prepared to die, not to mention kill indiscriminately by the million.

I think this view of the matter held apparently almost without question throughout the Western world to be false and productive of disastrous consequences. The Marxist version of this doctrine differs of course in the economic emphases it places on the role of capitalism and communism respectively in determining issues of equality and freedom, but it resembles the Western view in that it derives legitimacy of governmental power from the consent of the people. I think this view is accordingly also false, and equally productive of disastrous consequences.

Whether a man lives in a State that is allegedly democratic or autocratic, he will in either case be given no option as to his membership. If it were the case that men were conscripted into autocratic States, but in 'democratic' States membership was purely voluntary, the difference between the two would indeed be the difference between servitude and freedom. But no man is ever given any alternative to 'joining' the State where he happens to be born. All States are coercive by nature, otherwise they would not be sovereign. A man without a country, that is to say, a free man, nowhere exists. It is not permitted for the simple reason that the existence of one free man would imperil the structure of obedience for all, and the existence of Power itself would be threatened. Consequently, all States, including the most 'democratic', are based ultimately on force, and were originally created out of the spoils of war. Britain, the USA, the USSR, Albania, Belgium, China, France, Venezuela *et alii* may exist as geographical entities, but as political categories they are inseparable from the activities of war out of which they were forged, and they maintain their separate political existence only in so far as they are backed by the appropriate military force.

Although people living in 'democratic' States are not permitted to not assume or to renounce citizenship, they are subjected to ceaseless propaganda which tacitly assures them that although they are coerced, they are free because indirectly they are only being coerced by themselves, since they are represented in the governing body that coerces them. But this argument is obviously fraudulent. A 'general will' expressive of the united will of all members of a State made up of millions of adults is obviously not possible. This is generally conceded, but then the principle of majority right is asserted. But no majority ever has an indefeasible monopoly of the truth—quite the contrary! And even if it had, if I am in the minority, the majority will to which I am being subjected is clearly not my will.

It will sometimes be conceded that, logically speaking, this is undeniable, but that 'democracy' in practice justifies itself by its superior results. It is thought likely to be productive of wiser policies and to be generally more accommodating, flexible and tolerant than non-democracies. But what evidence is there of this?

No test of the quality of a community can be more significant than that of its relations with other communities. How does the behaviour of 'democratic' States compare with that of non-democratic States in the sphere of international relations? Do democratic States spend less on the insane armaments race now threatening the peace of all mankind than do the non-democratic States? They spend more; and are just as intransigent and evasive as their enemies when disarmament steps are proposed as they are from time to time in order to maintain the public pretence that governments share the public's concern about the dangers of the arms race. Earlier in the century it was quite genuinely, however naïvely, believed in democratic Labour circles that disarmament could be achieved if a government truly representative of the people could be elected; if, that is to say, a Labour Government committed to disarmament were to be returned. On this assumption an enormous amount of effort was put into obtaining a majority in favour of unilateral nuclear disarmament in the British Labour Party. The majority was in due course obtained at the historic Scarborough Annual Conference of 1960. Its only consequence was to prove empirically and decisively that even the principle of majority rule only counts when it obeys the logic of existing economic and military power, a fact of life which every professional politician must imbibe almost in infancy if he is to survive a day in his profession. What happened was simply that the party leader defied the majority vote, as must any party leader who is a serious contender for sovereign political power. Ministers of Disarmament are no more than a macabre joke wherewith to deceive the gullible.

Are the 'democracies' more just or more humane in their relations with other States? The greatest single atrocity committed by one nation against another in recent times is that committed by the United

States against Vietnam. Whatever the 'justifications' or rationalizations, the horrifying facts are incontrovertible. Second in infamy was the indirect responsibility of the British (and to a much lesser extent the USSR) in arming the Nigerian government to destroy and starve to death the Biafrans. Shortly before that the British and French had joined Israel to wage an unashamedly aggressive war against Egypt. The United States had likewise intervened to overthrow by violence the governments of Guatemala and San Domingo. There is, of course no lack of outrages committed by non-democratic States, ranging from Tibet to Hungary and Czechoslovakia. My only point is that 'democracies' are not only not innocent; they have in recent times been more guilty than the others.

The other important issue to be considered is the recognition and protection of civil rights. It is here that democrats feel themselves to be on strong ground. Minorities and private individuals are freer under 'democracy' than under 'autocracy', for example, in Britain or the USA as against the USSR. In the matter of civil liberties and as regards white citzens of the USA this is surely undeniable. But two things need to be said: (i) the extent of the contrast has been enormously exaggerated by Western ideologues and pressmen, and (ii) the reason for the superior protection of civil rights in 'democracies' is not to be found in the array of institutions which purport to constitute democracy.

For example, in the West a dissident writer need not fear incarceration, as was experienced by Solzhenitsyn under Stalin. Today Solzhenitsyn is free, but permitted to publish his writings only in *samizdat*. But only the naïve would suppose that if the West were fortunate enough to possess a writer of such calibre, and he were to tell the truth about the exercise of power in our own society, he would be granted the kind of publicity necessary to enable him to reach the general reading public. It needs also to be said that a Solzhenitsyn in gaol for speaking the truth, while his lot may be extremely harsh, is nevertheless freer by far than Western democrats who compromise their own beliefs by obedience to laws they deem false on the grounds that the laws were made by governments allegedly representing them.

It may be said that this is to overlook the vital role of 'Her Majesty's loyal Opposition' or the minority party in a 'democratic' State, in protecting civil liberties and minority rights generally. But members of the 'Opposition' are, no less than members of the majority party, attracted by the lure of power, and behave in accordance with the logic of power. If a man persists in defying that logic, he will ultimately be despatched from the political scene, as was George Lansbury in 1935, who after being the victim of a brutal attack by Ernest Bevin was denied even the right of reply. It is not the case that Parliamentary benches of the Left or still less the Right in any country attract the wisest and most selfless men. Political parties generally exhibit frequent and bitter factional struggles—caucuses, intrigues, expulsions and threats of expulsion, abuse of opponents, and ceaseless propaganda designed to distract the unsuspecting from their constant and real goal, the acquisition, consolidation and, if possible, expansion of their own power. In a general election, each contending party automatically assures the voters that their opponents are unfit to govern, and in this at least they are always right. 'The price of liberty is eternal vigilance' has become so hackneyed as to lose its vitality, but it is nevertheless true; but that vigilance must be exercised by the free individual, for no one else can be counted upon to stand in for him. There is, for instance, no more vital freedom than the simple right to be let alone. Yet in Britain in 1971 the government prosecuted and convicted people who were not willing to disclose to them such personal and private matters as their academic or professional qualifications, their hours of work, mode of transport. As a token of their liberal good faith, the Government stated that people would not be compelled to answer questions about their health. This outrageous violation of the elementary human right to a private life was enacted with scarcely a ripple of discussion by a freely elected Parliament in which the ultra-loyal Opposition was strongly represented. This occurred in a 'democracy', not an 'autocracy'. Fortunately for the civil liberties of the English people, over 3,000 recusants risked the penalities and simply defied the unjust law. That is to say, they defended freedom in the only way in which it can be effectively defended by disobeying non-violently those who make unjust demands.

'Democratic' governments, then, have in general a record in international relations that is rarely superior to that of 'autocracies' and frequently much worse. Secondly, in domestic affairs, while they are generally not as repressive as 'autocracies', the reason for this is not attributable to the institutions of democracy but to the refusal of the citizens to obey unjust laws.

It is quite wrong to suppose that freedom consists of being able to do what the government, allegedly representing us, permits us to do. This is not freedom, but voluntary servitude. When we obey the government, any government, we obey not ourselves, but other men, and therefore are to that extent not free. We are free when we obey our own consciences which subject us to a universal law, which is not man's law but God's law, namely, that we should not do to others what we would not want done to ourselves, and that we should love our neighbour as ourselves. The theory of democracy is not only false, but it has the most pernicious consequences. A man is deceived when he allows himself to be persuaded that it is his duty to obey not his conscience but the will of the government on the grounds that under democratic conditions the government represents his own real will or at any rate should be obeyed because it was freely elected. The gravity of this is twofold: (*a*) it fatally undermines the original source of manhood and independence, viz. conviction born of strenuous struggle with and faith in conscience, and (*b*) it ensures that potential opposition to power is snuffed out, since no matter how much lip service is paid to participation, a man holding to the theory of democracy will both as a matter of theory and practice never disobey government. It is true that even Dicey, the author of the classic liberal, conservative interpretation of the English Constitution, argued that if the Government were to go mad and order the murder of all blue-eyed babies, citizens who did not disobey would themselves be out of their minds. But anyone holding to Dicey's false theory of the legitimacy of government would be very unlikely to disobey even in that improbable eventuality. During Cuba week in 1962, it was not solely the blue-eyed babies who were threatened with imminent extermination but all of us; and even then only the smallest handful of people proceeded to active civil disobedience.

Finally, it may be objected that even if the truth of the above analysis is conceded, the facts of power remain unchanged, and the grounds for fear of the consequent peril have not been removed. But, of course, the existing dangers require for their continuance a rationale whereby one's own side is held to be innocent and the enemy guilty. The truth, by exposing the hollowness of this fabrication, exposes also where the true enemy always lies, at home in one's midst. And it is there that the struggle for liberation against the tyranny of power by non-violent disobedience must be undertaken in all countries throughout the world, if mankind is ever to achieve a stable and peaceful existence. Freedom begins and ends with the individual, and the individual must first overcome the will to power within his own breast in order effectively to counter its effects in others.

8

Epilogue

The generally accepted view on which our society and culture are based is that the legitimacy of government derives from the consent of the governed in geographical communities which are united by historic ties, mutual loyalties, common literature, customs and institutions, and generally though not always common language. This view of the matter claims to be in accordance with the facts and also to be morally valid as well as providing the most adequate explanation of what is happening in the world and why. For example, men living according to this theory are free as contrasted with those who do not live in accordance with democratic belief or where the consent of the governed is held to be not genuine through intimidation or manipulation. And free men naturally feel threatened by unfree men and must therefore arm against them. This is why we must arm—in order to defend freedom. If the bill for world arms expenditure is currently running at $159,000 million and if the larger part of the earth's population live in hunger and destitution, this is, of course, to be regretted; but it is the price of freedom, and no one pretends that the world is perfect.

I think that this view—the view based on democracy within the framework of nation states—is false, and therefore is leading, and is bound to lead to ever-growing disaster. In order to restore hope to mankind, as signs multiply of a general succumbing to bewilderment and despair, it is urgently necessary to reject this false theory and substitute for it the true view of the matter.

The true view is that human history is the resultant of the conflict between the forces of good and evil. The evil is made up of the will to power in man, expressed in the coercion or domination of man by man. And the good consists of the renunciation of that will and the consequent enlargement of the ability to love. Men, whether they will it or not, are members one of another, and ceaselessly interacting upon each other, influence each other for good or ill. Power exerts constant influence because it is both keenly desired and sharply feared. But love is universally respected; and men also wish to be in good standing with their fellows, for genuine, valid reasons as well as for reasons which will not bear close scrutiny. Genuine public opinion—not at all to be confused with the whims and caprices of fashion or the answers to opinion polls regarding the 'news' headlines of the moment—real public opinion, which is the true source of what happens in the world, is the outcome of the struggle between power and love.

When Prince Andrew Bolkonski joined Barclay de Tolly's army on the banks of the Drissa, he found a great many factions, proffering different military strategies, competing with one another for the Emperor's favour. But by far the largest group—'to the others as ninety-nine to one'—was interested not in questions of peace or war, of advancing or retreating, but in securing as much advantage for themselves as possible from the exceptional circumstances.

> All the men of this party were fishing for rubles, decorations, and pro-motions, and in this pursuit watched only the weathercock of imperial favour, and directly they noticed it turning in any direction, this whole drone-population of the army began blowing hard that way, so that it was all the harder for the Emperor to turn it elsewhere.[1]

This picture is true of more than those who pay court to Emperors, but all men are ultimately susceptible to feelings of shame, and need to think well of themselves. Hence the vital importance of the minority who can generally be relied upon to put principle above convenience or advantage. The influence of this relatively small group on the many is out of all proportion to its numbers, although in the nature of things, it is an indebtedness that is rarely if ever acknowledged. It is painful to be shamed or reminded that one is betraying one's better self. We do not therefore readily honour those who perform for us this task, rather are we likely instantly to relegate the process to the unconscious.

Over and over again the retort is made to the rigorous advocate of non-violence who rejects the legitimacy of all exercise of power by man over man that even if the theory is morally impregnable, it is wholly utopian, and one who holds to a view so far removed from actual human behaviour is simply condemning himself to a sterile irrelevance. But this cannot be so. Moral excellence is always moral excellence and must necessarily always exert an influence for good even or indeed especially in a debased moral climate. Moreover, those who out of a desire to be 'realistic' hold to a false view of the moral universe will find that they lose the means to understand what is happening in the real world and why. Tolstoy chose the Napoleonic invasion of Russia

[1] Tolstoy, *War and Peace*, op. cit., p. 701.

to illustrate how received opinion totally failed to grasp the significance of the events which unfolded in Europe during the years of Napoleon's ascendancy. I would like to conclude this present analysis of the nature of power and its vital connection with the cause of war with a brief résumé of a contemporary episode, the thirteen days' Cuban missile crisis of 1962, as reported by one of the leading *dramatis personae*, the late Robert Kennedy.

The conventional Western view can not unfairly be summarized as follows: Mr Khrushchev in a bid to extend the sphere of Soviet Communist power put missiles with atomic warheads into Cuba, and thereby threatened the peace of the world. Mr John F. Kennedy, by his sober restraint and iron nerves, refused to be blackmailed into either capitulation or provocative retaliation, and so not only saved the peace but successfully defended the freedom of the free, that is to say, democratic world. At least this is the view put out for public consumption and widely accepted. And there is the clear implication, sometimes made explicit, that the fate of the world's billions of people depended on the judgement and will of these two men. Had we, for instance, not had the good fortune to have John Kennedy as our leader, we might not be here today.

It is difficult even now—nearly a decade later—to write calmly about an incident which so sharply exhibited the extent of the humiliation of mankind. For what other word can reasonably be used to describe a situation in which the life of mankind could even appear to be directly threatened by decisions, the ultimate responsibility for which lay with two men, one in the Kremlin and one in the White House? The situation could only have come about as a result of the willingness of immense numbers of people to subject themselves to a virtually absolute regimentation, so that on both sides absolute obedience can be relied upon from large numbers—indistinguishable in this respect from machines—no matter how humanly atrocious the orders received by them. It is this extraordinary degree of regimentation made possible by the combination of advanced technology and the despiritualization of men through mechanization which constituted the basis of the extraordinary power temporarily and apparently wielded by Khrushchev and Kennedy. Robert Kennedy states that these hour-to-hour decisions made by the President determined whether the peoples of the world should live or die. But this is pure illusion. That the power exists to destroy mankind, that the machinery for this end has been elaborately worked out, created and set up, that

the danger that it will be used is very real—all this is incontrovertible
and inexpressibly shameful. But it is illusion that this fantastic power
resides in the hands of an individual or group of individuals. Even if
an accident were to occur or a madman in a key position were to inflict
untold damage, the responsibility for such acts would clearly still
belong to all those who set up or authorize the setting up or even
passively acquiesce in the setting up of such diabolical machinery.

Let us look at the nature of the power as it appeared to a first hand
witness of the Cuban crisis, while first noting that of these two men
allegedly wielding power of life and death over mankind, one, the
leader of the 'autocracy', was constitutionally relieved of his office and
forced into retirement within two years, the other, the leader of the
'democracy', was relieved of office within a year—by a murderer's
bullet. It is not possible to prove that either of these two events were
directly linked with the Cuban missile crisis. Nevertheless, it should
be noted that, as far as the power forces on both sides were concerned,
both men, by refusing to be provoked into taking the ultimate and
irretrievable step in the horrifying circumstances, had failed to secure
the aims of supreme power, which were of course necessarily mutually
contradictory—the securing of a missile base in Cuba by the USSR
on the one side and the invasion of Cuba to destroy both the missile
sites and the Castro régime by the USA on the other.

On each side the play of forces was exactly the same, although we
can only infer the intensity of the struggle on the Russian side. On
behalf of the USSR Khrushchev exercised 'moderation', offering to do
a deal whereby the missiles would be removed in return for an
American pledge not to participate in an invasion of Cuba and the
lifting of the blockade. On the other hand, the Kremlin Foreign Office
sought to make the missile withdrawal conditional upon a parallel US
withdrawal of the Vulcan missiles from Turkey's NATO bases.

Kennedy from the start was subjected to very strong pressure from
the military to respond to the Russian move by a surprise air strike
against the sites in Cuba, confident that that would be the end of the
matter. Kennedy at least understood that his opponents were under
exactly the same pressures that he was, unable to ignore the logic of
power other than by resignation, an alternative unthinkable by men
who play for such prodigious stakes. It is highly significant that notwithstanding all the ideological propaganda disseminated for public
consumption about the moral superiority of one's own side, the top
level professional exponents of *raison d'état* have themselves no

illusions that they must obey only the logic of *raison d'état*, the logic that is identical for all secular princes (and 'spiritual' princes too for that matter). In short, Kennedy rejected the military advice.

> They [the Russians], no more than we, can let these things go by without doing something. They can't, after all their statements, permit us to take out their missiles, kill a lot of Russians, and then do nothing. If they don't take action in Cuba, they certainly will in Berlin.[1]

In reviewing the President's experience throughout his conduct of the whole affair, Robert Kennedy gave this account of the President's 'distress' at the working of the minds of his senior military advisers, excepting only General Maxwell Taylor, for their indifference to the implications of the steps they recommended.

> They seemed always to assume that the Russians and the Cubans would not respond or, if they did, that a war was in our national interest. One of the Joint Chiefs of Staff once said to me he believed in a preventive attack against the Soviet Union. On that fateful Sunday morning when the Russians answered they were withdrawing their missiles it was suggested by one high military adviser that we attack Monday in any case. Another felt that we had in some way been betrayed.[2]

On the other hand, in resisting the proposals of the military, the President found political support, notably from Adlai Stevenson and also voices within the Executive Committee itself—a support which, if present, had not made itself articulate a year earlier when the President received unanimous advice to sponsor the Bay of Pigs invasion, itself the principal immediate cause of the Cuban missile crisis. Robert Kennedy, in discussing the vital importance of ensuring that a diversity of views be expressed to the President, throws an interesting light on the psychology of those whose will to power has succeeded in bringing them close to the levers of supreme power. After characterizing them as men of 'highest intelligence, industrious, courageous and dedicated to their country's well-being', he proceeds to emphasize that not one of them remained consistent in his judgement throughout the crisis. In the process of discussion some even changed from one extreme to the other, from support of an air attack at the beginning to advocacy of no action at all at the end. This, Robert Kennedy asserts, was no reflection on them, but a reflection of the difficulties and awesome responsibilities attaching to each of the alternative choices of their

[1] Robert F. Kennedy, *13 Days: The Cuban Missile Crisis, October 1962*, London 1969, pp. 39–40.
[2] Ibid., p. 117.

dilemma. In such circles, naturally, the thought could never arise that no man is entitled to put himself into a situation where his responsibilities require him to make choice between morally depraved alternatives. Nothing can alter the supreme value of moral clarity and consistency; no man is obliged to find himself in a situation where such virtue is by definition inaccessible. But men who pursue power have never been accustomed to expending excessive energies on moral issues; and no one knows this better than those who achieve supreme success. President Kennedy, his brother tells us, wisely decided not to attend all the meetings of the fourteen-man Executive Committee (plus occasionals), the reason being that:

> Personalities change when the President is present, and frequently even strong men make recommendations on the basis of what they believe the President wishes to hear.[1]

This point is given renewed emphasis in the conclusion to Kennedy's account of the crisis, where he dilates upon the gravity of the risks arising from the sycophancy or, as he puts it, 'awe' of power, of officials themselves near the apex of power and therefore with much to lose. And it is clear that Kennedy is speaking not only from his experience of the Cuban crisis but from his political experience in general, and in the light in particular of hindsight resulting from the unanimity of advice tendered to the President over the disastrous Bay of Pigs affair. The President's brother concludes of the Presidential office:

> His office creates such respect and awe that it has almost a cowering effect on men. Frequently I saw advisers adapt their opinions to what they believed President Kennedy and, later, President Johnson wished to hear.[2]

In illustration, he cites the case of a Cabinet officer agreeing with him (Kennedy) a recommendation, and within minutes 'vigorously and fervently' expressing the opposite point of view to the President, on learning that that was what the President wanted to hear.[3]

In order to 'succeed' in life, and nowhere more so than in politics,

---

[1] Robert F. Kennedy, p. 37.   [2] Ibid., p. 109.

[3] The effect of Power on a power seeker's ability to maintain stability of judgement is also illustrated by Tolstoy. Compare, for example, Robert Kennedy's account of the Presidential milieu with Tolstoy's description of the behaviour of the Polish ambassador when given audience by the Tsar, Nicholas I: 'The Ambassador, having exchanged a rapid glance with the aide-de-camp—to whom he

it is above all necessary not to fall foul of those in whom power resides. All office seekers and holders know this intuitively, it is the rule by which they live. What they most fear is to be caught publicly in a situation where they are compelled to choose between their constant private loyalty to power and the claims of morality. When that happens, it sometimes occurs even amongst power men that they find that they have limits beyond which their consciences will not permit them to go. But then the price of virtue is remorselessly exacted. For example, at the time of Suez in 1956, this buccaneering exploit was too much to stomach for five Conservative MPs, who were not lost to honour, and who accordingly opposed their party leader's decision to commit an act of aggression against Egypt. That they were right to do so would no longer be disputed other than by party bigots, but their political careers were none the less irretrievably ruined. For they had offended against the logic of power and in so doing had alienated the guardians of that power, who set loyalty to it far above any possible moral consideration or often even of long-term political wisdom.

It was President Kennedy's tragedy that he happened to be President at a time when the conflict between power and even a relative morality forced him to commit himself publicly to decisions offending against the logic of naked power. When he had attempted privately to use his personal judgement against even the *appearance* of the logic of power by ordering the withdrawal of the Vulcan missiles from Turkey on the grounds that their 'deterrent' value was only apparent, since they had been superseded by Polaris-carrying submarines in the Atlantic, he had only discovered his own impotence as President of the United States. Earlier in 1962 he had made repeated attempts to secure via the State Department the withdrawal of the obsolete missiles, but to no avail. Robert Kennedy comments:

> The President believed he was President and that, his wishes made clear, they would be followed and the missiles removed. He therefore dismissed the matter from his mind.[1]

That he dismissed from his mind the matter of his discovery that he was President only in name, we may take leave to doubt, although we

---

had only that morning spoken about Nicholas's unfortunate weakness for considering himself a great strategist—warmly praised this plan which once more demonstrated Nicholas's great strategic ability.' (*Hadji Murad*, Ivan Ilych and Hadji Murad, World's Classics 1951, pp. 327–8.)

[1] Robert F. Kennedy, op. cit., p. 93.

can well believe that he was 'angry' (as Robert Kennedy asserts) when the Russians threatened to make the removal of the Turkish missiles a *quid pro quo* for the removal of the Cuban missiles.

At the missile crisis, Kennedy's 'restraint' prevailed because the crisis was played out in the full light of the public view, and the moral forces of mankind prevailed over the power forces. This was fortunate for mankind, fortunate too for the reputations of the two principal power protagonists, but apparently fatal to their continued power careers. They each offended against the logic of power; they each were shortly afterwards removed from power.

The Cuban crisis ostensibly was a struggle between two giants for supreme power. Each giant claimed that he was a good giant and his enemy a bad giant, for this is the way of giants. And the substance of this projection of the nature of the conflict has to be accepted by the mass of the people attached to each giant in order to make the conflict possible. The ideologies in terms of which this is done are false. The true conflict is that being waged inside each and every camp between the forces of power on the one hand and the forces of love, co-operation and trust on the other. At Cuba, it would be too much to say that the latter forces prevailed, but not too much to say that the former forces were defeated.

In this brief discussion of the Cuban missile crisis, on which so much has been written, I have merely drawn attention to certain remarks in an account by one of the participants. It seemed to me worth doing in this context, because that crisis represents the supreme symbol of the importance which Power has come to assume in the common culture of mankind as a whole. It could not have come to assume such importance if men had even begun to pay serious attention to the problem of Power and to analyse the enormity and universality of the deceit upon which it rests. Cuba week ought to represent a turning point in the history of mankind, if mankind is to survive. But it will only constitute such a turning point if the correct essential conclusion is drawn from it. Most of the discussion of these events is couched in terms which suggest explicitly or implicitly that mankind succeeded in emerging relatively unscathed from the crisis due to the wisdom, prudence, insight, statecraft of Kennedy and his advisers or/ and Khrushchev and his advisers. It is important that we understand that the Cuban missile crisis with its immediate threat to the life of mankind was primarily the responsibility of the people of the USA and of the USSR and indirectly of the peoples of all the other countries indirectly involved for being so forgetful of their duty and dignity as individuals as to abdicate control over their lives to other men no different from themselves. That we survived the missile crisis is due in no way to the statecraft of Kennedy or Khrushchev—both of them principal actors in the series of events which led up to and caused the crisis. We survived thanks to those anonymous people in the USA and in the USSR, and in the other countries involved, who long before the crisis, during the crisis, and continuing after the crisis, had never ceased to struggle against the forces of power within their respective societies and within themselves.

To put an end to power may not be possible. But to change men's values concerning power—so that they stop admiring that which is the reverse of admirable—is certainly possible. Moreover, it is indispensable to continued human survival on this planet, and will therefore be accomplished. Man is not going to commit suicide in order to please Caesar. However 'natural' —and this is a proposition open to endless disputation—power, that is the domination of man by man, is not, never has been and never can be legitimate. When men finally come to understand this, it will be the most momentous revolution in the history of mankind, and we shall enter an altogether new era. Such an era will naturally be long in being born. In a real sense, it began to be born with the emergence of the teaching of Jesus, although he, too, of course, built on the work of his predecessors. Today the disastrous consequences of ignoring the evil nature of power are so obvious that it requires the expenditure of considerable energies not to see it. Nevertheless, the struggle can still be expected to be long and protracted, because the will to power in man has put down deep roots and has been allowed to go unchallenged for so long. Moreover, power men everywhere in all walks of life demonstrate complete solidarity in wielding their power to prevent the truth so fatal to their aspirations from being heard. But because the truth is the truth, it will continue to be heard. Humanity continues to burn, bomb, destroy, imprison, torture, banish, repress, but however much and however long it goes on, the truth that love is good, imperishably good and that power is evil, is indestructible.

According to the way we live now, each child is sedulously taught throughout his educative years that the purpose of life is so far as possible to excel others. In the past this was tempered by a certain amount of lip service to Christian virtues like humility, service, cooperation and loving one's neighbour. Today we are less tolerant of cant and therefore dispense with the lip service. Each of us is taught simply to succeed, so far as possible in a well-mannered fashion, but essentially to succeed and not to fail. Such an ethic obviously generates enormous problems in every walk of life. The successful naturally want the best accommodation in the most salubrious areas; they want the best education for their children; they want the most healthy resorts and finest hotels for their vacations; they want the swiftest, most up-to-date and luxurious means of transport, preferably at their exclusive disposal when they travel; they want the richest foods and wines to cheer them when they dine, and the best medical skills, as well as privacy and comfort, when they are ill, as they not infrequently are.

Since this competition is not confined to any one country but is on the contrary world-wide in its ramifications, and since to produce wealth on a scale appropriate to meet the stimulated demand of so many appetites very large-scale organization is necessary, it follows that those who control this vast organization are very powerful within their own sphere, and fear those of like power to themselves in areas as yet beyond their control. So that in addition to all their other 'needs', they also have an over-riding need for the most up-to-date armaments and the most efficiently trained soldiers, sailors and airmen to deploy them as the strategy of fear should indicate. Economic demand is accordingly insatiable both for material consumer goods and for the 'protective' means of destruction. But supply of goods and labour is naturally severely limited. Therefore in every field of consumption, in housing, education, transportation, hospitals, vacation provision, land utilization—demand is satisfied in proportion to the power of the competitor. The competitors' power consists of many things—fortune of inherited position, money, skill, energy, cultural background, practical intelligence, knowledge, ruthlessness, social connections, and not least race and nationality. Those possessed of most power get most, those possessed of least get least.

Inevitably in such a system problems grow with mushroom-like rapidity, and are soon cumulative in effect in every sphere of life. The next step, therefore, is to assert that society must establish the necessary power to deal with its manifold and pressing problems. Because people live in fear, Ministries of Armaments must be set up to organize their 'protection'; when the resultant arms race generates in its turn another set of fears, it becomes necessary to set up next door to the Ministers of Armaments Ministers of Disarmament in order to appear to be concerned about those fears. The people at the end of the competitive queue in housing, education, nourishment, transport, medical aid and so on will all generate problems, and so corresponding Ministries with large bureaucratic staffs are set up. And since those at the bottom of any one queue will naturally tend to be near the bottom of other if not all queues—the connections between unstable homes, over-crowded slums, illiteracy, poverty and ill health do not need to be demonstrated—it follows that an ever-increasing number realize that the lawful means of success in the great competition are for ever beyond their reach. They can choose between an endless, broken-down struggle for impoverished if not destitute survival or the hazards of an unlawful short-cut to success—crime, theft, burglary, violence. Given the amount of violence society is busy accumulating in its military arsenals to protect the wealth and power of the rulers, it is in a very poor position to address pious moral exhortations to its ne'er-do-wells at the bottom. And to be fair, not overmuch exhortation is addressed. More Ministries are set up—the ministries of courts and police and prisons—in order to maintain law and order and internal deterrence to match the external deterrence. The latest refinement is the growth of additional private armies to guard the more vulnerable targets for plunder in the shape of banks and offices. In a decade in Britain *Securicor*, an organization of private armed guards, has increased its annual turnover from half a million sterling to £26 million. Insanity Fair is scarcely the correct image for lunacy on so grotesque a scale. Rather is it that of a ship heading for a hurricane, with all its stop-cocks wide open, the captain busy not in ensuring that they be closed but that more and more of the crew be offered more and more incentives to bale out.

I am not of course suggesting that there is moral innocence at the bottom of the social pyramid and a monopoly of guilt at the summit. Still less am I suggesting that there is any easy solution for problems so vast. But in order to make any real headway in the right direction, it is necessary first to destroy the great central illusion, namely, that problems which have all been caused by the will to aggrandisement and power in man can be solved by a further application of power. They cannot; they can only be aggravated. The people who are allegedly helping to solve the problems by the wisdom of their policies imposed and executed by means of power—the legislators, the generals, the Ministers, the Bishops, the Managing Directors, the Judges, the Professors, the Press Lords—are themselves by the consistency of their life-long will to power, without which they would not hold the positions they do, a major cause of the problems their offices exist to 'solve'. If they are sincere in their wish to help, let them get off the backs of the multitudes by whose toil they are borne up.

It will be objected that rulers are not necessarily personally wealthy or selfish men. Were not Calvin, Cromwell, Robespierre, Lenin personally men of great simplicity, even austerity in their lives? That is so. But in the first place, they were in this matter exceptional. And in the second place, they were highly dangerous exceptions. Their appetites for comfort, wealth, luxury had been eliminated only to be re-channelled into the single desire for power. Genuine exceptions are singularly hard to come by. Sir Thomas More is one. He held the office of Lord Chancellor, from which position he sent men to their deaths by execution; and yet retained a sufficiently true religious sense to forfeit his own head rather than obey sovereign power in violation of his conscience. An astonishing example, perhaps unique to a period in which a unified Catholic Christendom yielded to the modern secular sovereign, nation state.

It is interesting in the light of this discussion to take a look at how the distribution of patronage and power in contemporary England appears to a distinguished Oxford historian. A. J. P. Taylor, reviewing the period 1914–1945 writes:

> The system of patronage was a cheap way of getting public work done . . . It was also conservative, though not entirely in a party sense. Rewards went, on the whole, to the conformists, those who saw nothing but good in the British way of life.
>
> The men in public life were not, however, merely the most dutiful members of the community. They were usually also the most conscientious. Nearly all of them wanted to leave their country a better place than they found it.[1]

Taylor's observation is no doubt just—taking a generous view—so far as conscious motivation is concerned. The unconscious motivation, viz. will to power, Taylor does not appear to be significantly aware of. Almost certainly he would consider it to be so universal as to be not worth mentioning. The will to power in public figures is accepted by radicals as well as conservatives as natural and inevitable, and therefore as quasi-legitimate.

Modern man's thinking is so closely geared to conceiving all meaningful purpose in terms of power—conservative, reformer and revolutionary alike—that the supposition that life should not be lived on this

[1] *The Oxford History of England*, Vol. XV, 1965, pp. 175–6.

basis appears tantamount to the suggestion that life itself should cease, that we might just as well be dead, it is even said. He who seeks to oppose this force is like King Canute ordering the waves to go back.

Nevertheless, the goals of life should be the attainment of excellence in the realization of right values, whereas the goals of competition are simply to excel all others. We are emotionally geared to the values of the competitive system from our earliest years. Children are even bribed with material rewards, but more effectively motivated with emotional approval or disappointment by parents compulsively anxious for their children to succeed, that is to say, to oust their rivals in the competition. School curricula directly or indirectly are shaped by the demands of the competition which determines the duration and type and frequently even place of education for each child. The values to which such children are exposed are almost exclusively hierarchical values. Esteem and approbation are gained by being higher up a list of marks than others; those who are in the higher brackets go to preferred institutions with superior facilities; continued success opens up broader fields of opportunity to be placed in the higher brackets in more prestigeful competitions. Those who survive to reach what is politely termed 'higher education' find that curricula there too reflect the unquestioned axiom that inequality must inform all institutions and culture. The mere suggestion that economics should be about equality of economic distribution, politics about 'anarchy', history about the activities of everyone equally, philosophy about the metaphysics of equality, psychology about the relations between power and equality in the human soul, sociology with the problem of how to overcome discrimination in social, class and racial spheres, would be considered at best wildly eccentric. Yet, what in all conscience is odd about the demand that all sciences should be humanly committed to advance the welfare of all human beings equally?

The children of our culture are so thoroughly conditioned to find security in success in competition that for the rest of their lives they are prone to react with symptoms of severe anxiety to anything or anyone who appears to threaten the hierarchical system of values by which they live and which has made them what they are. It is not therefore surprising that we are emotionally seemingly incapable of conceiving any problem in other than power terms. If things in the body politic are seen to be less than desirable, then what is necessary is to devise fresh public policies, perhaps to change the men at the top for more able, efficient or better-trained or charismatically gifted men, in short, to effect significant change in large numbers of controlled men rapidly by means of externally applied power. And this fantastic conceptual framework is common to virtually all thinking, responsible men. Indeed it is taken for granted as the primary test of responsibility. No wonder that resistance goes so deep and is so nearly universal to a truthful analysis of the nature of power. For such analysis demonstrates clearly that power is not only morally illegitimate but also morally self-defeating; that men cannot be changed for the better by external coercive or power means; that the only way genuine improvement can be brought about is by each person bringing about the kind of change that *is* legitimate, that is not *ultra vires*, namely, change within him or herself. However radical, eccentric or revolutionary one's views, provided one retains some allegiance to violence, however small or conditional, one is still political, and therefore viable in the existing society. In short, you can reasonably expect to be heard. But to admit no violence whatever as legitimate is to repudiate all politics, all power, and thus expose to the light of day the unwanted truth that the responsibility for ending the evils in the body politic rests inescapably on each one of us, who can only contribute to moral progress by mending his own life. Those who make this truth clear are apt to experience difficulty in getting their voices heard anywhere.

Yet the true way to live is also the most rewarding—here on this earth, the only earth we know. But to apply one's energies to the multiplicity of creative activities open to a human being for their own sake, requires as well as knowledge of what Blake called the 'Minute Particulars' a share in the vision that can see 'a world in a Grain of Sand and a Heaven in a Wild Flower'. This is a gift, but it is not necessarily a natural one; it can with strenuous effort and much patience be acquired. We cannot all be born Thoreaus or Blakes, but their values are not esoteric ones. In so far as they lead to life—and to a life bearing within it the joy of endless renewal without robbing anyone else of a like joy—they are values which are desirable for their own sake and attainable by all alike.

Index

ABOUT THE AUTHOR

R. V. Sampson has been Lecturer in Politics at Bristol University since 1953. Born in 1918, he studied at Keble College, Oxford, before and after his service in World War II, and did post-graduate work at Nuffield College, Oxford. He spent 1951-1952 as a John Hay Whitney Visiting Fellow to the United States, and then taught for one year at Durham University. R. V. Sampson is also the author of *Progress in the Age of Reason* and *The Psychology of Power*.